SRI SHUKADEVA SPEAKS SRIMAD BHAGAVATAM

PART-1

Narottam Gaan

BLUEROSE PUBLISHERS
India | U.K.

Copyright © Narottam Gaan 2024

All rights reserved by author. No part of this publication may be reproduced, stored in a retrieval system or transmitted in any form or by any means, electronic, mechanical, photocopying, recording or otherwise, without the prior permission of the author. Although every precaution has been taken to verify the accuracy of the information contained herein, the publisher assumes no responsibility for any errors or omissions. No liability is assumed for damages that may result from the use of information contained within.

BlueRose Publishers takes no responsibility for any damages, losses, or liabilities that may arise from the use or misuse of the information, products, or services provided in this publication.

For permissions requests or inquiries regarding this publication, please contact:

BLUEROSE PUBLISHERS
www.BlueRoseONE.com
info@bluerosepublishers.com
+91 8882 898 898
+4407342408967

ISBN: 978-93-5989-194-1

Cover design: Shivam
Typesetting: Namrata Saini

First Edition: July 2024

Dedication

Guru is adored in India as Lord Brahma, Lord Vishnu, and Lord Shiva. He is the direct Supreme Brahma, the God. Guru and God are one. Abiding in us, He is the sole doer. The ideas, thoughts, interpretations, and narrations are his. Being a mere instrument, I owe everything that is written in this book to him. This book contains the knowledge, ideas, thoughts, words of wisdom, discourses, writings, and speeches I have garnered from my revered Gurudeva Paramahamsa Hariharananda and Sri Gurujee Paramahamsa Prajnanananda from time to time. In reality, this does not belong to me at all. It is exclusively a flower of their design unfolded out of a tiny bud of their ideas nestled in me. In the journey of life, I seek earnestly their blessings and inspiration for making my life blissful. I deem it a God-given privilege to consecrate this at their Lotus Feet.

With humble prostrations

Narottam

Acknowledgement

Human life is a life of gratitude and gratefulness with all humility and dedication. Our lives have been shaped by borrowing and acquiring things, ideas, thoughts, inspiration, and feelings from others and the outside universe. Life remains unfulfilled and imperfect if this gratitude is not paid to all around us in every moment for our deeds, thinking, and living. Unknowingly or knowingly, we have been inspired or enriched with knowledge and subjected to the influences of many sources, many of which we have come into contact with. I must remain in deepest gratitude to my revered and loving parents, who are now in eternity and instrumental in the hands of God for giving me birth and shaping my life. My heartfelt thanks go to Reena, Tattwamasi, and Yogeswar for their cooperation and inspiration. We in our home every evening used to recite and discuss Srimad Bhagavatam, authored by Maharshi Vyasadeva, venerated as an incarnation of Lord Krishna, and its Odia version by Jagannath Das (Das means a servant of God), a great renunciant widely adored and known for his love and bhakti for God. Being inspired by the nectar of love flowing in every page for Lord Krishna, I ventured into this uphill task of translating it into English, which has now taken the form of a book by the divine grace of God. Devarshi Narada, Maharshi Vyasadeva, his son Sri Shukadeva, Sri Jagannath Das, Paramhamsa

Hariharananda, my revered Gurudeva, and our most beloved and adored Sri Gurujee, Paramahamsa Prajnanananda. All these things that are put forth in this book are their words of wisdom and interpretations. I have just borrowed and imbibed from them. In great acknowledgement of this, very humbly speaking, I am just an insignificant and ignoble dust under their divine feet with heartfelt gratitude and love.

With love and reverence

Narottam

Contents

1. Despondency of Sage Vyasadeva: Origin of Srimad Bhagavatam 1
2. End of the Mahabharat war and birth of Parikshita, the king and devotee 39
3. Coronation of Parikshita as King and Pandavas ascension to Heaven 72
4. Arrival of Kali Yuga and conversation among Dharma, mother Earth and king Parikshita 89
5. King Parikshita cursed to death by snake Takshyaka 111
6. Jaya and Vijaya cursed to born as demons on the earth 148
7. Discourses by Kapil Muni to Devahuti 176
8. Extermination of the demon Hiranyaksha 246
9. The King Pruthu and Prithivi (Mother Earth) 259

1

Despondency of Sage Vyasadeva: Origin of Srimad Bhagavatam

The indelible history of Indian undying civilisation when unfolded throws glimpses into its glorious saga of greatness not in military conquests, atrocities, plundering, religious wars, or annexation of others' territory but in its inexhaustible search for the ultimate truth. Its history has been bedecked with the lofty ideals and spiritual achievements of its God realised masters, seers, sages and saints. For this reason, India has been since aeons called as Bharat. It connotes Bha plus rata. Bha means indivisible and ineffable divine light and rata means to be engrossed with. In other words, the inhabitants of Bharat were always engrossed in divine light not lured by the worldly delusions.

Maharshi Vyasadeva was one such sage who stands preeminent among sages and saints of India. He was otherwise known as Krishna Dvipyayana meaning the incarnation of Lord Krishna. Sage Vyasadeva, the son of sage Parashara and mother Satyavati, widely known as Padmagandha (lotus fragranced) or Yojangandha (fragranced to long distances). Mother Satyavati was the daughter of a fisherman. Before she came in contact with sage Parashara her body was stinking fishy smell out to the aversion of many people going nearby or even at a long distance. She was contemptuously known as Matsya gandha (smell of a rotten fish). But coming in contact with sage Parashara she was transformed into Padmagandha and Yojangandha. Fishy smell represents the bad and negative attributes ingrained in human beings through many births in the past born out of desires and karmas. But contact with Guru Preceptor and constant practice of what Guru has instructed one to do make one transformed into padmagandha. It means negative attributes give way to divine attributes. Sage Vyasadeva was born out of the union of Satyavati with sage Parashara. It means the union of the embodied Self (Jivatma) with the supreme Self (the disembodied Self). Through the constant realisation of the union of the Self with the supreme Self in all one's actions and thoughts under the supervision of the Guru Preceptor one reaches the stage of wisdom (prajnaghana). This stage of wisdom is represented by the sage Vyasadeva. Author of countless scriptures on Sanatan Dharma, Puranas editor of *Vedas*, he has left nothing or no aspect of divinity to the posterity to be written or filled up. It is venerably said whoever has written anything on God after him has added nothing new to the cornucopia of Indian knowledge but only reiterated or reaffirmed what sage Vyasadeva has already scripted. He was able to know the past and future. Towards the end of Tretaya Yuga and in the beginning of Dvapara Yuga he manifested on the earth as a divine incarnation.

One day in the early morning after taking a dip in the holy river Saraswati he was sitting in a secluded place in Badarikashram contemplating on the all-devouring Kala (Time Spirit) which leaves no one to escape its invincible jaws. Very invisibly, the life, energy and strength of all living being are eroded away by its unparallel corrosive powers. By throwing his clairvoyant glimpses into the future happenings through his yogic contemplation he was grieved to see the gloomy pictures of people in Kali Yuga being degenerated into the hell of delusion, ignorance and error, materially attached and forgetful of divinity. People will be short lived and ill-fated because of their according a very insignificant and subordinate place to God in their materially engrossed life.

Pondering over that very deeply he carved out ways to give liberation to the mundane bound people in Kali Yuga by dividing the *Vedas* into four parts for the convenient practice of the people according to the prescribed nuances of the *Vedas*. He accordingly distributed the *Vedas* among his disciples to teach people in terms of their attributes as pertains to their division into four categories: Brahmana, Kshyatriya, Vaisya and Sudra. He gave Rig *Veda* to Paila Muni, Yajur to Vaisampayana, Sama to Jaimini and Atharva *Veda* to Angira Muni. Sage Vyasadeva created the fifth *Veda* known as eighteen puranas which were given to sage Romaharsana. Gradually, the *Vedas* distributed thus were further divided by their disciples and passed on from disciple to disciple. Without being well established strongly in the divinity the *Vedas* were divided and misinterpreted further according to their little knowledge and feeble realisation of the Self. Taking the essence of all *Vedas* as the source sage Vysadeva scripted Puranas for the liberation of the entire mankind who were even staying at the lower strata of the society.

After doing all these out of compassion for humankind his mind was not remaining tranquil, still, calm and quiet. In spite of doing constant practice of Yoga his mind was wavering and restless. His mind was constantly smitten by countless thoughts. He continued to think that the path of knowledge he sought in accordance with *Vedas* was not free from delusion (Maya). How the bewitching forces of delusion and illusion will be perished permanently through the path of Bhakti (Love) and Yoga, he persisted in thinking over this.

Having authored so many scriptures on Jnana and Yoga he felt his mind was not under his control. It was in stage of vacillation, restlessness and agitation. He was perturbed by lack of inner peace and mind being not still and merged in divinity. Sage Vyasadeva was really in a state of despondency. Arjuna asked Lord Srikrishna about the restlessness of mind and his inability to control it (*Srimad Bhagavad Gita*, 6:34):

> canchalam hi manah Krishna
> pramathi balavad drham
> tasya ham nigraham manye
> bayor iva suduskaram

O Krishna! Mind is very restless and uncontrollable. It is very strong and determined in a very wrong way. To control it is as difficult as it is to control air in the sky.

Lord Krishna has himself admitted to the fact that mind is really restless and very difficult to control. It is by constant practice and detachment to the world, to the material and desire bound body and mind, it can be subject to control (*Srimad Bhagavad Gita*, 6:35).

Though a person of irrefutable knowledge and a versatile spiritual genius in inking innumerable scriptures on God, Vyasadeva was not completely detached to the world. His only son Shukadeva just after birth was on his heels and sage Vyasadeva was running after calling him by his name. Shukadeva was detached, constantly day and night engrossed in the Almighty God. Without any sense of body and mind he was always roaming naked. He was in the world but nothing he was beholding except Lord Krishna. Even minded and having equanimity of vision and insight and free from delusion and illusion he moved like an ignorant. To him Lord Krishna is in all and everywhere. He was seeing everywhere only Lord Krishna nothing else. Nobody was in a position to measure the fathomless depth of his love and surrender to God. When he was running away followed by his father sage Vyasa, the celestial nymphs were taking bath naked in the nearby river. Beholding Shukadeva coming they all came up the river bank without feeling any shame to pay homage to the naked Shukadeva. But when they saw sage

Vyasadeva following him they suddenly pushed themselves back into the water. Seeing this strange change in behaviour of celestial beings, he asked them the reason: "My son was young and naked but you all did not hesitate to come up water to pay homage to him. On the contrary, in my case I am very old and you all with exhibited shame left immediately to enter the river water". Hearing this, the celestials responded with humble respect to him:

"Shukadeva does not know the world. He is in the world but his heart is not smeared by the delusion and illusion of the world, He is completely detached and merged in God. He has no knowledge of who is male and female. Bereft of any sense of duality he thinks all as Lord Krishna and nothing else. On the other hand, you say you are old but you are attached to the world and you have body consciousness and knowledge of duality. This is the difference".

This was the state of sage Vyasadeva smarting from the pain of being restless, perplexed and despondent like Arjuna in the Mahabharat war and the king Suratha and Samadhi Vaisya in Saptasati Candi purana. This was the state of Lord Rama. As described in Yoga Vasista Ramayana when he accepted sage Vasista as his guru Preceptor all his despondency got obliterated from his mind. This is the state of every worldly attached human being. When Arjuna accepted Lord Krishna as Guru Preceptor and followed him all his despondency and delusion wiped out. Similar was the case with Suratha king and Samadhi Vaisya. When they came in contact with Medha rishi and accepted him as Guru

Preceptor all their mental agony disappeared and they became realized and liberated.

When sage Vyasadeva was desperate and despondent not being able to rein in the restless mind and fervently in quest for peace, bliss and joy, he heard the melodious song of Devarshi Narada approaching him. He immediately woke up and went some steps ahead to receive him with all humility and reverence. Holding his hand, he with all adoration and devotion received him and made him seated on a very respectable place as due to a very venerable guest. Touching his feet with his head he paid homage to him. It is very auspicious and exhilarating on the part of a person who is despondent and bewildered to see a great sage arrive at his place unexpectedly. It was a matter of unspeakably joyful solace to him. When mind was wavering like a leaf in the wind beyond his control, he was feeling a gnawing search within his heart for a preceptor in whom he will take the ultimate refuge and who will show him the way for controlling the mind.

The situation changed from a heart wrenching supplication to the fulfilment of the prayer. Devarshi Narada was in the seat of a Guru preceptor and sage Vyasadeva was eager to listen to him. By the way of conversation between the two sages, Narada said, addressing him as the son of sage Parashara. The word Parashara in Sanskrit means paran vyastanati hinasti iti. One who has subdued his enemies is Parashara. Being the son of sage Parashara, he has not been able to control and subdue the enemies within which make the mind restless. On contemplation "I could presage your mind being restless and agitated even after writing so many scriptures and distributing *Vedas* among your disciples and nuancing Dharma for the common humanity, you are not getting peace and your mind has not become still and quiet despite your indefatigable trying". In reply sage Vyasadeva said, "you are fully right in knowing beforehand the condition of my mind". Sage Vyasadeva expressed his deepest gratitude to Narada for coming to him in right time when he was in adversity. "Without God who can control my mind? Without love and devotion to Lord Krishna my mind cannot be controlled. Nobody knows better than you about the God's all pervading, omniscient and omnipotent nature moving like sun everywhere, shedding light and heat on all without being attached. Like air blowing everywhere inside and outside He is not touched by anything. He remains as a witness to what one does and thinks bad or good, sinful or virtuous without being attached by the fruits thereof". Sri Krishna said, "O Arjuna:

na mam karmani limpanti

na me karmaphale sprha (*Bhagavad Gita*, 4:14)

I am not attached to any work and I am also indifferent to the fruits of the work.

Again, in chapter 7 (12th verse) Lord Krishna said:

ye caiva sattvika bhaba rajasas tamasas ca ye

matta eve ti tan viddhi na tv aham tesu te mayi

Know that all sattvik, rajashik and tamasik attributes originate from Me. But I am not in these nor these are in Me.

Sage Vyasadeva continued saying "I am every moment taking dip in the water of yoga, meditation and other rituals as prescribed by *Vedas* and realising the coolness and warmth of the water divine. In spite of doing all these, mind is not contented, peaceful, still and calm. It is because of my fleeting mind. There is nobody other than you who knows the glorified greatness of Lord Krishna".

He entreated him with all humility to reveal before him the ways to quiet his mind.

Devarshi Narada replied:

"I know you are not happy and your mind is not still, calm and quiet. The spiritual path which Lord Krishna does not relish is not true spiritual path or dharma. You have written voluminous on dharma, artha, kama and mokshya from Vedas. Had you practiced in every moment of your life the majestic glories of Lord Krishna, you would have got immensely peace and calmness of mind. If your tongue does not speak the divine deeds of Lord Krishna which liberate human beings and speaks non-divine things, then these words are like the cacophonous voice of the crows. Where this voice is heard is like a place of stinking dirt, leftover food scrubs where crows meet to eat (kaka tirtha). Holy pilgrimage is one where sages and saints meet and sing the glories of God. Therein taking bath splashed with deep waters of love to God all sins, mental turmoil and agony vanish. If every moment of human life is not spent in His thought and feelings of love, human life becomes useless.

Engrossed in worldly desires and karmas in total forgetfulness of God is like a boat floating in deep sea unable to cross the ocean and reach the shore in the tempest of attachment to the fruits of one's deeds".

Addressing sage Vyasadeva as supreme soul, Devarshi Narada continued, *"You are pure, truthful and determined, you know the effulgent glories and splendid majesties of Krishna. You know what is nivriti and pravriti – the two ways of knowing God. You are a wonderful realised soul of knowledge and wisdom. You can be able to write a scripture as Srimad Bhagavatam – a receptacle of epitomic love for Lord Sri Krishna. Let an emblematic inscription of love in every page of human life be the essence of this monumental scripture (purana)". Immersing oneself completely in the ocean of love to Lord Krishna one will get liberation and all the fruits of his karmas performed in the past lives will be burnt and he will be free from the bondage of sins and liberated for ever from the circuits of birth and death. Leaving aside all the ways if one surrenders to God he or she will be indubitably exonerated from all sins.*

Lord Sri Krishna said to Arjuna:

sarvadharman parityajya mam ekam saranam vraja

aham tva sarvapapebhyo mokshyayisyami ma sucah
(*Bhagavad Gita* 18:66).

"You take refuge in Me with surrender of your own self by renouncing all other ways. Be certain that I will decimate all your sins".

Narada continued:

"All are under the supreme reign of Kala (Time spirit). Prey to the inexorable laws of karma all living beings take birth

after birth to enjoy the fruits of their karmas, evil and good, happiness and sorrows in dyads like day and night coming alternately. Those who have sought ultimate refuge and found goal and sole doer in Lord Krishna intoxicated with whole hearted love and devotion, know nothing except Thee in all their actions and thoughts through constant practice. They always remain merged in Him by drinking the nectar of His love secreted from His lotus feet. He is the creator, sustainer and destroyer of the universe. Without Him where is the creation? The entire cosmos springs from Him but He is not within the cosmos. He is the ultimate destination, abode, refuge, solace, witness, the emancipator, lord, and sustainer of the creation. He is the primordial seed from which the entire creation has sprung up".

Expatiating on the ineffable and effulgent glory of Lord Krishna, Devarshi Narada addressed Vyasadeva:

"O supreme sage! You are omniscient and God incarnate. Intoxicated with the drink of nectar of love streaming from the euphoric joy of being engrossed with the indwelling self, the embodiment of Lord Krishna, you reminisce the cosmic play of God in all its beauties and serenity and put into a form to be called Srimad Bhagavatam. This will be an epithet of divine love – the essence of all Vedas and all scriptures for the liberation of human kind. All yogas, penance, meditation, tapasya and all kinds of worship and yajnas will be worthless without this divine love".

He narrated before him the story of his ordeal and suffering he passed through in his previous births to be ultimately privileged to drink the nectar of divine love which his parched heart was in earnest quest for".

Narada said, O great sage, the whole creation revolves in a cycle through a triad process: creation, sustenance and dissolution. This was the beginning of creation: Narada, Vasistha and Marichi etc were first to come out from the mouth of Lord Brahma. The task of creation was shouldered upon Lord Brahma by God. Lord Brahma desired that his sons would carry on the process by leading a married household life which Narada in his heart of heart was averse to. He was concerned with the ultimate goal of God realisation without being shackled by the fetters of the simmering mundane life full of delusion, illusion and attachment. He was boisterous and joyful in his approach to life and setting the unswerving goal for him to be attended to. Knowing his adamantine approach his father having four faces reciting *Vedas* and meditating on and born from the navel of Lord Vishnu, called for him. Without making any tarry Narada presented himself before his adored father and noticed his father discontent and enraged. With reverence Narada, the first-born child asked the reasons of his being summoned. From the very birth Narada was gifted with divine wisdom. He thought, there was nothing negative in him that would anger his father. It is not unexpected of any father to wish that his son follow his footsteps. The very nature of Narada was to love God and over and above everything that was mundane he was always joyful to have surrendered his life to the love for God. For this reason, the strings of his piano were always resonant with the illuminating glories and elegant majesties of God streaming through his lips in his sweet and melodious voices. But his father wanted him to be an ideal householder which he considered an impediment to his cherished spiritual life.

Sensing his deep-seated distaste for worldly and household life and relentless refusal to tread on the path as directed by his father, Lord Brahma summoned his other sons. A person of God realisation sincerely wishes that all worldly people get liberation following his way. He wants to distribute selflessly the nectar of wisdom among all. He wants to trail the blaze for the worldly people to ride on the crest of divinity. He considers it as his sole duty to dissuade others from walking the worldly way and engage in deed that is sreya for them (sarva bhuta hite ratah). Considering it his primary duty he instructed his brothers not to get involved in mundane life. Worldly life is one of attachment, delusion and error, the fruits of which would become the seeds of numerous births one after another. It would be an endless journey in the worldly life tied tightly in the vicious chain of life after life. It is said in *Mundaka Upanishad* (1:1:4):

> dve vidye veditabye iti ha sma yat
>
> brahmavido badanti para caiva apara ca

One should know two types of knowledge: supreme knowledge (knowledge of Supreme Self or God) and the relative knowledge (knowledge of the worldly life).

Narada said to his brothers, *"is it not wise on their parts to shun the path as shown by their father and bring an end* to this torturous journey birth after birth? What will add beauty and joy to life is the life of love, devotion and wisdom surrendered at the feet of the Almighty Father. The pleasure, merrymaking and amusement in the attachment to the worldly life are perishable and momentary like bubble in the water. Seek what is permanent, imperishable, eternal and ultimate truth ever full of joy and bliss".

Hearing this, his brothers in total disregard of what Lord Brahma advised them to do, walked into the forest to meditate. The unthought-of conduct on the part of Narada annoyed his father. With a tone of chagrin, he said "Narada, you are throwing spanners into the great deeds of the divine plan. Why you are standing in the way of the cosmic plan being worked out? How God's plan to continue creation through me will go on? Do you think the Divine will is subordinate to your will? You did not obey my instructions. On the other hand, you dissuaded your brothers from walking on my path. Instead of joining hands with me in the divine act of procreation you are standing in the way. You are behaving like a fool".

Getting a raw deal from his father, Narada felt humiliated by his spiteful words which hurt his ego. Boastful of his mission to guide the people on the path of divinity, he replied, "I was spreading the message of truth". His father said, "he who tenders advice without being sought for is a fool. Your brothers did not seek advice from you".

In rebuttal of the logic and arguments of his father, Narada replied:

"Father and mother have given birth to their children. They are born out of blood and flesh. But the real birth is that *they should be born of spirit or the supreme self. That is every man's birth right. A guru preceptor gives man his second birth, gives him the knowledge of God, the Supreme Self, liberates him from the bondage of karma and implants in him love, devotion and surrender at the feet of the Lord. Guru preceptor is the true father, mother and guru. I have played that role. You on the other hand, instead of leading them on the path of the Divine, you are putting on them fetters of bondage by engaging them in the act of creation and procreation. You are throwing them into the muddy waters of worldly life for countless births. Like a mother offering candy to the child, you are pandering them to the ephemeral taste of senses. Like a guru preceptor I admonished them not to choose the most tortuous, troublesome, hazardous and delusive path of worldly life which is far away from the path of divinity. A guru preceptor has the ability to liberate humans from the shackles of bondage which the parents do not have. I do not think in that sense I am impolite and I have committed any wrong".*

Lord Brahma, his adorable father taking exception to his stubborn, disobedient and improper attitude lost his temper and wanted to punish him. He cursed him saying, "Narada, because of your arrogant and inflated egoistic behaviour you will be reborn in a family of celestial artists (gandharvas) and fritter away a lot of time in company of women. Your egoistical dislike for women and the life of householder will make you an amorous husband in complete oblivious of your so-called divine knowledge. In due course of time coming in company with devotees of the Lord you regain your status as my son".

It was already too late to understand the folly Narada committed. Humility is the pathway to knowledge. Men of wisdom like a fruit laden tree bends down. In *Bhagavad Gita* it is said by the Lord to Arjuna (13:7):

amanitvam adambhitvam ahimasa ksyantir arjavam

A person of wisdom is free from ego and pride. He is non-violent and forgiving in his attitude.

One has to reap the consequences of one's actions. With a deep sense of contrition, he bowed at the feet of his father for his impropriety, egoism and pride of his knowledge left his body and reborn as a gandharva. He got married to fifty beautiful daughters of Chitrarath, the chief of gandharvas and enjoyed life in sensual pleasures and merry making forgetting his knowledge of the divine, his past and his friends and relatives. In this amorous enjoyment of life, he also became an expert in the profession of gandharvas.

Time rolled on. Once, he was invited to perform a programme in the august presence of all the celestials, sages and Lord Brahma. In the initial play of the divine life of Lord Krishna he did well to the high applause of all. In the next play due to his ego, he committed some silly mistakes to the utter displeasure and wrath of all present. He was on the verge of being cursed again by all. Sensing this beforehand he prayed Lord Vishnu beseechingly for respite from this predicament. If the imploring is sincere, deep and heart rending it will not go unanswered. Lord Vishnu out of mercy, compassion and forgiveness appeared before him and said, "You will reborn in the family of a maid servant. With the blessings and company of some devotees you will be fortunate to behold my vision. After this you will be exonerated forever from excruciating suffering and regain your previous status as the son of Lord Brahma".

The seeds of one's karma are bound to germinate into new trees of life in coming births to bear fruits. This is the mysterious law of karma. As a result of his action Narada was reborn as the son of a very poor maidservant. To sustain livelihood and finding no other way she had to employ herself in the house of a wealthy man of his village. She had to work day and night in the house of that villager. As he was the only child, he had to accompany her to the rich man's house every day. While her mother was engaged in household chores, he was busy playing in the backyard. His mother was not leaving him alone even for a moment. Since he was her only hope, a strong bond of attachment mother developed towards him.

One day, the monsoon arrived with new drops of water to wash out the dirt and simmering heat of the summer and enliven the parched and dried trees and plants with green leaves, flowers and fruits creating new hopes and aspirations in the people. The rains were a metaphorical expression of quenching the thirst of a parched heart of love for his Lord which was latent in Narada as a little boy carried from his past life and in quest for a proper environment to bloom. The monsoon unfolded that opportunity. A group of monks arrived in the village and the rich man implored them with intense love and devotion to stay in his house for these four rainy months to observe chaturmasya brata. He prayed them saying, "O supreme souls, my life today has been gratified by your holy presence. If you are all compassionate to me kindly bless me to stay these four months in my house".

In a traditional monastic life, the monks usually do not prefer to travel from place to place but stay in one place during the rainy season which starts from the full moon day of July and ends in full moon day of November. During their sojourn in one place they meditate, pray and teach the villagers in the evening. It is a rare and auspicious opportunity to the villagers and the host villager to have a good company with sages and saints. The next eight months they travel from place to place not staying one night more in one village with a sense of detachment. The entire locality betrays an ambience of divinity vibrant with discourses on meditation, prayer and scriptural knowledge. By the company of these holy monks the villagers are inspired to lead a spiritually transformed life.

Perceiving the intense and earnest love of the rich man the monks consented to stay in his house for these four rainy months. His mother was assigned the task of serving the monks without any slightest inconvenience to the monks. The seeds of hidden love and devotion in his heart for his Lord got germinated with waters of company with the monks. With awe and curiosity, he started serving the monks day and night leaving aside his childish restlessness. Gradually his inexpressible love and devotion grew for them. With keen enthusiasm and interest, they discovered in him the intense love and devotion for them. Narada would collect flowers and fruits for them in the morning and follow them to the river for bath. He would join them on the worship and prayer. He would waste no opportunity to serve them at any cost. This devoted and dedicated service pleased them highly. Nothing is impossible to achieve with selfless service and humility. These are the quintessential for attaining Godhood. As a boy of five these two qualities were not dearth in Narada. By this he won the heart and love of the monks. The leftover food in the leaves after their eating was his only source of living. With a delighted heart he was relishing this as Prasad of the Lord. He was endowed with the opportunity to listen to the spiritual discourses delivered by them every evening. He was acquainted with listening to the prayer and devotional songs streaming out from their mouths. By their grace he memorised all the prayers and songs in praise of God. Every moment in the parchment of his memory the songs and hymns flitted through in praise and glory of the Lord. By the constant companion with the holy monks and dedicated service with humility and devotion his mind got rested in the thought of Lord Krishna. Nothing other than the Lord did dare to intrude into his mind. There is nothing other than the all-pervading Lord. The world is mere an illusion. The sheaths of attachment to the world vanished one after another. All the past impurities in his mind and heart were cleansed off. The little wind of spiritual awakening and love was transformed into an unmitigated tempest. By partaking of the leftover food and the food served to God his devotion to them developed a luxurious growth.

Constant good and divine company with holy monks creates a fertile field for spiritual harvest. The love, dedication and devotion with which they are served burn one's ego to ashes. By that he wins the heart and love of these holy monks. What pleases the realised souls also pleases God. The love and service for them are ultimately transmuted into love for the Lord. The love for and faith in God remains undeviating. By partaking of the leftover food and the food consecrated to the Lord the mind and heart are sanctified, became pure and unblemished. Food creates the mind. The sattvik food spiritualises the mind and heart. That food is God comes to the realisation of the devoted person. Memories of the Lord remove all worldly ties and attachment from the mind by constantly listening to their prayer, devotional songs and hymns in praise of Him and discourse on divinity. The spiritual awakening in one takes deep root. His heart cries for the union with the Lord.

By intuition and wisdom, the monks perceived in the boy Narada his pure and sanctified heart and stainless mind earnestly yearning for his beloved Lord. Having compassion on him the monks taught him the most secret and mysterious yogic technique of meditating on God and revealed the mantra through his ears. He was advised never to forget the mantra and chant it constantly. He was instructed not to forget the Lord and His presence in all his deeds and thoughts. By removing the sheaths of delusion, illusion and error (Maya) he was advised to behold the all-effulgent Lord in all His beauty and majesty through constant practice of meditation and recitation of mantra every moment. He was taught that by constant practice of meditation and remembrance of the mantra given at initiation the knowledge of the indwelling soul manifests with its illumination. The monks said to Narada "In this state all karmas performed with total surrender to the Lord the bondage to the world will be snapped forever and the raging agony of the gross body, subtle body and causal body will be burnt. It is like the food that causes disease when mixed with other thing acts as the panacea for the disease. In the same sense if karmas are surrendered to the Lord, the disease of worldly delusion will be cured forever. If you drift into the euphoric joy by drinking the nectar of love secreted from your being transfixed in the Lord, you will be able to cross the worldly ocean easily or else you will be slipped away swiftly into the dungeon of worldly delusion itinerating from womb to womb". Narada revealed to Sage Vyasadeva, "it is due to my company with the holy monks for four months it dawned on me that all karmas done with the knowledge and realisation of the indwelling self and surrendered to the Lord with devotion and love (bhakti) will be the funeral of all sorrows born of desires, delusion and attachment to the world". It is revealed in Mahanirvan Tantra:

bahu janmarijitaih punyaih sadguru yadi labhyate

tada tat vaktrato labdhva janma saphalyam apnuyat

"Due to the profound virtuous deeds of a previous life, when one is fortunate to get a qualified guru, one is able to transform life and achieve success through his instructions".

The virtuous deeds of Narada being the son of Lord Brahma for the liberation of his brothers though irked his father but were very much deposited in his divine accounts. The result was he came in contact and company with the holy monks.

The final date of the painful departure of the holy monks after four rainy months ultimately arrived to the indescribable shock of the lad Narada. He felt as if heaven falling to the earth. He was not prepared to see an end to his privileged company with them so soon. He remained for some time speechless. With tears rolling down his face to drop down on their feet very entreatingly he expressed the voice within his heart that he wanted to accompany them. Having treasured the divine wealth of love for God from them he was not ready to part company with them. Very lovingly with a tone of consolation they said, "You are too small to accompany us and go a long way on feet". But to his longing heart for company with them these words were unconvincing as he said, "age is not the criteria to love God". Finding him unmovable from his stance the holy monks through their power of intuition said, "You have some karma and responsibility to your mother since you are the lone child of her. At this stage it will not be wise to leave her alone. The opportune moment will come one day when your cherished desire will sail you to the shore of God realisation from the deep sea of worldly delusion". Assuring thus, they proceeded towards the north. Metaphorically it means, they journeyed to the fontanel, the uppermost part of the head (Sahasrar). Though they departed towards the north, their destined goal the spiritual seed they implanted in him was soon blossomed into a very beautiful divine tree with fruits and flowers of love for God. His life was transformed. He was no longer attached to the world. His mind and heart were always anchored in God. Thought of the Lord was always in his every breath. Neither his mother nor his villagers did understand or measure the depth of his love in his heart for God.

On being asked by sage Vyasadeva about what happened after the holy monks giving him the supreme knowledge left, Narada said, "while my mind was at the feet of the Lord, my mother was engaged in rich man's house for food and our living. Since I was the love of her heart, whatever little she was getting, first she would feed me and if something left over, she would relish very contently".

Narada had never forgotten a moment to meditate, pray and chant as taught by his gurus. Nothing of the world interested him. The sweet name and thought of God consumed all his time. Though he was a child of five years, he was wise enough by the company with holy monks never to forget the intrinsic worth of human life meant for God realisation only. Narada said, "I felt the world is like a wooden lifeless statue in the hands of the Divine. It is like a cog in the vast mechanical structure of His thought. Being with the mother in rich man's house my mind was always roaming mirthfully in the thought of God. All my attention was in the direction of the north towards which my holy monks travelled". It means his attention was always in the fontanel where his gurus and God are staying in union.

A child is very simple, pure, serene and soft in his heart. Pride, anger, ego, vanity, fear, hatred, like or dislike and jealousy have not touched him yet. He is like a lump of clay to be modelled into any shape as the potter wants. The holy monks were like divine potters who shaped Narada into a very beautiful divine being. Many centuries later in *Bible* (Matthew 18:3) Jesus said, if we want to go to heaven, we must become like children. Narada ceaselessly waited for the predicted opportune time to be dawned upon him for his ultimate sojourn with the Divine. The sky surfeit with heavy clouds when bursts out with torrents of rain in great sighs of relief it renders immaculate joy to the mother earth. Similarly, a heart heavy with longing, crying, imploring and prayers for the Lord when bursts out at the sight of the Lord divine solace of relief from the worldly snares overwhelms him with intoxicating joy.

Then Narada said:

"God listened to my deep prayer for Him. While my mother was milking the cow of the rich man, a poisonous snake bit my mother to death. I was reared in the lap of my mother without my father. I was her everything. The last cord of bondage to my mother was torn asunder forever. I remained highly grateful to God for having opened my ways to leave

the world and search for Him. After finishing the funeral rites and rituals I stood up and looked back to the world full of delusion, illusion and error with gratitude to God for having made me free from the shackles of worldly attachment. When the villagers were thinking of the deplorable plight of an orphan boy out of sympathy, my heart was dancing with unbounded joy within at the thought of leaving the world at this moment. Considering the demise of my mother as a blessing of God in store for me I instantly moved towards the north which direction the holy monks travelled in. I took complete refuge in God. Surrendering everything of mine to Him and disrobed of worldly cares and ties I moved on carelessly and freely like a bird flying in high heaven without being haunted by the uncertain future. Keeping in mind the thought of my preceptor and God as my sole treasure-trove I crossed villages, groves, meadows, ridges, mountains, lakes, rivers, streams and dense forests one after another. No obstacle proved insurmountable to me".

Glancing at the surprising and awesome look of sage Vyasadeva I continued:

"The turtous paths I crossed past were wafted through busting open the breast of high mountains and forests. The natural beauty of these deep forests and high range mountains full of trees laden with varieties of flowers and fruits amidst lakes, rivers and springs running across these resembled that of the heavenly abode reserved for devas, celestials, saints and sages. These forests infested with wild and ferocious animals like tigers, elephants, lions, bears, wolves, jackals and serpents failed to deter me from my onward journey towards my destined goal. Thirsty and famished I entered into the sweet and cold water of a river.

Taking a dip in and drinking the water to my content I came out energised and rejuvenated. Beholding this place as one of solitude, tranquility and serenity without any footsteps of human beings, I came under a holy peepal tree and started meditating on the Lord with deep prayer as taught by my Gurus – the holy monks. My meditation grew intensely deeper and deeper with overwhelming love and devotion and I was submerged in the ocean of God consciousness. The sense of body-mind existence and ego got dissolved in my flight into and merge with the infinite Divine. I got the vision of the Divine indescribable in words and incomprehensive to the mind. My heart was filled with enraptured joy. With tears of love streaming down from my eyes and enthralling my whole body and mind I lost my existence in the ocean of divine bliss and joy. I transcended time and space. The vision of the Divine was for a moment. Crestfallen and dejected at not getting a vision of Him again I dived deep into the cave of my heart with more concentration and determination. Everything outside looked enveloped in darkness. Not inside and outside I could be able to get even a glimpse of Him. My heart pained heavily with the agony of the sudden departure of my Lord. A grave voice from the infinite sky I heard: "My child, in this life you will not be able to behold me. Who are not perfected in yoga and are attached to the world and not free from the impurities and fruits of past karmas stored in from previous births are not able to behold Me. It is because of your company with divine beings you are able to get a vision of Me. With unswerving devotion and refuge in Me continue your practice in the company of sages and saints. After end of this life, you will come to Me and remain as My devoted attendant. You will not face any difficulty and nothing untoward will touch you. By My grace you will regain knowledge. With these words of bliss and grace the voice melted away into the Infinite. I bowed down at His feet with deepest gratitude. From that day onwards I know nothing except the Lord. Enthralled always by the beatific magnificence of His nature and majestic glories and enthroning Him in my lotus petalled heart I roamed from place to place singing His infinite names. My God permeated heart and mind became pure and unsullied devoid of the delusive world. The time for my departure arrived. I left the body with the vision of the Lord. With a new divine form, I entered into the body of the Lord sleeping deeply in the milk ocean on the bed of the infinite hooded divine serpent. After thousand- and hundred-years Lord Brahma was born from the naval centre of the Lord to create the universe. I was born from the lap of Lord Brahma and the seven sons Marichi, Pulasthya, Pulaha, Kratu, Atri, Angira and Vasistha were born from His different parts of his body".

Narada continued saying: "With my mind and heart exuberant with love and devotion and transfixed in the Lord and perceiving Him every moment, day and night, everywhere, inside and outside I wander in three worlds (Lokas: bhu, bhuba and sva). Staying with Devas (gods) I dance and sing the glory of the Lord in a very sweet and melodious tone. Seeing me sing and dance in so marvellous voice enraptured in the Divine that touches every being, the gods gave me a violin. In its strings the resonance of my sonorous voices in seven rhythms with harmony and symphony on the glories of the Lord along with dance bewitches everybody into a divine exultation".

Reflections

What is discerned from the story of Narada's life? Though he was destined to be born to a maid servant, he was fully aware of his heredity that he was the son of the Lord Brahma. Heredity plays an important role in shaping the spiritual being of a person. It was lying latent in him. A proper environment is necessary to activate the potential heredity in him. Through his mother he was brought to the earth and very lovingly she nourished him at the cost of her life. She was employed in a spiritually inclined rich man's family to sustain their livelihood. The stay of holy monks in rich man's house for four months created the proper environment for him to be closely associated with them. It was the spiritual company with holy monks that helped the divine bud in him blossom into a very beautiful flower of love to be proffered to his Lord. It is declared in Tantra scriptures:

> satsangena bhavet muktih asatsangena bandhanam
> asatsanga mudranam yat tanmudra parikirtitam

"Good company is the cause of liberation whereas bad company creates bondage. The art of renouncing bad company is known as mudra".

The good company with holy monks untied the fetters put on Narada by the worldly delusion and sparked the divine quest in him to seek earnestly liberation from this mundane life and return to His Lord.

By serving them with dedication and love, listening to their discourses, following their meditation on and worship of the Lord, memorizing certain mantras and verses of the scriptures and eating their leftover food ignited in him the spark of his heredity that his sojourn on this earth was very ephemeral. He realised that he did not belong to the world. He was living in a tent house. Once his tenure was over, he had to leave to His Father's home.

This was many centuries later echoed in the *Holy Bible*. St Peter and St Paul made reference to a tent:

"... if the earthly tent we live in is destroyed, we have a building from God, an eternal house in heaven...." (Corinthians 5:1).

Accepting the holy monks and sages as guru preceptor means to surrender everything and hand over your own self to them. By virtue of this the guru preceptor keeps a watch on your footsteps, activities and thoughts. By watching on him continuously the adorable monks could perceive his spiritual thirst, his devotion and love to them and the Lord and his past life and destiny. By bestowing upon him their grace and blessings they became his guru preceptor and taught techniques of meditation and mantra to be chanted every moment in every breath. Then he strived heard to get knowledge of the Lord in all His beatitude and magnificence who resides in us through meditation, prayer and chanting of the mantra. This is karma. Serving the adorable monks and practicing meditation is karma. Realisation of the indwelling self is knowledge (jnana). Through karma and knowledge, he started offering them and God his indivisible love and devotion every moment and in every breath. Unless karma, knowledge and bhakti are not integrated in unison and felt in one's every breath, perfection will not come to one's life. Karma, jnana and bhakti are causally connected and integrated. Feeling the integration of the three in simultaneity every moment and in every breath opens the doors to liberation.

When one is intensely ebullient with love and devotion to the Lord and Guru Preceptor the Lord's blessings and compassion alight on him. It is said in scriptures when God becomes kind and compassionate to you, He takes away everything of yours, so that you will be His and He will be solely yours. Except the Lord nothing belongs to him. His fountain of kindness was showered upon him when his mother died of snake bite. His last shackle to the world was shattered to pieces and led him free to go in the direction of the holy monks".

It is said in the Mahabharat "mahajana jena gatah sa pantha". That means the seekers should always follow the footprints and path blazed by the seers and realised masters. For this reason, Narada walked the masters' way.

The path to God realisation is always strewn with dangers, difficulties and pitfalls. It is not a straight way. These difficulties and dangers are not obstacles but the crucible to test the intensity of the seeker's quest and depth of his love and the immutability of his determination to attain Godhood. It is pronounced in *Katha Upanishad*:

ksurasya dhara nisita duratyaya; durgam pathas tat kavayo vadanti (I,3 14)

Sharp as the edge of the razor and hard to cross, difficult to tread is that path (so) sages declare.

In the same vein centuries later, Jesus said in the *Holy Bible*:

"Strive to enter in at the strait gate, for narrow is the gate and straitened the way that leads to life, and few be they that find it" (Matthew VII.14).

The royal road to God realisation is the spine which ends in the medulla oblongata (Ajna chakra). The holy monks and Narada went in the direction of the north. It means the north in the body is the top of the head, sahasrar. It is written in *Purusha Sukta* (mantra 1, *Veda*):

> sahasrar purushah sahasrakshya sahasrapat
> sa bhumim visvato abrutva
> atya tista dasangulam

The Purusha (the Supreme Being) has a thousand eyes and a thousand feet. He has enveloped this world from all sides and has transcended it by ten fingers (angulis). He is hiding in this human body, ten fingers above eye brows. The place between eye brows (Ajna chakra) and Sahasrara is the abode of God. The path elongates from muladhara chakra (coccygeal) to the fontanel (sahasrar). This path as walked on by Narada is infested with dangers at various chakras of the spine. In Yoga Shastra the base of the spine is muladhara or coccegeal centre. It is called annamaya kosha (sheath). It is also called wealth centre because all material wealth is of the earth (kshitti element). This is a knot blocking the passage of kundalini power lying latent in the muladhara centre. The mind engrossed in material wealth at this centre is deluded. Narada considered the material wealth as nothing but flippant and temporary. He was not deluded by the temptation and lure of material wealth. He was concerned with paramartha (divine wealth). The next knot is swadhistan chakra (sacral) It is called pranamaya kosha, the life centre, because every human being is born by sex pleasure. It is natural that all human beings run after sensual pleasures. Once the mind is engaged in that centre, the divine energy flowing upward from muladhara is stopped. Man is put in worldly bondage. The lumbar centre (Manipur or navel centre) is called manomaya kosha. Mind is formed in this centre. In every matter and foodstuff there is energy. The life force and soul fire when combined together by techniques of Yoga man feels real energy in his whole body and mind. God as vaisvanara agni (divine fire) digests the food in this centre. It is said in *Upanishads*: annam brahmam vrajanat iti. Food is God. In this centre mind is formed into two parts depending on the nature of food whether it is sattvik, rajasik or tamasik. It is declared in *Amritabindu Upanishad* (mantra 2):

mana eva manusyanam karanam bandha moksayoh
bandhyaya visayasaktam muktam nirvisayam
smrutam

Mind is the cause of bondage and is the cause of liberation. A mind engrossed in the material world is in bondage and a detached mind is in the state of liberation.

The mind can lead a man to hell in the coccygeal and sacral centres where he is after money and sex. The humankind in general is engrossed in amassment of wealth, power and pleasure of senses. They remain captive to the material world forgetting the Divine in the matter also. Born of this being steeped deeply in materialism are anger, passion, attachment, avarice, greediness, enmity, egoism, doubts, diseases, difficulties, worries, woes and sorrows.

Had Narada's mother been alive, he would have been tempted into a married household life. His long-cherished desire to return to the abode of his Lord would have ended in fiasco. God was extremely kind to him by taking his mother away from him permanently.

Narada was taking every day the leftover food from the plate of his guru preceptor – the holy monks as her mother had nothing to offer him. The food he was partaking was sattvik and divine. So, his mind turned God ward not towards the material world.

The heart centre is known as dorsal centre (anahat). It is known as vijnanamaya kosha. Ignorance and knowledge are both coming from the heart centre. Hatred, love, compassion, cruelty, friendship and enmity, ego and humbleness do come from this centre. Both negative and positive attributes coexist here. Love for God and love for material world comes from this centre. This is the most dangerous centre.

The path Narada travelled on was infested with wild animals. It means these aforementioned negative attributes from muladhar (coccygeal) centre to the heart centre (dorsal) are animal propensities. These are as dangerous and ferocious as the wild animals in the jungle. They create obstacles in the path of pursuit of the Lord. These animal attributes are like nooses binding the man to the deluded world. The *Kularnava Tantra* (13:70-71) says:

> lajja ghrna bhayam krodhah/sanka jugupsa ceti pancakam
>
> kulam silam tatha jatih astau pashah parikirtitah
>
> pasabaddho pasurjneyah pasamukto mahesvarah
>
> pasabaddho bhavet jivah pasamukto sadasivah
>
> tasmat pasaharo yastu sa guruh paramo matah

"Shyness, dislike, fear, anger, or doubt, disgust, family, nobility, and gender or castes are the eight nooses. One who is bound with these eight nooses is a fettered being living like an animal, and one who is free from them is Lord Shiva or God".

By the constant practice of meditation under the guidance of realised masters these nooses creating obstacles in the path of God realisation can be untied.

The cervical centre is the Visuddha (neck) centre. If man remains in this centre, he feels extreme detachment in the midst of attachment. The sixth centre is called Ajna chakra (pituitary), the place of sat-chit-ananda. Above this centre is the fontanel (sahasra dala padma). This is also called cortical centre. From Ajna to Sahasrar is called anandamaya kosha. God abides here in the body temple.

Coming under the direct tutelage and guidance of a realised master the practice of meditation following the techniques as taught by Lord Krishna to Arjuna a seeker can realise God. By the constant practice the real divine path known as susumna opens from Muladhara to Sahasrar by pushing the Ida nadi and Pingala nadi aside facilitating the unobstructed passage of the kundalini power from the coccygeal to the Sahasrar. The seeker is fixed in Sahasrar and attains Samadhi stage free forever from the deluded world. This is the stage of jivanmukta.

Through the proper process of breath control and purification of the chakras in the spine one opens the path of sushumna. The subtle breath control flows in this opened passage. Thus, the mind becomes tranquil and still. Then, all the actions of the knower of yoga are like life giving nectar. It brings immortality.

Narada coming in contact with the holy sages remained detached to the material world. Later on, initiated by them into the path of God realisation with certain yogic techniques (kriya yoga) of doing meditation he left the world and later on became God realised and merged with the Lord.

Teaching Bhagavatam to sage Vyasadeva

Narada narrated to him, "Om is the single syllable Brahman - the root of everything - creation, knowledge, dissolution and liberation. This primordial sound manifested from the Lord and was heard by Ananta, the divine serpent who explained it in fourteen syllables to Lord Brahma, my adorable father. He later divulged it in four verses to Nara and Narayan the divine incarnations meditating in the Himalayas. That revelation is known as Bhagavatam in four verses. Both Nara and Narayan meditated on it and explained to me in ten verses".

Very consolingly Narada said, O sage Vyasadeva, "*I divulged before you my past life to show you how love and devotion are quintessential for God realisation. Karma, Jnana and Bhakti are integrated and causally connected. Without love life is imperfect and strive for union with the Lord will not be successful. Love is like the sweetness of the sugarcane and honey. It is that bewitching power of divinity that binds one ultimately forever with the Lord. It behoves you not to feel dejected and bewildered being a person of supreme knowledge. You lack divine love within you. This Bhagavatam is the epitome of divine love. Write and meditate on it for the benefit of humankind. Karma and knowledge interspersed with divine love brings fulfilment to life. Your writings on it will enkindle the spark of love within one's heart for the Lord. Hundred and thousand earnest seekers will be inspired to propel safely to the shore of the Lord by the boat of divine love stuck in the maelstroms of high seas of worldly illusion, delusion and error*".

Devarshi Narada taught sage Vyasadeva Bhagavatam in one hundred verses. All doubts nested in the mind of the sage Vyasadeva vanished with the teachings of Narada. Taking a bath in the holy river Saraswati in the early morning flowing in the forest Badari wherein was situated sage Vyasadeva's ashram, he deeply meditated on the Lord with love and devotion and got the vision of the Lord along with Maya (illusive power). After deeply meditating on what Narada had taught him, he started writing Bhagavatam. It was completed in eighteen thousand verses. Sage Vyasadeva was transformed by the divine magic wand of Bhagavatam taught by Narada.

Srimad Bhagavatam is reflection of a very beautiful blend of karma, jnana and bhakti. If Bhagavatam is compared to a nice tapestry the threads are karma and action but the weaving itself is bhakti. Knowledge and action have been explained in terms of love (bhakti). The divine play and incarnations of the Lord to protect dharma on the earth, the exemplary lives and teachings of devotees, sages and saints have been narrated in heart touching words of love. Srimad Bhagavatam was the last illustrious creation of sage Vyasadeva. Later on, he taught Bhagavatam to his worthy son Shukadeva who remained in mother's womb for sixteen years. When sage Vyasadeva asked him to come out otherwise it would be painful to mother. He replied, "I am not coming out the reason being I do not want to come to the world which is full of illusions. On earnest request he came out at last and started walking straight into the forest. Later on, Shukadeva told Bhagavatam to the king

Parikshita who was cursed by rishi Srungi to die weekend by the bite of the snake Takshyak in the congregation of sages and saints on the bank of the holy river mother Ganges.

The question crops up in the mind what is the need of Bhagavatam to Shukadeva who is always engrossed in God and whom the delusive Maya failed to drag him into its invincible snare. He is a completely detached Yogi always remaining immersed in the ocean of divine bliss and joy. An embodiment of love and roaming in the divine meadows without any sense of body and mind Shukadeva was chosen by his father preceptor to distribute the kernel of love embodied in the Bhagavatam among the devotees and earnest seekers of God for their spiritual advancement.

2

End of the Mahabharat war and birth of Parikshita, the king and devotee

The curtain on the last scene of the epochal Mahabharat war went up to show how prince Duryodhan, the eldest son of Dhritarashtra escaped into the Vyasa Pond to hide himself out of fear with his thigh harshly broken by Bhima. In the next morning he was seen crying aloud wrenched with pain. Asvathama, the only son of Guru Dronacharya spotting him on the shore said, "You did not make me the chief commander of our side, otherwise I would have seated you back on the throne by decimating all Pandavas". Being consoled and inspired by his words Duryodhan made him the chief commander and directed him to kill all Pandavas. Without a second thought Asvathama immediately shot an invincible arrow in the night with recitation of a mantra towards the camp of Pandavas. With a thunderous sound the arrow killed the five sons of Pandavas who were sleeping then. This atrocious and barbarous deed brought tears into the eyes of the grief-stricken mother Draupadi and Pandavas. Her heart busted with inconsolable cries at the grief-stricken loss of her sons. Consoling her Arjun promised to present the beheaded body of

Asvathama very soon. Arjuna said to Draupadi, "it is not a sin to kill a person who has gone astray being a Brahmin and who is an assassin." Riding in his chariot known as Kapidhvaja with his Gandiva bow Arjuna hurriedly went out in search of Asvathama. On seeing Arjuna follow him, Asvathama escaped into the forest in great fear and eerie as there was nobody alive to help him out. The horse carrying him was not able to move even a step ahead out of hunger. Without finding a way out in order to save his life Asvathama shot the 'Brahmasira' weapon at Arjuna without knowing how to withdraw it. Arjuna trembled at the light and heat of the weapon equal to that of the sun and sought refuge in Lord Krishna falling at His feet with the following words of supplication:

"O Krishna Yogeshwar, you are the remover of the fear of those who are insecure. People adore you as the sole and only protector against the simmering fire of the worldly delusion. You bestow upon those few the bliss of liberation who sought ultimate refuge in Thee. You are primordial non-dual and absolute Brahma beyond the knowledge and comprehension of the people. Covered under the veil of bewitching illusion (maya) the worldly people are not able to behold your real nature. Your incarnation is to lessen the burden of sin on the earth. I am completely benumbed with fear and dreaded at the ever-blazing light and heat of the weapon. What shall I do? I am at my tether's end. Without You I have no other way".

Sri Krishna making Arjuna fearless said, "Out of fear Asvathama did a very inhuman deed. Without knowing how to withdraw it he shot it at you. Nobody knows how to withdraw it except you. You know everything. Out of fear you are not conscious of your knowledge. By the use of Brahma weapon, you negate it".

Hearing these words from the Lord, Arjuna without making any tarry shot the Brahma weapon by reciting the mantra learnt from his Guru Drona. These two Brahma weapons shot against each other made the entire world enshrouded by the inflaming fire as if a great havoc was being wreaked upon to burn the earth. People trembled at the ferocious and all enveloping fire advancing towards them. Krishna advised Arjuna to negate it by his weapon. After the negation of the weapon, Arjuna alighted from his chariot and out of compassion caught hold of Asvathama by his hair and with the noose of Varuna, put fetters on his legs and hands as done to a beast and tied him to the post of the chariot. When Arjun was ready to move towards the camp, Sri Krishna intervened saying:

"He is a Brahmin gone astray who feels no compunction in killing the sleeping innocent children. Without delay and thinking anything you kill him. Who kills a drunkard, careless without sense and a mad, children, girl, people in sleep, refugee, a warrior without chariot, and people fearful of war, is considered dead even before he dies. The wise says in the Vedas it is virtuous to kill a person who takes pride and satisfies revengeful ego in taking away the lives of others. You have promised before Draupadi to behead Asvathama and surrender his head at her feet. I have heard this. Reneging on your words you out of compassion saved his life. Without delay take away the life of the sinner

Asvathama. Groomed from his childhood under the panoply of Duryodhan's compassion and protection in the palace he enjoyed all royal privileges and amenities of a very luxurious living along with other princes. But in the end, he perpetrated a heinous deed which even would not please Duryodhana. Being an accomplice in the sinful deed of decimating the Kaurava dynasty from its root, he deserves not to be saved but to be killed".

Advising Arjun from various perspectives, Sri Krishna put him in a dilemma of what to do. Without listening further, Arjuna showing compassion on Asvathama being the son of his own Guru went back to the camp in the battle field and surrendered him before Draupadi with these words "I put before you your enemy for disposition". Looking to the pale and gloomy face of the derided Asvathama, Draupadi became compassionate and soft hearted. Being the son of Guru Drona, she paid homage to him within. With folded hands she entreated Arjuna to untie Asvathama from the shackles with these words in great solemnity, *"Guru Drona, a Brahmin taught you the secrets of all the art and techniques of warfare through various weapons with the power to shoot and withdraw the arrow, even the knowledge of countering and negating a Brahma weapon. He is his son, born of his soul. His mother Goutami is virtuous and embodiment of chastity, austerity and sacredness and religiously loyal to her husband. She did not consecrate herself in the funeral pyre of her husband as she had the only son Asvathama alive with her. "O Arjuna, you are divine and conscientious. He does not deserve to be punished. As I am bereaved and grief stricken at the loss of my sons, let her mother not suffer from the same agony of losing her only son. If out of ignorance and anger a kshyatriya kills a Brahmin, the fire of that anger and revenge will burn to ashes the entire clan".*

Listening thus to the words of wisdom, rightful and conscientious judgment, all assembled there including King Yudhishthira who looked elated, and his brothers, Satyaki, sons of Devaki, and mother Kunti and other women remained silent though they appreciated the truth within. In a fury with red eyes Bhima looked at Asvathama and in inconsolable and plaintive words opined to kill him at once. If he was not beheaded how he would be exonerated from sins he incurred by killing innocent and sleeping sons, asked Bhima?

Hearing from all Lord Sri Krishna said:

"I have already told that to kill a Brahmin is forbidden by scriptures. But to kill an assassin is permitted in scriptures. He is worth being killed". O Arjuna, Sri Krishnan said, you have promised to Draupadi to submit the slain head of the culprit for attenuation of her grief who has killed our five sons. Then, you do one thing. You withdraw the mysterious and illuminating gem within his forehead by weapon and make him dead like. Let him live a dead life immortally with humiliation divested of the illuminating gem. This will extinguish the simmering sorrows of the bereaved heart of Draupadi and satisfy Bhima".

In great appreciation of and obeisance to Lord Krishna Arjuna caught hold of Asvathama by his hair and removed the brilliant gem from inside his forehead by his sharp sword. With the removal of this divine gem Asvathama looked dark and pale without any glaze in his visage. With his head tonsured and punished to live like a dead forever he was removed from the country.

All the Pandavas, Kunti, Draupadi, Gandhari, Dhritarashtra and others mourning inextinguishably in grief and sorrows accompanied by Lord Krishna, sage Vyasadeva and many other sages and saints assembled at the bank of the holy river to offer consecration of rice and water to the deceased and slain sons. To assuage their sorrows Lord Krishna told them about the ephemeral world full of illusion, delusion, ignorance and error. Attachment to the world is like running after transient mirages. All are the toys in the hands of God. Taking refuge in the Almighty Father, to cross the worldly ocean will not be insurmountable. Speaking thus, Lord Krishna assuaged them wiping out their sorrows. The prince Duryodhana in company with the bad and wicked friends by machination, falsehood and unfair and foul play of dice deprived Yudhishthira, the eldest son of king Pandu of his rightful claim to the throne in Hastinapur.

With decimation of the Kauravas in the Mahabharat war Yudhishthira was enthroned as the king of Hastinapur likened to that of Indra, the king of devas by Lord Krishna. The name and fame of king Yudhishthira wafted to all parts of the country with performance of three Asvamedha Yajna at the behest of Lord Krishna. The five Pandavas in company with Uddhava, Satvaki, sage Vyasa and other sages and saints worshipped Lord Krishna seeking His blessings with all love and devotion. With completion of His mission Lord Krishna was getting ready to leave for Dwaraka.

Uttara, the wife of the deceased Abhimanyu did not consecrate herself into the funeral pyre of her husband being pregnant. Asvathama humiliated and disarmed of the divine gem hidden inside his forehead was in great fury of anger. Without brooking a moment with water of the holy Ganges in his palm he uttered the mantra and shot the Brahma weapon directing it to destroy the Pandavas. With the inflaming light like that of the all illuminating sun the weapon encompassed the entire earth and proceeded towards Uttara and Pandavas. Trembled with fear at the imminent holocaust the Brahman weapon was proceeding to wreck upon, she ran out with her both hands raised above with supplication to Lord Krishna for ultimate respite. With handful of tears gathered from her weeping eyes she prayed:

"You are the supreme Deva and Lord of the universe (Jagannath). You are incarnated to destroy the demonic and save the righteous. You are the Lord of those who seek refuge in you. I do not know anybody other than you. You are the fearless to those who fear and remover of all dangers. This deadly weapon is fast running to destroy the Pandavas from its root. I take refuge in you for saving the last Pandav in my womb. Let my life be sacrificed for the protection of the womb".

A prayer with complete surrender and devotion never goes unheard by Lord Krishna. He knew immediately the barbarous deed of Asvathama. Without any tarry

He directed His Sudarshan Chakra (disc) to go and save the Pandavas. The Chakra immediately went and enwrapped the five Pandavas with a wall of darkness which the Brahma weapon could not penetrate, and rushed back to the hand of Lord Krishna. With the Chakra Lord Krishna entered into the womb. With the all-effulgent light of His Chakra, He negated the Brahma weapon and saved the womb. God himself is the creator, sustainer and destroyer. Who can understand His Maya when He Himself does not know His own Maya? To save the Pandavas and the womb of Uttara is not at all surprising. To do what is not possible is surprising, but before God what is impossible? Everything is mere a part of His play. God Himself is the most surprising of all. Whom God will save what harm the other can do? Kunti with Draupadi and Uttara keeping her five sons in the front prostrated themselves at the feet of Lord Krishna. Kunti with folded hands full of gratitude and love and in a sobbing tone prayed Him:

"O Lord we are always at your lotus feet. You are the primordial and the most ancient Purusha and Lord of the universe. You are above the Prakriti beyond the knowledge of the mundane people. You reside inside and outside of the beings. But for You there is nothing. You are alone the ultimate reality and truth. You have created Maya that remains like a veil between You and the rest of the creation. You are the sole doer and actor. You are imperishable, immortal and the embodied self in every being and remain detached. How can one know Thee unless the veil of delusion, illusion and ignorance is penetrated? The people deeply embedded in the delusive world cannot be able to

know Your true nature. Like a director enacting a drama with many actors to play different imaginary roles for the entertainment and amusement of the audience on themes highly fictitious and concocted, you have created the universe giving different roles to human beings to play on themes full of illusion and delusion. But in reality, these are not true. But people out of ignorance and delusion, develop deep attachment to the conjectured play and forget the ultimate truth and reality. In this incarnation being born to Vasudeva you are adored as Vasudeva. As a young child and boy, you spent your infancy days with Gopis in the family of king Nanda in Gopapur. You saved Gopapur, its people, wealth and cows under the hill Gobardhan by keeping it up by your left-hand smallest finger like a panoply against the calamitous thunder, lightning and torrential rains of infuriated Indra, the king of devas. For this people adore you as Govinda. By annihilating the demon Kansa, you released your mother Devaki and father Vasudeva from the prison. When I was with my sons in great adversities and roaming in deep forests you saved us and treated me like Devaki. It is you who saved Bhima from poison mixed with sweet and saved my five sons and me from the fire of jatu griha (wax smeared with animal tallows which immediately catches fire) building in Varunabanta. You saved us from the crocodile demon in the water and also from many demons like Hidimba. When Draupadi was forced to be disrobed in the court of Dhritarashtra by Duryodhana led Kauravas after Pandavas lost the game of dice, you came to her rescue. You are always with us in our sorrows and difficulties. It is because of you we came out victorious in the Mahabharat war and in overcoming the insurmountable difficulties."

Adversities and sorrows are not the negative aspects of human life. These are not the signs of being ill fated. Rather, they are like treasure-trove that helps one to be in close association with the Lord. It is these that not estrange you from God, it brings one closer to the Divine. In adversities and difficulties man remains always in God consciousness. That's why it is yoga that unites one with God. It is in the muddy waters of sorrows the lotus of divinity blossoms with its full grandeur and beauty. Instead of blaming the providence for all the difficulties the Pandeva's were put into, they found in these a rare opportunity to be with Lord Krishna. In *Bhagavad Gita* (7:16) Lord Krishna said to Arjuna:

caturvidha bhajante mam janah sukrtino 'rjuna

arto jinjasur artharthi jnani ca bharatarsabha

O Arjuna! O Bharatarshabha (Lord of the Bharatas)! There are four types of devotees who are noble in deed and who meditate upon Me: the man in distress, the seeker of knowledge, the person with desire for material possession, and the man of knowledge and wisdom.

Out of these four noble persons one in deep distress seeks refuge in God. Pandavas thrown into excruciating distress very earnestly sought God and remained with Him. Instead of being bewildered and crestfallen by distress and adversities the Pandavas remained steadfast, calm and quiet in their loyalty and devotion to Lord Krishna. While singing praises of Lord Krishna as a sign of her undeviating gratitude, Kunti prayed O Krishna!

"Since I am seeing you in every moment of our distress, let this distress be every aspect and goal of my life. By getting the sight of yours I will get a place in the Supreme Abode. People steeped in inflated egoism for their high birth, elite life, erudition and abundance of wealth will not get you. You are the seed and life force of the entire creation; you are the treasure-trove of the earnest seekers, the poor and the humble. You are far away from those who are very poor in their love and seeking for you. You are without beginning and end. You are immortal and imperishable. For the emancipation of human beings, you have taken birth on this earth. You have no distinction between foe and friend. You are abiding in all animate and inanimate, living and non-living. Where you are not? You are timeless spirit (Mahakala). You are the abode of peace for my sons. They know none but you. Like senses becoming impotent without You I am nothing without You. Born to your Brishni dynasty I have attachment to this and to the world. I pray you to earnestly to sever the last cord of my attachment to this mundane life and world. Let me be established in You and at Your feet forever like eternal flow of water in the holy Ganges River. As rivers rest in the ocean, let me rest in You".

Hearing the love-soaked words of entreaties from Kunti as a testament to her heart felt gratitude for saving the life of Pandavas, Lord Krishna with a divine smile said, "I will do what you earnestly seek for". Visiting everybody in Hastinapur palace Lord Krishna assuaged them all with peace, joy and happiness.

Reflections

The epochal Mahabharat war was not only a description of the battle that took place outside between Pandavas and Kauravas but is a description of the battle that takes place within each human life every moment. Pandavas, the embodiment of divine attributes representing five elements (five tattwas) khiti (earth), apa (water), teja (fire), marut (air) and vyoma (space) stand for purity, honesty, love, simplicity, truth and humbleness. The Kauravas, on the other represent the demonic propensities like anger, pride, ego, jealousy, envy, hypocrisy and slander. These two opposite propensities – divine and demonic are more or less present in every one of us. In order to accelerate human evolution and transformation of human life from animality to rationality and thence to divinity, each person needs to subdue and overcome the demonic Kaurava propensities by the forces of divine Pandava propensities under the direct tutelage of God realised masters always pointing to the Lord as the sole purpose of life like a navigation compass directing to the north. This struggle or battle is taking place both outside and inside. The battle inside is more complex taking place constantly till man joins the Lord. If we will be sincere, staunch follower, dedicated and devoted, humble and constant practitioner of Yoga and meditation with unflinching love like Arjuna to the Lord Krishna, victory will be ours.

The evil propensities represented by Kauravas have beguiled human beings into the invincible snares of delusion, illusion and error. Each human being tries to win the battle with weapons of jealousy, anger, passion, desire, avarice, envy, ego and slander in complete forgetfulness of the Divine. This brings them into inescapable bondage and cycle of birth and death. On the other, the Pandavas represent the knowledge side and the five gross elements. They were constantly after the Lord Krishna for liberation. The few sadhakas and seekers who are earnestly seeking God as their ultimate goal of life are metaphorical representation of the Pandavas. Though they were five in different forms, they were feeling and living like one with one mind and one soul. These five gross elements need to be merged in the infinitude for God realisation. These five gross elements known as Prakriti are not in reality different, they are one. These five elements are in five chakras situated inside the spine of human beings.

The Muladhara chakra (coccygeal centre) represents earth, the Svadhisthan (sacral centre) the water, the Manipur chakra (lumbar centre) fire, the Anahat chakra (dorsal centre) air and the Visuddha chakra (cervical centre) represents the space. They are to be merged in the soul. It is said in *Taittiriya Upanishad* (2:1.1):

> tasmad va etasmad atman akasas sambhutah,
> akasad vayuh, vayur agnih, agner apah, adbhyah
> prithivi, prithivya osadhayah osodhibhyo annam,
> annata purushah

From this Self, verily arose ether, from ether air, from air fire, from the fire water, from water earth, and so on.

In other words, creation starts from the principle of universal consciousness (Brahman). From it first arises space and the primary matter or ether whose quality is sound. From this etheric state successively arise grosser elements of air, fire, water and earth.

A spiritual seeker should raise consciousness from the Muladhara chakra to the soul centre (Ajna chakra) and ultimately to Sahasrara chakra which is beyond any tattwa and is referred to as tattvatita. In Shiva Samhita (1:78) it is said:

> prithvi shirna jale magna jalam magna ca tejasi
> linam vayum tatha tejo vyomni vato layam yayau
> avidyayam mahakasho liyate parame pade

"When the earth dissolves in water, water merges in fire, fire merges into air, and air disappears in space, one transcends ignorance and gets merged at the feet of the Supreme".

This is like rising up and swimming against the current of the water as the deluded people (Kauravas) are generally swept away into the sway of time (kala). Instead of descending from the top (Sahasrara chakra, crown of the head) to the bottom, one (Pandavas) who is aspiring for God realisation has to climb up from bottom to the top.

What is the meaning of Draupadi whom five Pandavas married? How is that? In the words of our beloved Gurudev Paramahamsa Hariharananda, Draupadi symbolises shakti (power). This life force is in five gross elements. Shakti is the life that sprouts from five gross elements symbolised by the five brothers. This is the union between shakti and five gross elements which symbolically represents that five Pandava brothers got married with Draupadi.

In the *Bhagavad Gita* Lord Krishna said to Arjuna:

bhumir apo nalo vayuh kham mano buddhir eva ca

ahamkara iti 'yam me bhinna prakritir astadha (7:4)

"Earth, water, fire, air, ether, mind, intellect, and ego are the eightfold divisions of My nature".

God is all pervading. The entire creation is His manifestation. Hence God and universe are one. Everything manifested in the universe is mother nature or Prakriti. The body is also the manifestation of mother nature. Every human body is a little universe, a microcosm. It is said, what is in the universe is also in the human body. Whatever man does outside or inside his body and thinks is the play of the indwelling self. Whatever is seen or perceived in the universe, in mother nature or even the body nature all belong to the eightfold principles.

Apart from these five gross elements in the five lower centres there are three elements present in the Ajna chakra (pituitary): mana (mind), buddhi (intellect) and ahamkara (ego). In the Yogic scriptures it is mentioned that mind is associated with moon, the intellect with sun and the ego with darkness. During meditation following the path of Yoga as taught by the Guru Preceptor when attention is fixed in the ajna chakra, one perceives the light of moon, the light of sun and the darkness.

In the next verse Lord Krishna continued:

apare 'yam itas tv anyam prakritim viddhi me param

jivabhutam mahabaho yaye 'dam dharyate jagat (7:5)

"O Mahabahu (mighty armed Arjuna) this is My lower material nature. Apart from this, I have My higher spiritual nature, which is the soul, by which the whole universe is sustained."

Mighty armed means strong arms and hands with immeasurable strength. Arms and hands are the organs of action and dominated by the air element. Who has through control over breath or mastered the art of controlling breath through the practice of Yoga and meditation, can be said as mighty armed one. Arjuna metaphorically represents that power.

As interpreted by our Sri Gurudeva, the Lord explains para and apara are the two aspects of nature. Para is the spiritual element and apara is the lower and material element. Apara prakriti or material nature is extrovert, restless and kinetic. Para is introvert, silent and static. The material nature is the cause of all extrovert activities and also of bondage, while the para nature is the cause of liberation. The Kauravas represent the material nature and the Pandavas the para nature.

This jagat or material universe is nothing but the five centres, the five gross elements and mind, intellect and ego. Jagat means, gamayet gachhate iti, that which is constantly changing. That means, what is found at this moment is not found the next moment or tomorrow. It is in a state of constant ebb and flow.

But this material universe is sustained by the para prakriti (spiritual nature).

In the yogic scriptures it is said: pranena dharyate lokah sarvam pranayama jagat. The prana, the vital breath sustains the universe and is the manifestation of the whole universe. Every human body can be divided into two parts. From the ajna chakra down, the eightfold nature predominates, namely apara prakriti. From the ajna chakra to the fontanel is para prakriti or the spiritual nature. Apara prakriti, material nature, is maya: delusion, illusion, and error. Para prakriti, spiritual nature is disillusion. Each gross breath goes into the body and merges with vital breath, prana which goes into the lungs. On the other, the causal or finest breath merges with the inner vital breath. This is called sthira prana, tranquil vital breath. The material nature is the cause of restlessness, bondage and attachment represented by Kauravas. In the material nature the breath is restless. The spiritual nature represented by Pandavas is the cause of liberation and realisation. In the spiritual nature the breath is tranquil and even ceases when one attains samadhi. It is breathlessness stage.

The union between para prakriti and apara prakriti is creation. It is pronounced in *Srimad Bhagavad Gita*:

etadyonini bhutani
sarvani 'ty upadharaya (7:6)

"Know clearly that all living beings are born from the union between these two natures."

That means, the union between para prakriti, spiritual nature and the apara prakriti, the material nature is yoni, the place of origin. Many things are born in the external universe, including the human body; many thoughts are born in the mind every moment. Different perceptions are generated in the sense organs. Sight of different things and persons is born in the eyes, sound and hearing of many things bad and good is born in the ears, smell of good fragrance and bad odor is born in the nose, taste of all kinds of things is born in the mouth, speech is born in the tongue, sex sensations are born in the sex organs and touch sensation is born in the skin. Every part of the body is like a yoni or womb from which innumerable thoughts, perceptions and feelings spring. The breath is the spiritual nature. The joining of the two natures body and breath is the place of creation. Without the breath body is dead and no creation is possible. The spiritual source or nature breath or spiritus is masculine and the body is feminine. Creation requires the union between the feminine and the masculine. It is declared in *Katha Upanishad*:

yad idam kin ca jagat sarvam prana ejati nihsrtam (II.3.2)

"The whole world, whatever exists, springs from and moves in breath."

God is the source of all creation. He is the seed. He breathes His own breath of life into the nostrils of human beings. If God does not take breath entire creation is dissolved and no creation is possible.

Without the breath the material gross body and mental body – the six centres from Muladhara to Ajna cannot be activated. Nature is the field and God is the seed of all creation. Lord Krishna said to Arjuna: "bijam mam sarvabhutanam" (*Bhagavad Gita*, 7:10). I am the eternal seed of all beings.

In perception of this Pandavas were always with Lord Krishna. That means, they were well established in Him through each and every breath in all thoughts and actions. The shakti (Draupadi) is immanent in Pandavas, all creation, thoughts, actions and deeds.

Each human being has embodied both negative and positive qualities. Both the Kauravas and Pandavas are allegorically held as representing two kinds of trees having different types of fruits. In the Adi Parva (1:110-111) of the Mahabharat it is described:

> duryodhano manyumayo mahadrumah
> skandhah karnah sakunih tasya sakhah
> duhsasanah puspaphale samrddhe
> mulam raja dhritarashtrah amanist

"Duryodhana is a huge tree (manyu) of anger, distress, and meanness. Karna is its trunk, Shakuni the branches. This tree is loaded with flowers and fruits like Dushasana. The root is King Dhritarashtra who considered himself a wise person."

> yudhishthiro dharmamayo mahadrumah
> skandhah arjunah bhimaseno asya sakhah
> madrisutau puspaphale samrddhe
> mulam krsnah brahma ca brahmanasca

"Yudhishthira is a huge tree of (dharma) values, virtues, and righteousness. Arjuna is its trunk; Bhima is its branches. The tree is loaded with flowers and fruits like Nakula and Sahadeva. Its root is Lord Krishna who is none but Brahman and representing brahmins".

The Mahabharat war is a constant battle between two forces – demonic and divine forces within a human being. Lord Krishna residing in Ajna chakra is the compassionate and detached conductor of these two forces.

Lost in the dice game to the Kauravas who played tricks under the direction of Shakuni, the Pandavas along with Draupadi as per the terms and conditions of the game went into exile in forests for twelve years and one more year exile incognito. After successful completion of the exile, the Pandavas returned to Indraprastha. Those who are virtuous, noble, righteous and divine always want peace, stillness of mind and tranquility for God realisation amidst suffering, travails and difficulties. The crooked and demonic people are always restless and unsteady and turbulent in their mind because of their inflated egoism, anger, jealousy, passion and avarice.

In order to avoid the inevitability of war the Pandavas wanted sincerely peace. After much consultation it was decided that Lord Krishna would go as a mediator to resolve the conflict between the Kauravas and Pandavas through talk and dialogue. At least, history would not blame the Pandavas that they had not tried the last efforts for peace. In the assemblage of all, the king Dhritrashtra, Kauravas led by Duryodhana, Karna, and Shakuni, and others like Bhisma, Kripa, Vidura, Dronacharya and sages and saints like Narada, Parashurama, Lord Krishna narrated very beautifully the imperatives for peace and truce to the greatest joy and happiness of all except to Duryodhan, his brothers and advisors Shakuni and Karna. Devarshi Narada, Parashurama, Vidura, Bhisma, Dronacharya and king Dritarashtra all tried to convince Duryodhan but to no avail. The revelation of His cosmic form by Lord Krishna did not bring any change in the adamantine attitude of Duryodhana. Warning him about the inevitability of the decimation of Kauravas if they did not follow the path of good and virtues, Krishna asked him to give at least five villages to Pandavas that would usher in permanently peace between the two sides and the Pandavas and Kauravas living together in peace would be the invincible force in the world in all their glories, valour and majesties. All elders present there advised him to accept what Lord Krishna proposed. Taking this approach as sign of weakness of Pandavas, Duryodhan point blank rebuffed the proposal with a great pride in his own superior strength. Quite ignorant of Krishna as the Lord of the entire universe and the sole doer of everything inside and outside, he made a boastful declaration:

> yavat hi sucyah tiksnaya viddhyet agrena marisa
> tavadapya parityajyam bhumernah pandavan prati
> (Mahabharata, Udyoga Parva 58:18).

"O venerable one, I will not surrender to the Pandavas even that much land, which may be covered by the sharp point of a needle."

Prey to egotism, proud and arrogance, brute force, indulgence in lust and anger, self-conceited and deluded people like Duryodhan discard God totally forgetting that He dwells in them as well as in others. They think that they are their masters. In the *Shwetashwetara Upanishad* (6:11), it is said:

eko devas sarva – bhutesu gudhah sarva-vyapi sarva bhutantar-atma karmadhyaksah sarva-bhutadhivasah saksi ceta kevola nirgunas ca

"One God hides in all beings, all pervading, the inner self of all beings, the ordainer of all deeds, who dwells in all beings as the witness, the knower, the only one, devoid of qualities".

Similarly, the *Bhagavad Gita* (10:20) states, "I am the soul present in all living beings. I am in the beginning, in the middle, and in the end."

Intoxicated with stubbornness, arrogance and egoism such people think that they are the doer, sole giver and nobody on this earth matches their wealth, possession, honour and position and power. Thinking this way, Duryodhan vehemently declared, I will not even give land equal to the sharp point of the needle what to speak of five villages.

When man's attention remains engrossed in centres descending from the Ajna chakra to Muladhara he is drowned in delusion, illusion and error. He forgets God as the sole doer. He is not able to fix his attention in the atom point (bindu) of the Sahasrar. Mind wavers towards egoism, food, sex, wealth, passion and attachment. This is the meaning of Duryodhana denying to give Pandavas land equal to the needle point. The sadhakas and earnest seekers like Pandavas always try to stay above Ajna chakra and remain fixed in Sahasrar. The atom point is smaller than the needle point. It is the door to the abode of God. It is subtler than the subtle (anor aniyamsam). In *Katha Upanishad* it is stated:

anor aniyan mahato mahiyan, atmasya jantor nihito guhayam (I.2. 20)

Smaller than the small and greater than the great the self is residing in every creature. He is held as of the size of a thumb residing in human body ("angustha matrah puruso", Katha *Upanishad* I.1, 12).

Undeviating attention constantly on the atom point of the Sahasrara in all actions, deeds and thoughts enabling the seeker to enter into the stage of *samadhi* will be the death of all demonic attributes and the worldly delusion, illusion and error. Unless one is permanently established in the Sahasrara, the demonic propensities symbolically represented by Duryodhan will dominate and deflect one's concentration away from the Sahasrara. It is the demonic forces that deny one the atom point, which is like the sharp point of the needle.

On the last day of the Mahabharat war, Duryodhan was lying very painfully on the ground to breath his last being wrecked with a deadly blow on his thigh by Bhima with his mace. The thigh was the weakest part of Duryodhana. Before the war his mother Gandhari said to Duryodhana "you come naked to me in the night and if I will stare at you by removing the cover from my eyes your body will be impregnable no weapon will be able to penetrate your body. It will be an invincible shield against all kinds of threats from weapons." Accordingly, while Duryodhana was moving towards her mother completely disrobed, Lord Krishna seeing him thus, laughed at him and advised Duryodhana to cover the part of the thigh before approaching the mother. His entire body was made invulnerable by the gaze of his mother except the thigh which Duryodhana covered. That was the Achilles heel of Duryodhana which was hit hard by Bhima for the death of the former. Duryodhana stands for desire, passion or kama: insatiable desire for material things or sex. Bhima, the son of Vayu devata is situated in the heart centre (Anahat). If by the practice of kriya yoga one withdraws one's mind from the lower centres to the Sahasrara his passion and desire will be transformed into divinity.

By the practice of this, emotions, desires and ego are completely destroyed. By withdrawing the senses into the soul, all material ambitions will be burned to ashes. In *Bhagavad Gita* (4:37) it is said:

<blockquote>
yatha 'dhamsi samiddho 'gnir
bhasmasat kurute arjuna
jnanagnih sarvakarmani bhasmasat kurute tatha
</blockquote>

O Arjuna, "Like fire burning wood into ashes, the knowledge of the inner soul burns all actions".

Thus, killing of Duryodhana means decimation of all ambitions, desires, passion and kama through the practice of special technique of breath control as taught in Kriya Yoga.

The actions of various body parts are connected with the five gross elements. Feet is connected with space. It is because of space the feet enable one to move ahead or backward. Feet are the end part of the leg which begins from the base of the thigh. At the base of the thigh are situated the Muladhara and Swadhistan - two lower centres. If mind remains fixed in these two centres, man always moves after wealth, name and fame and sexual desires. These carnal desires deflect man from seeking God. Instead of moving upward for God realisation man moves down for these demonic desires which Duryodhana was craving for. It is stated in Devi Kavacam of Sri Durga Saptasati:

> katyam bhagavati rakset januni vindhyavasini
> janghe mahabala rakset sarvakamapradayini

Let Bhagavati protect the waist; Vindhyavasini, the knees; Mahabala, who fulfils all desires, the thighs (31).

All carnal and animal desires are created in the thighs which means in the Muladhara and Svadhisthan centres. The seeker prays Mother Durga for transforming these base desires into noble and divine desires. By Her grace the seeker's noble desire for divinity is fulfilled. It means the killing of Duryodhana by Bhimasena hitting his thighs. Bhimasena represents breath. Unless one attains breathlessness (samadhi) stage through the practice of breath control he/she cannot be able to free himself/herself from being fallen prey to the carnal desires.

Wreaking a hard blow on his thigh to death with the mace by Bhima means complete control over these desires and moving upward to the space beyond the Sahasrara. If the seeker of God roams in the space, he/she will be able to hear divine sound constantly.

Dronacharya was an excellent teacher, the guru of both the Pandavas and Kauravas. Before the beginning of the Mahabharat war he knew very much that if Lord Krishna and Arjuna stayed together no power in the world was able to vanquish them. Initially, he expressed his desire to show allegiance to the Pandavas. Knowing this Duryodhan became extremely unhappy and said to him, "my father has brought up your family with food, money, comfort and shelter by appointing you as our teacher. Instead of showing gratitude to us you are determined to be on the side of the Pandavas". On hearing this Dronacharya immediately changed his mind and remained on the side of the Kauravas. This was the propensities of Dronacharya to be fickle after knowing the truth that victory would be to the Pandavas.

As explained by Paramahamsa Hariharananda, people are having the vacillating tendencies of

Dronacharya. They know very much what Truth is and they are able to distinguish between truth and falsehood like Dronacharya but due to fickleness of mind they do the opposite. They do not seek God or walk on the path of self-realisation. The word 'Dronacharya' comes from the root *druban* which means to roll on like water from one side to another on a lotus leaf according to the wind. Metaphorically speaking, it means vacillating and wavering temperament. Knowing the truth that God or the indwelling soul is the sole doer and realisation of the self is the goal of human life, people of this fickleness temperament do the opposite and remain away from the path of self-realisation.

Ashwatthama being the only son of Dronacharya also stands for fickleness and vacillation of mind. He had many plans up his sleeve to kill the Pandavas but he did not stick to one and wavered from one to another without being successful. Similarly, human beings have endless desires. One after another takes birth in him without giving any satisfaction. Desires are the arch hurdles in the path of God realisation. They prevent man from perceiving the Ultimate Reality.

In another interpretation, Paramahamsa Prajnanananda explained, the word ashvatthama is composed of four syllables: a means not, shva means until "tomorrow", ttha means to exit or to remain and ma means not. Two negatives in the beginning and in the end makes it positive. Thus, it means that which will remain until tomorrow. Glory, fame and name will remain until tomorrow. In that sense it is immortal. For this reason, Ashvatthama was immortal. It is the belief till today that he is still alive. It means in all people the negative attributes represented by him are always alive until decimated by proper sadhana. He was always relishing self-eulogization. He was always wishing to bash in self-glory. In the Mahabharat war he was always boasting of his own valour and strength. Good deeds, fame, name and glory of few are always venerably emulated and remembered by people. Being dead they remain always alive in the memory of the people for their good and adorable deeds. For the bad deeds of revenge Ashvatthama is disdainfully denounced and remembered for ever. In *Gita* Dhyana it is pronounced:

> ashvatthama bikarna ghora makara
> duryodhanavarttini

Here Asvatthama is considered as a dreaded crocodile ever ready to devour whoever comes within its grasp. When a crocodile devours a living being tears rolls down giving the impression that it is repenting for its cruel deeds. It is not actually that. Tears in its eyes symbolise enjoyment not repentance. Asvatthama as discussed earlier was presented before Draupadi for punishment for killing the five sons of Pandavas. Out of compassion and deep respect for the son of Guru Dronacharya he was left unpunished with only the dazzling gem hidden in his forehead removed. Instead of being repentant his anger and revenge increased and he attempted to kill five Pandavas and the son of Uttara in the womb by his Brahma weapon but failed by the grace of Lord Krishna. If one is completely established in the Lord all negative attributes like that of Asvatthama will be overcome.

Some people are also remembered disdainfully for their misdeeds like that of Kansa and Ravana. Ashvatthama is remembered for his cowardly deed. In the negative sense he is immortal for his moral turpitude, bad reputation and vain glory. Those who have negative qualities like that of the Kauravas want to glorify themselves and sing their own glory. This is the manifestation of one's egoism and pride. This is why Ashvatthama joined the side of the Kauravas. Spiritual people and seekers of God are averse to self-glorification. They are known for their exemplary humbleness and simplicity.

On the last day of the Mahabharat war when Duryodhan was even on his last breath, he evinced the last desire to kill the Pandavas being assured by Ashvatthama and accordingly, he was anointed as commander in chief by Duryodhana. Unless man is completely anchored in the Divine, his desires will continue to stand in his way to self-realisation. Until the seeker reaches the last summit of God realisation, i.e., *nirvikalpa samadhi* he is likely to fall down by a single desire. Falling down is easier and speedier than climbing up. The death of Duryodhana means having mastery over the senses leading to self-control.

Ashvatthama was so hell bent to annihilate the Pandavas that he forgot all righteousness and nuances observed during the course of the war. In the night when war was forbidden, he killed the five sons of the Pandavas while they were asleep thinking that they were Pandavas who were with Lord Krishna at that time. To kill Pandavas means the demonic qualities like self-glory, egoism, self-conceit and endless desires represented by Ashvatthama are unlidded that put hurdles in the path of God realisation. Once, the seekers like Pandavas are fully established in the Lord, these evil forces will on the other hand, stand negated.

The five sons of Draupadi were also known as Draupadeyah. From each Pandava was born a son. In this way from five Pandavas, she begot five sons. She married to five Pandavas and as per conditions she will stay with one Pandava for one year only. After self-purification by performing a yajna, she will stay with another Pandava, in this way she gave birth to five sons. Prativindhya was the son of Yudhishthira which means he was steady and still like the mountain Vindhya. He represents firmness in intellect. Sutosoma was the son of Bhima representing clear mind. Shrutakarma or Shrutakirti was the son of Arjuna representing glorious action as mighty and powerful like his father. Shatanik born to Nakula means immeasurable strength and from Sahadeva was born Shrutasena which means mastery over senses. Killing of all five sons implies when desires, egoism, self-glorification and lucre for fame and name overcome the seeker, he will lose the steadiness and firmness of mind. His intellect, wisdom and memory are easily lost to him (*Gita* 2: 62-67). The seeker's mind is clear and not filled with abuses of desires. His mastery over senses will be loosened and he will remain captive to the senses.

The immeasurable spiritual strength will be taken away by the beguiling senses. He will no longer have the pinpointed attention on the Brahma.

Birth of Parikshita, the king and devotee

Finding in Lord Krishna, the ultimate saviour, supreme goal, the sustainer, the witness, the abode, the refuge, and the compassion, the Pandavas along with Kunti and Uttara prayed Him with their hearts suffused with love and devotion for protection of their child in the womb of Uttara from the invincible and dreaded weapon of Asvatthama. God never wants that His devotees fall into trouble. Instantly, He entered into the womb of Uttara just in the size of a thumb with Sudarshan chakra in His hands adorned with ear rings, waist chain and crown in the head that were resplendent with light before which the sun will look gloomy. Looking awe and superb in all His splendour and grandeur in His four hands He held lotus flower, conch, mace and chakra. By the sight of His reddish eyes in anger and light emitted out of the mace and chakra which will put millions of suns to shame, the deadly Brahma arrow dissipated like the lotus flower withered away by the advent of the sun. With the negation of the Brahma arrow, Lord Krishna vanished. Parikshita as a child in the womb was privileged to behold the divine majesties of Lord Krishna.

When the planets and stars were in propitious and high positions the child came out of the womb of the mother to the unspeakable joy and happiness of all the Pandavas. In between the birth of the child and severing of the umbilical cord king Yudhishthira offered and gave away gold, jewels, cows, wealth and villages to many amidst the pomp and ceremony that took place to celebrate the birth of new born child. After the functions were over, the king Yudhishthira invited men of wisdom to his palace for making and study of the horoscope of the son born to Uttara and Abhimanyu. The child filled with all noble and divine qualities was given the name Vishnurata being given the second life by the Lord. The only successor to the Pandavas, the king was very much concerned and worried about the future of the son. He asked the wise men, "since nothing is unknown to you all, the future, past and present as well, please tell me by proper calculation whether the son will rule the kingdom in all righteousness".

In reply, the Brahmins and men of wisdom said,

"O king, the son of Dharma, listen to our blissful words. Like Ekshyaku, the son of Manu he will devote himself for the welfare of the people. His name and fame will spread throughout like that of Sri Rama, the successor to Raghu dynasty. He will match the king Shibi in giving away wealth to the poor, distressed and the needy and showing compassion to all. He will be like Bharata in performance of yajnas and like warrior Arjuna in archery. He will be as brilliant as the burning fire. He will be as deep and fathomless as the immeasurable ocean. He will be as ferocious and powerful as the lion. He will be the refuge of all like that of the mountain where all can find shelter. He will be as still, balanced and unperturbed as the earth and he will be as patient and tolerant as parents. Like Providence he will be equal to all. Like God he will be kind

enough to give boons. He will be refuge of all living beings like Lord Shiva in the world. He will be equal to Lord Krishna in all divine qualities. He will be as determined and staunch in adhering to the path of Truth. He will be as compassionate as Rantideva. He will be as spiritual as the king Yajati. He will be calm and quiet like the king Bali and Prahalada. He will be adept in performing Asvamedha Yajna. He will serve the old. He will be the destroyer of the wicked and for the protection of Dharma he will fetter the Kali. In his young age he will be cursed by a Brahmin to death by the bite of a snake named Takshyaka. He will be divinely privileged to have the holy company of Mahamuni Shukadeva and other sages on the bank of the Ganges. On listening to the glory of Lord Krishna and following the path as will be taught by Shuka muni he will be God realised and leave the mortal body in a stage of bliss and joy".

Witnessing the Lord in the womb the king Parikshita started perceiving Lord Krishna in all after coming out of his mother's womb. He tested himself whether the same Lord was abiding in all or not. After that he was widely adored as Parikshita (testified in God realisation).

3

Coronation of Parikshita as King and Pandavas ascension to Heaven

The great Mahabharata war came to an end with the decimation of Kauravas, and victory of Pandavas with the blessings of Lord Krishna, and Yudhishthira, the eldest Pandava was enthroned as king of Indraprastha. Mustering the support and strength of his brothers he reigned with righteousness and dharma. An incarnation of dharma he won the heart of the subjects of his kingdom. The people of his kingdom were highly content with his rule. With the end of the mission of upholding dharma, the incarnation of Lord Krishna was about to be wrapped up. Lord Krishna left His mortal body as destined to be shot by an arrow from Jara sabara(tribal). The Jadava dynasty as cursed by the sages and wished by the Providence was ruined by internal squabbles and internecine fighting among themselves.

Before the eternal departure of Lord Krishna to His ultimate abode Arjuna went to Dvaraka to comprehend and perceive directly His supreme Self and glory in His company not even knowable to Lord Brahma and Lord Shiva and other sages and saints. He stayed with Him some months. King

Yudhishthira felt restless in his mind without getting Arjuna near him for several months. Nobody knows which direction Kala (Time Spirit) is moving in. The king was shocked to see some unseen and ominous things started happening. The mind of the people began to do unrighteous deeds being deluded by anger, passion, lust and ego. Deceptive to friends, kith and kin and other well-wishing persons they had been in constant quarrel and conflict with their family members throughout day and night. Calling Bhima beside him he asked:

"Why Arjuna has delayed his return? Since Devarshi Narada had told me about the imminent end of the Dvapara Yuga and advent of Kali Yuga, I fear that day has arrived. For unspeakable love of Lord Krishna, I sat in the throne leaving everything to Him. By His grace and blessings all have been well. But you see how darkness has enveloped the sky with many untoward climatic convulsions happening. All living beings along with the earth and sky are shivering out of fear. Like the banana tree uprooted by the tempest my mind and intelligence are being agitated. My thighs, left eye and hands are shivering. On the eve of sun rise the jackals are shouting facing the east with fire coming out of their mouths. The dogs are fearlessly barking at my face. All my elephants and horses are looking at my eyes with their eyes moist with tears. The owls sitting in my front are shouting aloud. All the ten directions are looking smoky. The whole earth and the mountains are shirking ferociously. Hot wind is blowing and without clouds in the sky there is rain of blood with lightning and thunder. The earth gives out a stench of rotten fish. The rivers and rivulets are roaring like seas. It seems as if in the sky the planets and

stars are fighting with their crackers. All these ominous signs signal the advent of Kali Yuga. The cows are not giving milk with their calves not sucking. The ox and oxen are not grazing with joy. All the villages, cities, houses, ashramas and hermitages and forests, wear a funeral and gloomy look. What I see in my eyes, I fear all these opposite signs auspicate the departure of Lord Krishna from the earth with the completion of His mission for which He incarnated'.

While conversation was going on between Yudhishthira and Bhima, Arjuna arrived with tears flooding out from his eyes and sweats prespring in his body, and sobbingly prostrated himself at the feet of the king. Seeing him fatigued and enervated Yudhishthira with remembrance of the Lord in his heart and Devarshi Narada's words, caught hold of Arjuna's hands and asked,

O Arjuna, are all our kith and kin and friends in Dvarakapur well?".

He asked about all starting from uncle Basudeva, grandmother, Devaki and other sixteen hundred wives of the Lord and other women, Balarama, Satyaki, Devaka, Ugrasena, Pradyumna, Aniruddha Uddhava, Akrura to the warriors Susena, Sumitra, Rishava. The king consoled himself saying without waiting for the reply from Arjuna, all must be well remaining under the fearless canopy of Lord Krishna's blessings. At the same he glorified the Lord for His marvellous past deeds.

Staring at the face of Arjuna, the king was surprised and shocked at the same time and asked:

"Why you are looking crestfallen, gloomy and cowardice? What you have achieved and acquired, have gone where? Are you looking so shabby due to living in foreign land for a long period of time? Has anybody cursed you? Has anybody returned empty handed begging from you? Have you not been compassionate to old people, the diseased, brahmins, women, children, or cows or those who took refuge in you? For these reasons, do you look inauspicious?"

Further, he asked, *"Did you practice adultery with other women out of incest? Have you gone astray leaving aside the righteous path? Did someone vanquish you on the way? Without offering food to children and old people did you eat first? Did you commit any despised deed?"*

After asking all these questions the king Yudhishthira surmised, "I think Lord Krishna has left you. In His absence you look so bereaved and dejected. But I wish, this might not have happened."

With torrents of tears flushed out from his eyes and weeping aloud in a melancholic tone in reminiscence of all that Lord Krishna, his friend, guide, ultimate goal and refuge had done for him and Pandavas in their moments of adversities, joys and happiness, Arjuna failed to answer the questions raised by king Yudhishthira. In a choked voice interrupted by frequent sobbing he said:

"Sri Krishna, the friend of my life has left the world. I am now left forsaken and forlorn by His departure. Everything majestic, glorious, divine and brilliant in me have been lost. My valour and mighty incomprehensible to demons and gods went away with my Lord. My body is looking pale, dark

and sullen. I am looking like dead. The life force, the soul within me is no more. I am like a son feeling the agony of losing my father. Taking refuge in Him I was able to pierce into the eye of the whirling fish kept on the top of a pillar looking below its reflection in water tank in the palace of the king Drupada and betrothed Draupadi. It was Lord Krishna who helped me to burn to ashes the Khandava forest and get the demon Maya to build for us an exquisite palace not found even in three lokas. He brought all kings to your feet by arranging a rajasuya yajna. In the guise of brahmins we the two brothers and Sri Krishna were able to kill the most ferocious Jarasandha and release all kings imprisoned by him. It was our Lord who made it possible by directing all these kings to serve you. During the deceitful game of dice played between Kauravas and us Lord Krishna came to the rescue of Draupadi when we lost her in the game and Dushashana dragging by her hair to the presence of all assembled in Hasthinapur tried to disrobe her by the direction of king Duryodhan. During the time of our exile in the forest with the evil intention Duryodhana sent the sage Durvasa and his big troupe of disciples and saints to have food in our cottage. When they were taking baths in the river, knowing that we have finished food Lord Krishna arrived and partook a single boiled rice along with a green leave left over by chance in the cooking pot. By His blissful act the rishis taking bath in the river felt their stomach already filled with delicious food left elsewhere without coming to our cottage.

Blessed by His power I conquered Lord Shiva in the forest in a fight for which I was bestowed with Pasupat weapon and Mother Parvati gave me an imperishable shaft with unending arrows. Blessed by Him I was able to vanquish the demons in Heaven and Indra and other gods being pleased with me and my divinity adored me making me seated in the throne of Indra, the king of devas. In the Mahabharat war He became my charioteer and it was He who brought victory to us and it was because of His bliss and compassion no arrow pierced my chest and during the fight with Jayadratha when my horses became thirsty for water, I came down to the ground to fetch water for them, knowing this Sri Krishna entered into the mind of the Kauravas. Seeing me on the ground they did not raise any weapon against me. I was privileged to be with Him every time even whilst taking food, sleeping and walking and moving. I have moved with Him by holding His hands. Considering Him as my friend I have never behaved as due to my Lord. Without minding anything he has become tolerant of me as a friend tolerates his friend and a father tolerates son by his fathomless love. Today, I have come to naught without Him. I have become impotent without the Gandiva bow. I have been reduced to a mere lifeless body without valour, energy, strength. I am now directionless without a lodestar, guide and friend. I am like a seed left seething in a barren infertile and hard soil".

With these words of great remembrance of Lord Krishna's divine and glorious deeds Arjuna divulged everything about His ultimate departure from earth after finishing the works for which He was embodied on this earth. He narrated in details how the Jadu dynasty was razed to ground by the curse of sages and will of the Providence. Their incarnations on the earth in human forms to establish dharma under the direction of Lord Krishna were fulfilled.

The conditions into which Arjuna was put by the departure of his beloved, friend, guide, father and mother and everything of his life represent the conditions of a devotee who loves his Lord and has taken complete refuge in Him without whom there is nothing in his life and everything looks dark and meaningless. Human body is the temple of God. The indwelling self does everything in his actions, thinking and dispositions through every inhalation and exhalation. When the soul leaves the body temple, the human being turns into a corpse.

By devotedly remembering the deeds of Lord Krishna and his intimate and constant association with Him purified the mind of Arjuna. The mind was cleared of all the debris of worldliness, delusion and illusion by the thought of the Lord. He remained fixed at the feet of his beloved Lord. He was transformed into a state of quietness and calmness of mind, bliss and joy. The rivulets of love that spring from within his heart washed away all his agony and bereavement. The light of wisdom that manifested within him pierced through all the veils of ignorance and ferried him to the shore of divinity where being engrossed in the thought of the Lord, he remained tuned to the pearls of solemnised and sublime truths of *Gita* revealed to him by the Lord in the battlefield. His sense of and association with gross body vanished forever giving way to the complete elimination of duality, and ultimate identity with the soul.

Hearing from Arjuna the departure of Lord Krishna and end of Dvapara Yuga the king Yudhishthira and Pandavas decided to begin their eternal journey to mingle with the Divine by severing the last attachment to the body and world. Knowing the imminent arrival of their departure Yudhishthira coronated Parikshita as the king by performing all ceremonies and rituals associated with this on the advice of the sage Vyasadeva.

Ascension to Heaven

Led by Yudhishthira the Pandavas left the kingdom and did a pilgrimage to all holy places as advised by sage Vyasadeva attiring like the ascetics. The immortal and solemnised words of their mentor and divine Guru Lord Krishna in whom they had completely taken refuge were vibrating in their minds that nothing in this world is permanent and all are ephemeral. Nothing was seen to them except Lord Krishna. Their hearts were rending with tears of love and gratitude streaming out constantly in torrents to wash out the feet of their mentor Lord Krishna. In reminiscences of Lord Krishna and His unconditional love, insightful guidance and support in their adversities and saddening moments Yudhishthira followed by Bhima, Arjuna, Nakul Sahadeva and Draupadi at the rear could be able to scale the Himalayan ranges and its mountainous ridges, the invincible snow clad peaks forgetting the pains and suffering born of this arduous journey with the opportunity to get sight of many realised sages and saints deeply merged in divinity in the caverns of the Himalayas at Rishikesh and Badrinath, the abode of Nar and Narayan. While wading their ways through thorny and steep paths to reach Mount Meru the eternal abode of gods, the past acts of omission and commission which had stained their lives on earth flashed back in their minds with deep repentance and contrition for the sins they had committed and their inability to lead a perfect and sacred life. Their hearts cruised to fathomless humbleness and deepening imploring to seek forgiveness from the Lord for all the sins, were beseeching with love and devotion the all-compassionate Lord Krishna. In these thoughts and moorings one by one, first Draupadi followed by Nakula, Sahadeva, Arjuna and Bhima fell on the wayside dead. Yudhishthira was left with the faithful dog following him from the beginning of his journey. He did not look back even shed tears for the brothers and Draupadi falling dead on the way who stood with him in his adversities. Lord of righteousness and dharma he knew that all were guided and destined to be governed by the inexorable laws of karma. When one fell, others called him entreatingly to look back he did not look back and had not even a drop of tears of sorrow in his eyes. The death of his brothers and Draupadi who were once closest to his heart and were every moment at his beck and call did not deter him from his determined onward journey to the Ultimate.

As he was trekking up the lonely path in deep solitude with the dog following him, a flash of light from a sudden thunderous sky manifested before him with appearance of Indra as the king of devas (gods) in a chariot studded with efflorescent gold and gems, and addressed Yudhishthira, the lord of Dharma! "I have been ordained by the Almighty Lord that you shall ascend to heaven in human form in this chariot. You get into this chariot I have brought for you to ascend to heaven".

Yudhishthira asked, "what about my brothers and Draupadi who were my loved ones, and we had spent our lives together in our sorrows and happiness. I cannot go alone in this chariot unless my brothers and Draupadi accompany me in this chariot".

Indra said, "your beloved brothers and Draupadi have already reached the heaven before you. All that is needed is that you enter into heaven. You will join them in this abode of eternity".

On hearing these words of solace from the lips of Indra Yudhishthira bowed in deep gratitude and humbleness and while entering into the chariot signalled the dog to enter. But Indra forbade the dog to enter saying "heaven is not meant for the lowly creatures like dog. They are not noble souls like you. Leave it behind for it is ignorant of life eternal and truth".

Yudhishthira responded saying, *"this dog has shown me unquestioned loyalty and unshaken devotion from the start of my journey. It will be a heinous act perpetrated against all the nuances of dharma. How can I leave it behind when it has ensconced complete faith and refuge in me? All the virtues that I have earned throughout my life will be wasted in a single moment if I part company with it".*

Indra addressed Yudhishthira, *"You very much know that persons of impeccable virtues walking on the path of righteousness ascend to heaven which is realm of sacredness, purity and divinity. How a very ignoble creature like dog can aspire to dwell in heaven? The very presence of a dog will defile the sanctity and serenity of Heaven".*

Yudhishthira replied with all humbleness, *"it will be unworthy of me and the righteous path I have trodden unfailingly throughout my life to flat out abandon a creature who has followed me with the unbreakable trust in me. I am ready to sacrifice Heaven for the sake of the dog".*

At these words of determination and defiance to the admonition of Indra, the dog vanished and, in its place, appeared a divine being with brilliant illumination known as Dharma, the god of righteousness. He addressed Yudhishthira: *"You are the incarnation of Dharma. All glories and victory are to you. None in this earth can equal you. For an ignoble creature you are ready to sacrifice the Heaven the most cherished one by all".*

Then Yudhishthira seated himself in the chariot and landed in the Heaven. Alighting from the chariot and greeted by the celestials he was surprised and shocked to find not his brothers and Draupadi in the Heaven but the Kauravas and Karna who represented evil forces and injustice and unrighteousness. He said to Indra, the king of devas, *"Where are my beloved brothers and our consort Draupadi who wholeheartedly and devotedly supported me for the upliftment of Dharma, justice, truth and righteousness? Are they undergoing an ordeal of sufferings and travails? What kind of justice and righteousness reign in Heaven? Whereas my brothers and wife having sacrificed their lives for the cause of Dharma have had no place in Heaven but on the contrary, the Kauravas – the perpetrators of evil, injustice and unrighteousness and embodiment of adharma have been rewarded with berths in Heaven".*

Indra said, *"O King, the adorable one! This is the realm of eternal bliss and joy where there are no sorrows and grief and divine beings live. Everywhere you behold the dance and joy of celestial spirits. It is unbecoming of you not to unfetter your worldly ties and bonds. Your loved brothers and wife have ascended to the levels they deserve".*

Reacting sharply Yudhishthira said, *"I am not willing to live a moment here with the wrong doers without my brothers and wife. I knew that heaven is a place for the righteous one but I behold here the wrong doers are rewarded. I feel I do not deserve to live here with Duryodhana and his brothers and Karna. I strongly disapprove of your request to dwell here. I beseech you earnestly to take me to the place where my brothers and wife are sojourning".*

On the request of the king Yudhishthira, a celestial messenger was asked to lead him to the nether region where his brothers and Draupadi are living. The path to the nether realm was arduous, dreary, dangerous, gloomy and dark strewn with mortal remains of human bodies on both sides of the road and skeletons shrieking to create terror, trepidation, fear and shudder. More frightening was the blazing of fire on both sides of the road with stinging insects and flies flying across the body and face. Stenches of foul odours were spreading all around to make the stay even a moment hazardous. Then, they came upon a river which was flowing with boiling water. The very ground was made of hot iron. The leaves of the trees were as sharp as the swords. Clouds of vapour from cauldrons of burning oil in which mortal being were being tortured and boiled, darkened the place. Rivulets of blood and pus were flowing through. Yudhishthira was no longer willing to proceed further and felt like being in a dungeon.

The king Yudhishthira asked the messenger, "is it the place where my brothers and wife are living? The messenger replied, "this is the place you decide to move further in search of your brothers". Weary of the dreadful path and dangerous landscape around Yudhishthira was about to turn back, he heard wailings and crying wafting through the foul wind blowing across him. Do not leave us alone here in our misery. Our pain and agony have been lessened by your holy presence with us. "Do not deprive us of the radiance of your blissful presence that has cast a serenity of mellowing coolness and mitigation of suffering in this dreadful region". The very familiar voices of prayerful wailing were none than those of his brothers, Bhima, Arjuna, Nakul and Sahadeva and wife Draupadi. His steps hesitated to move forward. He stood still and cried out, "you are my Bhima, Arjuna, Nakula and Sahadeva and wife

Draupadi". In chorus the voice returned to him, "yes we are".

The king Yudhishthira beholding the miserable and painful plight of his brothers and wife asked the messenger to go back to your heaven, *"I will stay with my kinsmen. I do not want to go back to heaven where injustice is rewarded and justice is punished. There can be no better place than this where my salvation lies with those who are wretchedly mired in the hell. I will dwell with them so long as they are condemned to live here. It shall be as you wish, said the messenger".*

No sooner had the messenger vanished than the pale of gloom and darkness disappeared with resplendent light gushing through the manifestation of the devas in their celestial forms. Everything that appeared as hell to Yudhishthira was mere an illusion and mirage. The devas addressed the king as the most venerable and adorable one! *"You are welcome to the celestial abode of the gods where all of you, your brothers and Draupadi are rightly belonged to. Take a dip in the sacred river where you will divest yourself of your human body, grief, enmity and bondage. You are now risen to the divine realm of glory and bliss and eternal joy".* The God of Dharma said, *"O wisest one! I have put you to test for the third time. The first one was the dog, the second one you declined to stay in heaven without your kinsmen and the third one you preferred to stay with your kinsmen in hell. For the thirteenth part of a day, you are destined to spend in hell. Glories are unto you. Casting off his mortal frame and transfigured into divinity Yudhishthira sojourned in the Heaven – the eternal abode of bliss and joy".*

Metaphorical interpretation

The metaphorical interpretation of Pandavas' ascension to heaven through the Himalaya entails in yogic tradition that within the spine of the human beings there are seven chakras starting from Muladhara (coccygeal) – the base of the spine, then Swadhisthan (sacral), Manipur (lumbar), Anahata (dorsal), Vishuddha (cervical), Ajna (kutastha) and Sahasrara (fontanel or Brahma yoni) – the top of the head. Sahasrara is also called Himalaya. All these chakras represent five gross elements with their attributes or vrittis. Muladhara represents earth identified with Sahadeva. In this centre material desires – wealth, greed, name and fame are generated. Swadhisthan is identified with Nakul. It represents desire for sex and passion, physical pleasure, procreation. Manipur is the fire centre representing Arjuna. It is food centre which shapes mind and provides vital energy to the body. Bhima represents Anahata which is identified with air. Love, hatred, jealousy, enmity, compassion and sympathy, pride and ego are its attributes. Vishuddha centre represents space (ether) identified with Yudhishthira. It is otherwise known as centre of religion. Mind moves towards God. Ego about one's spirituality is its propensity. Ajna chakra is the abiding place of the soul. The seventh centre is the Sahasrara, the Unmanifest Infinity pervading the manifest infinity and remains compassionately detached. Ajna and Sahasrara are beyond the fusion of these gross elements found in lower centres. Draupadi symbolises the shakti (power or energy) without which nothing can be sprouted. Everything is dead. Draupadi also implies quickest movement or action. The *Vedas* say:

charan vai madhu vindati charan prahu samacharat
prithivya pasya sriyamana ye na tandrayate charan

"Through movement one attains immortality; move consciously. On this earth, those who practice avoiding laziness attain prosperity".

Life is short and uncertain. The journey for Godhood should begin at this moment without any procrastination or delay.

A spiritual seeker in order to be self-realised has to start his inner journey (movement) from Muladhara to Sahasrara and beyond through the practice of special breath technique as taught by self-realised masters in Kriya Yoga.

Through the proper process of breath control and purification of the chakras in the spine, one opens the path of the sushumna. The subtle breath flows in this opened passage. Thus, the mind becomes tranquil and still. Then all actions of the knower of yoga are burnt in the fire of wisdom. It brings immortality.

Through practice the seeker has to fuse Muladhara with Swadhisthan, Swadhisthan with Manipur, Manipur with Anahata, Anahat with Vishuddha, Vishuddha with Ajna and Ajna with Sahasrara and then beyond the infinite Brahman.

This happens within a moment. Sincere practice with love and devotion hastens the process of passage from mortality to immortality. The seeker reaches the breathlessness stage i.e., the Nirvikalpa samadhi. Here one attains to and merges with the Infinite Brahman. This is deathlessness stage. The fall of all Pandavas along with Draupadi means shunning of all attributes of the gross elements. At this stage of immortality all attributes and their corresponding deeds and thoughts remain baked in the fire of wisdom. It becomes a seedless stage leaving no scope for rebirth on the earth. Yudhishthira symbolises the seeker who attains to the Supreme through sincerest practice and with concentration, love and devotion. Space is the subtlest aspect which is all pervading and never attaches to anything and anywhere. The dog accompanying him throughout the journey symbolises Dharma. Yudhishthira known as Dharmaraj means he has never lived a moment without Dharma. Dharma means breath, it is the breath of God which remains with us from the very birth. It has never shunned us at any moment. The dog is loyal, dedicated, ever watchful and subservient to the master. The seeker must be watchful of his breath every moment in all his deeds, thoughts and dispositions.

4

Arrival of Kali Yuga and conversation among Dharma, mother Earth and king Parikshita

As foretold by Brahmins during his birth King Parikshita would be a man of immeasurable valour, power and strength and would be a great devotee of God and would always walk on the path of truth. Endeared to people and his unsullied name and fame would spread to all parts being the successor of the great Pandavas, son of Abhimanyu and grandson of Arjuna. After assuming the throne, he performed the *Veda* prescribed three Asvamedha Yajnas on the bank of the holy river Ganges presided over by the brahmins. At the end of yajnas he proffered gold, jewels, diamonds and other things to the brahmins, priests and others to their hearts' content.

On the eve of his first journey to reign victory over other kingdoms with his military forces and horses and elephants the king saw towards the end of the day Kali yuga in the guise of a sudra (lower caste) king with an iron club in his hands. Further, keeping in the front mother earth in the form of Dhenu (cow) and Dharma in the form of an ox, Kali Yuga was kicking the ground with sound. Without delay the king Parikshita caught hold of his hands and fettered him. Then, the king started his military adventure of conquering other kingdoms. No king was able to match his prowess and military might. All the kings in the entire Bharatasharva showed their allegiance to the king offering him plenty of wealth as a token of their unbreakable loyalty. During the course of his conquest, he heard from people about his grandparents and parents' long and constant association with Lord Krishna at every moment of their life and the king rejoiced in having romance with the Divine. The king started to imbibe the love, devotion and oneness that his predecessors had with Lord Krishna into his way of life. In all his actions, deeds and dispositions he tried always to remain at the feet of the Lord. With strong determination he remained unwavering in the thought of God. Nothing was seen to him except the Lord everywhere. Every moment he tested himself whether he was able to perceive Sri Krishna pervadingly residing in all.

One day, Dharma in the form an ox with one leg came near to mother earth who was in the form of a Dhenu (cow) crying in great sorrows and distress with tears in her eyes as if it had lost its calf. With deep faith and compassion Dharma asked her,

"O mother earth, tell me the truth. Why your entire body both inside and outside is diseased? Why your joyful face has turned pale, and looks mournful? Have you lost your son or your husband has gone away? Are you pondering over loss of your wealth? Are you worried for the sudras reigning you? Are you perplexed by the lack of Yajnas, for which Indra, king of gods being unhappy has stopped raining

causing death to the people? Thinking over the people that they will commit adultery by mixing with other women in the advent of Kali Yuga and children will be orphans, you are shedding tears. Are you saddening over the brahmins not doing proper worship as per the nuances of Vedas? Are you worried over the fallen Kshyatriya kings going astray not concerned with welfare of the people? Lord Krishna incarnated to alleviate the oppression and exploitation wrecked to you. Are you in great remembrance of His splendid deeds performed for establishment of Dharma and destruction of the evil and demonic forces? Recollecting His majestic play and deeds filled with compassion and love performed with His lotus feet on your bosom, are you afflicted by His departure with deep attachment to Him? Are people and gods showing dishonour to you, for which you are looking remorse and dejected?"

In reply mother earth said:

"O venerable Dharma, the answers to the volley of questions you asked are well known to you. Your four feet are the causes of happiness and joy. Before the advent of Kali Yuga divine attributes and virtues were prevailing everywhere. You were adorned with truth, purity, kindness, forgiveness, renunciation, contentment, simplicity, austerity, equanimity, self-control, quietness, detachment, divinity, knowledge of the self, strength, brahmacharya, divine effulgence, patience, softness, sweet words, lustrous body, humility and lack of egoism. With the end of Lord Krishna's incarnation on earth all these vanished and eclipsed. My sorrows are that the ominous eyes of Kali Yuga have fallen on earth. Pondering over this and adoring in great remembrance of all these attributes of Dharma I am crying very painfully and gravely shocked at your broken

legs. Disappearance of adherence to Varnashrama (four stages of human life) – Brahmacharya, grahasthya (family life), Vanaprastha (living in the forest) and Sannyasa pained me unremittingly. Sri Krishna left me in this mournful stage of distress and sorrows. The divine company that I have had with Him and other gods has become a nightmare for me. The divine imprints of His feet, deeds and movements on my breast were my ornaments adorning which I was looking serene and beatific. Keeping constantly attention at His holy Feet, words and deeds I was remaining always in divine euphoria. My whole body was resonant with melodious and sweet words of the Lord. Bereft of His presence on my bosom I have been divested of all that look glorious and divinely majestic. All my hope for liberation shattered and wrecked on the ridges of demonic attributes of Kali Yuga. With Lord Krishna leaving me alone I am looking forlorn, undignified and hapless. My whole body was covered with the beauty of the Lord. I was feeling holy and sacred by the touch of His feet. Every dust of my body was reflecting His image and presence. With His departure after establishing Dharma for the blissful life of the people I look defaced and defiled".

On return from his conquest of other kingdoms and subduing of all kings under his supremacy the rajarshi Parikshita alighted from his chariot on the bank of the holy river Sarasvati beholding a very shocking scene. Attired strangely like a joker and king in a sudra (Kali king) body with an iron club in his hand was beating harshly Dharma in the form of a one footed ox and mother earth in the form a dhenu (cow). With his excruciating beating the ox was shedding tears and trembling with fear defalcating and urinating. The cow was also crying and not able to stand even on its four legs. Surprised at this strange scene the king Parikshita making his bow and arrow ready to shoot asked him in a very humble and soft voice: *"What is the reason for your beating cruelly this hapless and innocent cow? What is your name and from where you have come donning a very strange dress and acting like a sudra though looking like a king? With departure of Lord Krishna and Arjuna you have arrived to do harm to the innocent and hapless beings knowing very much that they have become insecure and unprotected. Your stay on this earth has already come to an end".*

Turning towards the ox, the king asked, *"you look pure and white and you are moving on one foot. Why you have lost the other three feet? Which God you are in the guise of an ox. This looks strange and odd to me. You know that under the protective shield of Pandava kings nobody's tears were falling on earth".*

Again, shifting his attention to the cow the king asked, *"why you are crying and for what? You need not fear the king Kali. I am the annihilator of the wicked and demons. Where I am the king, there is no suffering for my subjects? In whose kingdom the subjects are committing cruelty and the king does not take appropriate and protective steps, where are the name and fame of the king? His longevity comes to an end and he enters the hell. The staple duty of the king is to kill the wicked and remove what is unrighteous from the righteous".*

Again, the king asked the Dharma in the form of the ox, *"in my kingdom always engrossed in the Lord, nobody remains in distress and sorrows. Your one footed body is a mark of great disgrace to the Pandava dynasty. The wicked and sinners tremble in horror hearing my name. The duty of the righteous king is to see that his people are treading on their respective rightful paths as chiselled by the four varna system".*

Highly content with the king's words of assurance, Dharma answered:

"O virtuous Purushottam (supreme among the people), "what you said is right. Pandavas are well acclaimed and adored for their yeoman's service and benevolent deeds for the distressed, diseased and helpless people. It was because of their virtuous deeds and nature Sri Krishna stayed with them as their friend, guide, philosopher, destination, goal and ultimate refuge and even became the charioteer of Arjuna in the Mahabharata war. The nature of one's dharma is the seed of his happiness or sorrows. How can one pierce into the veil of deluded words to know the nature of one's dharma? Some try to realise the indwelling self by the knowledge of the self. Some think that body is the alternative to soul. Some think that Providence or destiny is supreme. Some consider everything bad or good as the result of one's karma. Some think that all are due to man's nature. Others think that God is the sole doer. To speak about Dharma is beyond one's words but think that it is the description about the Lord".

Hearing the words from one footed ox as embodiment of Dharma all doubts of the king vanished like the fog by the touch of the sun. He was blessed to behold Dharma in His majestic manifestation with divine effulgence, four hands, matted hair, the mark of Sribatsa in his chest and moon in his body. At the sight of this divine manifestation the lamp of wisdom was lighted in him.

With folded hands the king very humbly asked:

"O venerable Dharma, you speak on dharma but why you are in the guise of an ox? The people doing works contrary to dharma and the people expressing against dharma by putting blame on others are both equally entitled to live in hell. I do not know why you have assumed such a form. Who can know the will of the Divine? By mere words it cannot be deciphered what is in your mind. But what I think in my judgment, your four feet represents tapa, purity, kindness, and truth as essence of the first yuga. With the departure of satya (truth) tapa went away. Purity went away with Tretaya yuga. Kindness disappeared with Dvapara yuga. Truth remains with Kaliyuga. Tapa (austere sadhana or meditation) was destroyed by pride and egoism. Purity was destroyed by attachment and delusion. Kindness was destroyed by pride and ego. This is the reason truth remains with Dharma as one foot. Its greatest foe is Kali yuga. Who loves truth begets Lord Krishna. Satya yuga was known for truth only. With the return of Lord Krishna to His abode, the mother earth looks shabby, shorn of her divine glories and virtues, gloomy and dejected taking the form of a cow. How painfully she is bemoaning that the sinful and wicked kings will combine together to exploit me".

Finding both Dharma and mother earth (basundhara) content and happy with his words, the king came forward with his sharp sword drawn from his sheath to the front of Kali. Shirking his dress of king, the kali fell at the feet of the king imploringly for forgiveness. Kind to those who seek refuge in him, the king desisted himself from killing the Kali and said to him:

"Since you have sought refuge in me being the heir of Arjuna, I will not kill you. You are the friend of the demonic, wicked and unrighteous forces. You have no place in my kingdom. You have places where there are unrighteousness, greed, falsehood, stealing, egoism, wickedness, cruelty, delusion and attachment. As these evil qualities are absent in my kingdom, you should not dare to enter my kingdom, if you venture, you will not escape without being beheaded. In this land of God (Brahmabarta) where the people are preforming their duties according to their position in the four varna system with complete surrender to the Lord and feeling His omnipresence everywhere inside and outside the body, you are forbidden to enter. God is the witness to what I said to you following the path of Dharma".

In reply to the king Parikshita Maharaja, Kali entreated with all humbleness, "I will obey your words but I entreat you to give me places where I can stay safely".

Satisfied with his prayer, the king offered him four places "where there is always play of evil forces – play of dice, women, drink and murder of living beings". Kali again begged for a fifth place to live in. The king offered him gold, the fifth place to reside.

Falsehood is embedded in the place of dice game. Passion and lust reside in women, drink of wine and attachment. Where rajasik qualities prevail, there is murder. In the place where there is gold, the thieves gather there with preying eyes. The wise person is one who never associates himself with these five foes. This is the strongest pillar of Dharma. Tapa, purity and kindness returned to Dharma and his four feet were restored. The mother earth was supported, sustained and nourished. Before their eternal journey to Heaven, Parikshita seated in the lap of king Yudhishthira was taught all that were quintessential for the dharmic duty of the king.

Reflections

Human beings are generally in delusion, illusion, ignorance and error while living in the world. They tend to forget their real nature that they are not mortal beings of perishable flesh and blood but immortal and imperishable souls, the children of the Almighty Father. The purpose for which they are born is easily forgotten being deluded by the snare of Maya. After death, they are again put back into the unending chain of birth and death. While in the wombs they remain like prisoners in the dungeon of darkness, unbearable pain bitten by various viruses, worms and insects surrounded by blood, pus and other pungent things. In the womb the child was constantly in communion with God. He was praying, "O God, release me from this condition. After taking birth I will never forget you". The past experiences with the Divine constantly made him aware of God. This hell like conditions impel them to be conscious of God and they pray very devotedly for liberation with the avowed determination that they will never again fall into the trap of the worldly delusion. The memory and picture of their past lives flash back in their minds by the grace of the Lord. All children in the womb are divine and identified with Brahma. But the moment they come out of the mother's womb and touch the world, they remain ignorant of God and the conditions of their miserable life in the womb and the reflections of their past lives as well in the womb.

The king Parikshita was divinely blessed to have the direct darshan (vision) of Lord Krishna in all His divine grandeur and effulgence in the womb when He protected him from the deadly Brahma weapon used by Asvatthama for his destruction. After his birth unlike the common human beings, king Parikshita remained conscious of the Lord. His name was given 'Parikshita' because he was always testing himself whether he had been successful in perceiving the same omnipotent Lord he beheld in the womb, everywhere and in everything both living and non-living and in all his actions, deeds, thinking and dispositions. Further, he was given a second birth by Lord Krishna in the womb. We are born out of blood and flesh by our parents. So, we are after pleasure of flesh and blood. God is the primordial seed that is in father and mother. Without God there is nothing. We must identify ourselves with God who is our Father and Mother. He has been residing in our body temple breathing His breath of life into our nostrils, thus giving us life. A spiritual seeker when remains engrossed in the Lord every moment and perceives Him everywhere, gets the second birth. This is the stage of dvija (tad dvitiyam janmam) implying to be ever with the Divine.

Apart from his direct meet with the Lord in the womb, what strengthens his love for Him was his own experience with the Lord in the womb, the experience of his grandfathers and the glorious talk and discussion among the people about his grand fathers and father's constant association with and total refuge in Lord Krishna which he heard to his overwhelming joy. The past guides the present and shapes the future. The divinely enriched legacy which he inherited nestled and nourished, engendered in him a nostalgic impetus to have a permanent divine romance with the Lord. Similarly, a spiritually inclined family provides a right environment and heredity to the earnest seekers of God for the quick evolution in divine path.

King Parikshita was the son of Subhadra and Abhimanyu (Saubhadra), the nephew of Lord Krishna. Abhimanyu very successfully penetrated into an invincible military strategic formation of the Kaurava army and killed innumerable soldiers. In the spinal canal of human beings are found millions of evil and demonic thoughts in each centre. In the coccygeal centre (Muladhara chakra) there is inexhaustible desire for money and material wealth. No man remains satisfied with what already he has. The more he is in possession of, the more he longs for more which goes on increasing. In the second centre sacral (Swadhisthana) the desire for sexual pleasure is endless. It is like ghee, the more it is added to the fire, its flames burn more brilliantly. It is never extinguished. The mind here goes extrovert. In the third centre (Manipura chakra) or navel centre is the desire for food. The more we eat the more we relish to eat without having control over it and the proper judgment over the quality and type of food we should take according to the requirement of a healthy body. Next centre is dorsal (Anahata chakra). In this centre is found endless desires. Demonic attributes like vanity, pride, egoism, jealousy, greed, hatred, anger and obstinacy and attachment arise here along with positive qualities like sympathy, forgiveness, compassion, love and tolerance. These innumerable evil desires represented by Kauravas were killed by Abhimanyu. Abhi means to destroy and manyu means evil desires.

Parikshita being the son of Abhimanyu represents the ability to kill evil and demonic desires in him. Every moment he was testifying himself whether he remained in God consciousness in all his deeds, thinking, perceptions, dispositions, and desires. Every moment is divine. In each and every breath one has to remain united with the indwelling soul.

After being coronated as king, Parikshita Maharaja annexed and integrated other territories into his kingdom by his military forces. The heads of these territories were subdued and showed allegiance to the king. All centres as discussed above in spinal canal of human beings represent various domains. By the practice of Kriya Yoga under the direct tutelage of self-realised masters the Muladhara is integrated with Swadhisthana, then navel with Anahata, Anahata with Visuddha and Visuddha with soul centre and ultimately in Sahasrara and then in the Infinity. That means the elements created out of the infinity in the beginning of creation are to go back to the source. If he remains constantly in the Infinity, he attains Godhood (nirvikalpa samadhi stage). With the attainment of this highest God realised stage, all desires and evil forces attached with these gross elements by human nature are killed. All these forces are transformed into divine forces. That means, Parikshita Maharaja by annexing and integrating all territories subdued the evil and demonic desires under his supremacy and transformed these into divinity.

It is narrated above that King Parikshita did three Asvamedha yajnas. This yajna was usually performed by kings to exercise their supremacy over other kings through a very rigorous and ritualistic practice. Asva means senses. Medha means to sacrifice. Asvamedha means to have through control over senses and offer these to God. In each and every sense realisation of God is Asvamedha yajna.

Asva means also horses. Horses represent senses or indriyas. The senses always move after objects for enjoyment. The ignorant thinks that he is the enjoyer but the real enjoyer is the soul or God. To feel the presence of God in the enjoyment of senses is asvamedha yajna. It is declared in Upanishads:

indriyani hayan ahur visayams tesu gocaran

atmendriya mano yuktam bhoktety ahur manisinah
(*Katha Upanishad* 1:3;4)

The senses are the horses; the objects of the senses the paths; the self-associated with the body, the senses and the mind, the wise say, is the enjoyer.

Another interpretation of senses is restlessness. Asvamedha yajna means to sacrifice restlessness at the altar of divinity to reap calmness and stillness of mind.

Asva also means seven which represent seven chakras. Remaining in God consciousness to sacrifice each and every chakra to God is asvamedha yajna. To realise in each centre the presence of God is asvamedha yajna.

As explained by Paramahamsa Prajnanananda, Asva is composed of two components: a + sva; a means not and sva means tomorrow. What does not exist for tomorrow is asva. Everything in this world is ephemeral. Only one thing is eternal and permanent. That is God. Nobody knows when this human body will perish. Its longevity pertains to one breath. Without waiting for the future or tomorrow which is uncertain, one should be concerned with the present moment. That moment is to be spent for realisation of God. This realisation of the Lord at the present moment in all actions, deeds, thinking and dispositions is asvamedha yajna. To realise God in every breath is yajna. To be constantly aware of the indwelling self through watching every inhalation and exhalation in all deeds, thoughts and dispositions is yajna.

King Parikshita performed three asvamedha yajnas. It implies the king sacrifices all desires in gross body by seeing the divine light throughout the body and world in meditation. In the astral body the desires are killed by perceiving the divine vibration in the body and everywhere. In the causal body desires are burnt completely by hearing the divine sound constantly. In the samadhi state the sadhaka completely merges with God and he becomes free from all desires as seeds of further births. He becomes a liberated soul.

The conversation between Dharma and mother earth on one side and the talk between the king and Dharma on the other hand describe the divine traits that the spiritual seeker should have. All these divine attributes are mostly found in people in Satya, Tretaya and Dvapara Yuga. But in Kali Yuga these attributes are absent. People will be distancing themselves from God by being deeply embedded in delusion, illusion, ignorance and error. For this reason, Dharma and mother earth were lamenting and feeling saddened with tears in latter's eyes and the former having lost three legs. These will be attributes of persons who are divine and perceive constantly that God is the sole doer in them in all their deeds and thinking.

The same thing has been enunciated by Lord Krishna when Arjuna, the grandfather of king Parikshita wanted to know from Him the divine attributes of those who are well established in God.

> sthitaprajnasya ka bhasa samadhisthasya kesava
> sthitadhih kim prabhaseta kim asita vrajeta kim

"O Keshava! What are the characteristics of those established in wisdom who have attained samadhi (whose mind remains in God consciousness)? How do those constantly merged in God speak? How do they sit? How do they walk?" (*Bhagavad Gita*, 2: 54).

Lord Krishna answered in details to Arjuna and all true seekers of God about the greatest and highest stage of God realisation, the divine attributes of these persons and way of talk and style of walk in subsequent verses of *Bhagavad Gita*. In chapter 12 from verse 13 to 20 and chapter 13 from verses 7 till the end, Lord Krishna has revealed the characteristics of those who are undeviating in their establishment in samadhi or God consciousness.

Dharma and mother earth are worried about the dearth of divine seekers in Kali Yuga where demonic attributes will be found in abundance in people. The deplorable description of mother earth about the impact of such demonic behaviour and attributes of people on her is being felt throughout the globe. The earth has been plundered, exploited and polluted by the people in disregard of the adoration that the ancient Indian people were offering her. The disastrous impact of the agonizing nature by the ruthless, inordinate and exorbitant behaviour of individuals on the globe has been painfully experienced by them in terms of climate change, water scarcity, pollution of atmosphere, incidence of diseases, sea level rise, storms and cyclones. The demonic characteristics of people infuriate and convulse the nature, the outcomes of which are being felt miserably by the people. The apocalyptic end of the globe is not far off if there has not been a transformation in the demonic nature of the people.

This sordid narrative of the mother earth to Dharma with tears has been exemplified at present in this materialistic and cause and effect bound scientific and technological development that has run predominantly into the very way of living of human beings at present.

King Parikshita assured mother earth and Dharma of proper protection against the advent of Kali Yuga and threatened Kali to death with his sword. If people will be on the divine path and will lead spiritual life as shown by the God realised masters Kali (demonic attributes) cannot dare to overpower them. The evil desires will be nipped in the bud as described above. The seeker has to kill these unwanted and evil attributes by the sword of wisdom. As beseeched by Kali the king offered him five places to live in. These are as discussed above, lust for women, wine, game of dice, place of murder and greed for gold.

It is not romance with women rather romance with God that should be the goal of human life. Mirabai, a great devotee of God was a renowned divine lover. Sensual pleasure is temporary and momentary. What is sweet in the beginning brings pain in the end. But what is bitter in the beginning brings in the end sweetness to life. The seeker of God perceives God everywhere and in all living and non-living. He bethinks women as his divine mother. It is stated in Saptasati Chandi (11:6):

> sthriyah samasthah sakala jagattsu
> tvayeikaya puritmambayeitat
> ca te sthutih sthabyapara paroktih

"O Devi Jagdamba! All women in this universe are your embodiment. There is none but You who pervades the entire universe".

The manifested creation is mother nature and the unmanifest is Purusha (Parambrahma). Seeing, hearing, eating, thinking walking and doing works, dreaming, sleeping and so on are manifestation of God. What is manifested is mother nature.

It is not wine or any drug that gives one peace and quietness to mind. People when get frustrated or dejected or coming in bad company get used to drinking as a panacea for their mental illness. Instead of giving supposedly peace to mind it disturbs mind and brain. The intoxication obtained from wanton drink is temporary and makes a person addicted to a bad habit. But the true spiritual seeker remains always engrossed in divine intoxication.

Murder or killing of human beings is a crime. It is heinous and inhuman. What is primary to a seeker is to murder or kill the internal enemies as narrated above to attain Godhood.

In the game of dice, the players toss their property or wealth for more unexpected gains. It is a risk-taking game. In this game total loss is more assured than any material gain. The spiritual seeker tosses with his attachment to the world in order to have union with God. Here there is no risk but the gain is divine bonanza. Once you are on divine path, union with God is assured without any risk.

Avarice for gold is intense and innate in human beings. For this gold there has been many bloodsheds and war among nations. In the past there has been many attacks on India from outsiders for gold and wealth. India was earlier known as gold producing country. Avarice for gold should be transformed into an avarice for attainment of inseparable union with God. It is pronounced in *Upanishad*:

hiranmayena patrena satyasyapihitam mukham
tat tvam pusan apavrnu satya-dharmaya drstaye

"The face of truth is covered with a golden disc. Unveil it, O pusan so that who love the truth may see it" (*Brhad-aranyak Upanishad*, V.15.1).

Being deluded by the glittering gold human beings forget to deeply penetrate into the veil of gold for attainment of indivisible union with Truth. The spiritual seekers instead of being stopped at the veil of bewitching gold, go beyond it by piercing it with sword of wisdom through constant practice of meditation and yoga as taught by the highly God realised masters.

As depicted by mother earth and Dharma, the people are not following the *varna system*. The four varnas are created by God on the basis of attributes and nature of karma. These are *Brahmin, Kshyatriya, Vaisya and Sudra*. These are not classification of people but classification of karma and characteristics. When we seek, worship and meditate on God and are spiritually inclined, we are playing the role of brahmins.

To be well established in God means to exercise supremacy over the enemies. The internal enemies like jealousy, greed, passion, desires, ego, pride, self-conceit, intolerance, attachment and delusion are to be wiped out from the very root. These internal foes are the shackles that bind us to the world and throw us into unending circuit of birth and death. The seeker has to annihilate these evil propensities through meditation under the able guidance of and company with God realised masters. Here, the seekers are doing the role of kshyatriyas.

Vaisya is concerned with cultivation, calculation of gain and loss and propelled into action or deeds by many desires. The spiritual seeker is to cultivate his body land properly. The spine and the seven chakras are to be cultivated to get the harvest of divine wealth. As seekers we have to calculate what is our gain by meditating and spiritual loss, we are incurring by wasting time. At the end of the day like the business man calculating his gain and loss, the spiritual seekers are to calculate what is their gain in terms of God realisation and what loss they incurred by not meditating or by wasting time with other trivial things not with God. In each and every desire the seeker perceives the presence of God. He has to cut asunder the fetters of endless desires (asapasasatair baddhah) and expectations that stand in the way of God realisation.

Sudra does not belong to low caste. As servant surrenders to the master and takes refuge in him as his sole sustainer, supporter and provider of his needs and requirements, the seeker surrenders completely to and takes ultimate refuge in God. As servant obeys the commands of the master, the seeker gets merged in Him always. It is the greatest stage of God realisation. The seekers who attain this highest stage sacrifices their life for the liberation of others like the servant sacrifices himself for the cause of the master. It is said in scriptures: parastheh prajnah

The men of wisdom exist for the other. They always love to serve the others (sarva bhuta hiteratah).

There were four foundations of Hindu life in ancient India which we have forgotten and are banished from our way of life. They are dharma, artha kama, mokshya.

Dharma is breath. To be conscious of breath every moment in all deeds, actions and thoughts is dharma. The seekers of Brahma remain always conscious of breath. Then the seekers are performing the role of Brahmins.

Artha means desire for money and earnings. Without breath there are no desires no earning for money and wealth. This desire is to be transformed into paramartha (supreme self) by remaining watchful of breath and surrendering all to God. Then we are Vaisyas.

Kama means desires, passion, all demonic and evil propensities. All these are the internal foes to be killed by the sword of wisdom. Every moment there is internal strife between the evil forces represented by Kauravas and divine forces represented by Pandavas with Krishna, the indwelling self as the sole conductor. So long as breath does not pass through the susumna passage – the royal divine road to Sahasrara by practice of Kriya Yoga under the guidance of the God realised Yogis, the evil forces are not to be easily crushed. Constant practice enables the seeker to play the role of true kshyatriya.

Mokshya is the ultimate liberation. After attainment of highest stage of God realisation (Nirvikalpa samadhi) the yogi behaves like a sudra and loves to serve others perceiving in them the existence of the all-compassionate God.

5

King Parikshita cursed to death by snake Takshyaka

Where is the fear to those who sing every moment the paeans about the heavenly majesties and beauty of Lord Krishna in solitude and stillness of mind and in synchrony with the rhythms of divine sound and with the lotus of their love and devotion blossoming in their hearts and with their nectar like words in reminiscence of His divine play on earth making them spiritually intoxicated and exalted to merge in Him? A seeker and lover of God taking ultimate refuge at His feet and getting united with Him every moment makes him immortal and imperishable like the space within the earthen jar when broken gets merged into the infinite all-pervading space.

The day Lord Krishna left His mortal body finishing His earthly incarnation and returned to His original abode, Kali, the embodiment of evil forces dared to enter into the world. But the King stopped his entry being the apostle of Dharma. Moved by his prayerful supplications, the king offered him five places to reside in. The Kali behaved like a bee eating away from within the essence of where it stays in. Those who think good of others without thinking anything for the future bear the fruits thereof. This is the attribute of Kali Yuga. Being kind-hearted and compassionate the king provided him his chosen places. Kali is powerless and fearful of those who are still and steadfast and established in God and behaves like a lion before the restless, agitated and deluded people.

One day, king Parikshita ventured into the deep forest for hunting deer. After long search in nook and cranny of the forest late into the day he failed to get even a single deer. Besides his dejected mood for the utter failure of his mission, what gnawed him more his hunger for food and thirst for water. Nowhere he uncovered a trace of food and water, he was in earnestly quest for. Moving here and there in the forest for these he lost the right way to go back to the palace. Wading his way through dense bushes and trees aimlessly he all of a sudden happened to see a sage named Angirasa (Shamika) in deep meditation with his eyes closed and body motionless and still and divine light haloing around his face and body rested on a mat of deer skin under a tree. The contemplating sage was betraying a sign of contentment and peace as witnessed by the king. The divine scene that was scripted by the sage with matted hair at that moment showed that he withdrawing his mind and intelligence from the nine doors of his body and the senses, was engrossed himself in the soul. Away from body and mind consciousness he was beyond the present, past and future completely merged in the Infinitude Ocean of the Divine. He was exuding an aura of immanent peace, bliss and joy quite ignorant of his existence and existence of the outside world.

To a hungry person perched with thirst, this blissful scene of divinity appeared meaningless and abstruse. The king only saw the picture of water overpowering his mind, intelligence and conscience. Looking at the sage in deep samadhi the king haunted by the thirst for water, beseeched water from him. The king in return for begging water to quench his thirst which had already dried up his throat, expected regal and warm welcome dignified to him from the sage who would come up and receive the king with due honours and soft and sweet words and a mat to sit on. Nothing happened belying his expectations. Even the much sought-after water seemed to be a far-flung thing. The indifference and nonresponse to the king's request for water strained his patience and defiled his conscience to assume that sage showed his disobedience and disrespect to him. The mind in a stage of quietness and calmness makes a person act conscientiously. But the sense of hunger led by his agitated mind affected his conscience. Long waiting and nonresponse infuriated the king. Under the spell of Kala (Time Spirit), the king riding high in the tempest of anger searched for something that would be a befitting reply to the callous, indifferent and adamant sage. When man is consumed by the fury of rage, he forgets his conscience to act in a gentle and humane way. All unvirtuous and immoral things are perpetrated at this stage of agitated mind. This happened to the king. While in search of something his eyes fell on a dead snake. He immediately caught hold of it by his arrow and put it around the neck of the divinely intoxicated sage like a garland. With this deprecatory nuisance done to the sage, the king returned to his palace without any second thought. While on his way the king started casting aspersion on the sage. He thought, the sage must be deceptively behaving like a yogi merged in samadhi. Had he been in samadhi, he would not have closed his eyes. Knowing beforehand the possible arrival of the king the sage might have feigned closing his eyes with the determination to show disrespect to the king. Being a human, he should not have shown so much disobedience to the king forgetting all etiquette due to a king. The sage Shamika did not know what wrong was done to him.

Time passed on. Shrungi, the son of sage Shamika was playing with his friends some distance away from the ashram quite ignorant of what happened in the ashram.

While playing he heard from his friends the wrong done to his father. This unethical and wrongful work done by the king fired Shrungi with anger who was glowing with divinity. He thought in his mind, the king who was supposed to sustain, support and respect Dharma, could be able to work in such a morally reproachable and unsustainable way. He acted like an ignorant and unrighteous being in total disrespect of what were adored as the nuances of a king described in scriptures and Vedas. When rishis and sages do the yajnas, they used to keep kshytriyas at the gate to give protection. With the departure of Lord Krishna this kind of unethical and immoral works were taking place. With this kind of kings on this earth there would be denigration of Dharma.

Saying this much to his friends in a fury he kept the water of the holy river Koushaki flowing nearby within his palm and with utterance of mantra and doing the necessary rituals of purifying him, and keeping in mind the king cursed him. "From this day on seventh day Takshyaka, the snake will bite the king to death. My words will never come untrue. Why a person showing dishonour to my father will survive?" After cursing the king very harshly, he rushed to the ashrama to meet his father. Beholding the dead snake on the neck of his father, he started crying aloud to such an extent that his father Shamika finishing the meditation opened his eyes to see the dead snake around his neck. He got up and throw away the snake from his body. Seeing his son in tears he asked his son, "why are you crying? Who brought tears in your eyes and for what reason?" Son Shrungi narrated everything to his father.

In a scathing and strongly worded rebuke to his son, sage Shamika chided his son:

"For a very trivial mistake you punished him so cruelly to death. Why you did so? He is divine and pure. He is an apostle of Dharma. This punishment you meted out to him is not fit for him. I was heavily shocked and saddened at your rude and cruel conduct. You cursed him to death on whom the people depend for protection of Dharma and living a very peaceful and contented life without any want and difficulty. He shows hatred towards none. An embodiment of God he upheld Dharma and after his demise Kali Yuga will enter unleashing the evil and unrighteous forces. People will live like flock of sheep without the shepherd. There will be burglary and theft of property and

wealth rampantly. People will enter into forests fearlessly and kill animals. Women will be subject to sexual exploitation. The world will be master less without the king. King has restored the four feet to Dharma by subduing Kali Yuga. With his death Dharma will lose all its feet. That means, people will not live and act according to the Varna system as enunciated by Vedas. Living aside Dharma and mokshya, the people will be engrossed in artha and kama. They will live like dogs and monkeys by renouncing Dharma. This king is divine, holy, pure and the direct embodiment of God. He is rajashri. He performed three asvamedha yajnas names as agama, nigama, and prasiddhi. He came to our ashram in great hunger and thirst. He sought water from us. Instead of serving him you cursed him. He is not entitled to be cursed by us as he is always governed by Dharma."

The rishi Shamika implored very earnestly to God:

"O God! You are the sole protector and saviour to the virtuous and spiritual. My son being unhappy with the conduct of the king and with little intelligence cursed your devotee to death. You are the ocean of compassion and kindness. I beseech you to excuse my son. Those who are your devotees never do harm to others. They are not jealous of others. They never use calumny against others. They never get angry and are always forgiving and tolerant of others' misdeeds. Their mind is always in Thee. I have done a very unkind deed of injustice. I am a sinner and unvirtuous. I have punished an innocent and faultless king. I am highly perturbed by such heinous deed which is against the Divine. I will suffer very soon in this adverse world".

The rishi praying God thus, got buried in deep repentance for his son. That the king committed a grave mistake, was not taken note of by him. He remained concerned with his son's mistake done to a divine king. In this mundane world, the self-realised masters like him never get angry and take seriously the mistakes of others. They remain always forgiving, compassionate and understanding. They are never overwhelmed with joy for praises. They remain above calumny and praises. They always feel for others. They perceive the same soul abiding in all.

While the sage Shamika was deeply repentant for the wrong done to the king by taking unto himself the blame, the king similarly sitting in solitude contemplated on the grave sin he perpetrated by putting a dead snake around the neck of the sage. After the fume of anger gone away and thirst for water quenched, the king came to the senses and in state of bewilderment and sorrowful mind thought to himself:

"I committed a deed that is deprecatory and opprobrious and contrary to the long established venerable Indian tradition and nuances of Vedas. *This is the result of my own earned karma as taught by my gurus. Like an uncultured and irreligious person, I did the work. Around the neck of an innocent sage, I put a snake. In acute thirst I lost my coolness and stillness of mind and power of discrimination to know that the sage was deeply immersed in contemplation. I did this to the discontentment of God. For this I have to face the consequences. Let death be unto me by Providence for bringing an end to my much-hated sin. In the fire of sage's rage let me along with my soul, my*

kingdom and my wealth be burnt to ashes so that I will never repeat this in future and act against the Vedic cows, Brahmin, and divine beings".

While scolding himself in a very remorseful mind, he found in his ears was resonating the ill spoken words about his imminent death by Takshyaka bite on seventh day being cursed by the son of the sage. Regaled himself with great joy he wished let the serpent devour him soon. He consoled him, "by this my dynasty and me will not fall into sorrows in this life and after life". Thinking this was irreversible and inevitable, he decided to leave the world along with his kingdom and take final refuge and rest at the feet of the Lord. This was the best option available to him, he thought. Without any further delay after making Janmajeya his son as the king on the advice of the sages, he very determinedly left everything dear to him and reached the bank of the holy river Ganges where he would breathe his last. He thought by sitting near the holy water of the mother Ganges flowing from the lotus feet of the Lord consecrated by the holy Tulasi leave on His feet, his life will be highly gratified by the grace of God. With this thought he engrossed himself at the feet of the Lord motionless, still and steadfast leaving completely water and food.

This news spread like a wild fire everywhere not barring the hermitages and ashramas in the forests. The sages, yogis and saints left their hermitages along with their disciples and moved towards Hasthinapur to meet the king on the bank of the mother Ganges. They included Devarshi, Maharshi, Brahmarshi and Rajarshi like Atri, Vasistha, Ristanemi, Chyavana,

Varadvaja, Vrugu, Angira, Parashara, Utathya, Visvamitra, Medhatithi, Indrapramada, Devala, Subahu, Goutama, Maitreya, Kabasha, Pipplayana, Ourva, Vyasa, Narada and Aasthya etc. Beholding them all assembled there king Parikshita with folded hands touching his forehead prostrated himself at their feet with tears of joy streaming down. Offering them mats to sit on, he in great adoration of the sages and saints present there with hymns of praises of their greatness and glories, Parikshita imploringly said:

"O Supreme ones! Today I know that being among the kings my life is highly gratified. On the very last moment of my life, the great sages and saints have arrived unexpectedly near me with joy. This place has become now sacred where I washed your feet and got the wash water as nectar and consecrated prasad. There is no greater privilege and destiny than this. What the gods have not obtained, today I was divinely privileged to get. It is my sin committed against the sage Shamika that enabled me to give up the world and sit at the feet of the Lord with wholeheartedness and detachment in the company of an assemblage of saints and sages at the very moment of my imminent death. The fire of the anger and curse of a sage burned my illusion, delusion error and ignorance to ashes and became very fortunately the root of my detachment and renunciation. I pray you all to be happy with my humble service and surrender and grace me so that mother Ganges will bless me to engross myself in the consciousness of Lord Krishna. Let Takshyaka devour me, I have no fear or I do not think of it at all. Let my mind be merged in Krishna consciousness. Where I will be born

in the next life according to the fruits of my karma, let me be the humble servant of Lord Krishna at His holy feet".

He prayed with all humbleness and tears of joy and love at the feet of the sages and saints, O great ones! Be all kind to me and bless me with what I am very earnestly cherishing".

Parikshita on the south bank of the river Ganges prepared a seat with kusha (a kind of grass used for worship and meditation) and putting it towards east he sat on it facing north for meditation on Lord Krishna. Without thinking anything his whole being merged in Krishna consciousness. The gods from above showered flowers on him with joy in praises of the king amidst various divine sounds that resonated the sky. The sages and saints assembled there also with great joy joined the chorus and started speaking to each other:

"This is astonishing that the pious and dharmic king will die at such an early age. Because of his destiny it is going to happen at the last moment of his departure that he is among a galaxy of sages and saints from various parts of the country. The king Parikshita to whom all kings bowed down and adored, will leave the body with God consciousness he has earned from his very childhood when he was in his mother's womb. So long as the king does not leave the body completely mingling with the Lord with enraptured joy, we will be here living on fruits and water as it is an altar devoid of any sorrow or attachment and delusion and the most sacred place. He is the supreme divine being among all and surely, he will attain the highest stage of God realisation".

The words from the mouth of the sages and saints were to the king as true and as sweet as nectar. All his doubts vanished. To be in euphoric joy in the thought of the Lord is the result of one's accumulated love for Him in his past life. What is not easily available to even Lord Shiva and Lord Brahma, has been available to a very fortunate few for having taken refuge in the Lord. The king thought to himself:

"It is because of my good fortune I have got the divine company of all sages and saints near me just on the eve of my death. As nuanced by Vedas, *the people reap happiness and sorrows as fruits of their karmas performed according to the Varna system in this life and after life. It is all of your mellowing hearts moistening for others that have made you gracious enough to come here. I am entreating you all what are the things I have to do at this moment for my liberation from this mundane world?"*

No sooner had the king finished his prayer seeking to know the way from the assembled sages and saints than the supreme yogi, the guru of all, Shuka Mahamuni with his horde of young disciples all looking like avadhuttas completely naked and looking very young and lustrous about sixteen years of age, stunningly elegant in beauty and glamour with a glowing aura of eternal joy and peace defeating Kamadeva and resembling that of Lord Krishna and the cynosure of all, arrived there. Stupefied at his indescribable and illuminating chiselled complexion resplendent with divinity all sages and saints including the king stood up in awe and reverence. The king Parikshita bowed down at his feet with all love and devotion worshipping him with flowers and all other things. Seated among the sages and saints near to the king, Shuka Mahamuni was resembling like a moon among the stars. Prostrating himself again and again at his feet with his folded hands the king prayed him:

Born in Kshatriya dynasty I made my life gratified by your holy presence at this moment. Getting such a Brahma rishi with a pure heart and mind my life has become gratified and sacred. By the very touch of your holy feet my body has been transformed into a place of pilgrimage. Remembering and keeping faith in you has made our worldly life holy. At the very sight of you all sins deposited in me have vanished. To get water that touches your feet is equal to all the good fruits that one will accrue by having pilgrimages to many holy places. Lord Krishna sojourned with Pandavas out of love, compassion and grace. Being born to them I have been graced by you to have your darshan. Company with you at the very last moment of my death will certainly enable me to cross the worldly ocean. You are the supreme Guru among the yogis like an immovable mountain. Nobody can be able to know you, your will and direction. You usually do not stay a moment at any body's door. Very fearful of this uncertainty I entreat you with a heaved heart that quests very solicitously within for a path that will liberate me from this worldly delusion. What sadhana I will do? What divine sound I will hear? On whom I will fix my mind? What I will invoke through my mouth? Whose feet I will worship? Whom I will remember in my mind?"

Moved by the heart-rending prayers of the king Parikshita, Mahamuni Shukadeva relapsed into the divine ocean of infinitute bliss of God in great ecstasy and explained to him in details about Srimad

Bhagavatam he has learnt from his father Maharshi Vyasadeva. He told the king about the omnipresent, omniscient and omnipotent and unmanifest God, the creator and His creation. He enkindled in him the knowledge of God and His embodiment as the indwelling self in all beings, both living and non-living. Through the practice of the eight limbs of yoga he taught him how to be established in God and how to realise Him everywhere. Within seven days through the active guidance of Mahamuni Shukadeva, the king passed through all the stages of God realisation as taught in Kriya Yoga until he attained the highest stage of God realisation (Nirvikalpa samadhi). He said to the king:

"With the attainment of this highest stage of God realisation, you have become immortal and conquered death. The fear of death will no longer touch you. The veil of ignorance has been removed and you have entered into the enlightened wisdom. You will not take birth again nor you were born in past nor you will die at present. Who has no origin will never perish. Nobody belongs to you. The space confined within the earthen pot mingles with the all-pervading infinite space when the pot is broken. Similarly, the indwelling soul will join the infinite God with the perish of your mortal body. Once, you are well established in God by the attainment of Nirvikalpa samadhi your body bitten by Takshyaka will be burnt to ashes. Since you are dissolved in God like the waves and ocean being one, you will not be able to feel the bite but you will remain just a witness to this act remaining merged in the cosmic consciousness. The deluded body will perish and you will be deathless. I have taught you the techniques of yoga the perfect practice of

which with love and devotion will lead you to complete liberation forever by snapping the snares of worldly delusion. Vasudeva (God) is none else than the indwelling soul in every being. Concentrating on Him through the practice of yoga you enter into the door of liberation".

Completely abreast of what Mahamuni Shukadeva instructed and taught him the means by which he will attain Godhood, the king with overwhelming tears of joy and his whole body and mind enraptured with gratitude laid himself down at the feet of Shukadeva and prayed with folded hands:

"O son of Maharshi Vyasadeva, you are supreme and glowing embodiment of wisdom. The entire universe is your manifested self. By your grace I have got permanent liberation from the shackles of the circuit of unending birth and death. The sublime truth gleaned from Srimad Bhagavatam, *you brought me to realisation as nothing but Lord Sri Krishna Himself. By the direct realisation of the Lord, I was made pure and unblemished. I have no longer the fear of death either from Takshyaka or anything else. All my ignorance, delusion, illusion, error and ignorance vanished by being united with the supreme, imperishable and unmanifest Brahma. I pray you to be kind and gracious to allow me to remain merged in the Lord by the practice of eight limbs of Yoga as taught by you in transcendence of the six chakras to be ultimately perched in the thousand petalled lotus chakra (Sahasrara) and go beyond into the Infinite. I am enthralled with divine euphoria to get merged at the most beseeched after the Feet of Lord Krishna".*

Shuka Mahamuni said, "O king, I bless you to attain Godhood and be free from the worldly delusion.

With our blessings you will soon reach the ultimate abode of the Lord".

With these words of blessings Shukadeva along with other congregated sages and saints in great joy left the place to Badarika leaving behind the king in solitude for ultimate dissolution in God.

As instructed by Mahamuni Shukadeva, in great divine exultation the king Parikshita relapsed into the cave of cranium (Sahasrara chakra) crossing the six chakras with the breath drawn through the sushumna nadi within the spine with the prayer to the Lord:

"O God you are the supreme. There is no end to Thy divine glories and majesties. You are known to yourself. There is no liberation without Thee. Let my mind be ever rested at your lotus feet. I take ultimate refuge in you. You are my destination, goal, and eternal abode. I implore you with all my body, mind and soul to enable me cross the worldly ocean".

By the practice of the technique of yoga as taught by Shukadeva the king released his embodied soul through the susumna path and merged it with the Infinite Supreme Paramabrahma from the sahasrara chakra, the Brahma door. The body remained motionless and still after the soul was released and the king entered into Nirviklapa samadhi, the attainment of deathlessness stage.

Takshhyaka bite the body of king Parikshita

On the seventh day while Takshyaka was rushing towards the king for killing him in the guise of a brahmana, he met on the way another brahmana named Kasyapa on his heels. On being asked by Takshyaka, the purpose for which he was going in a hurry, the brahmana replied, "I am going to revive the life of the king by withdrawing the poison from his body being bitten by Takshyaka for which I will be offered plenty of wealth, my name, fame and act of Dharma will reach the zenith".

Thus, heard from the mouth of Kasyapa, Takshyaka supplicated him, "O supreme being! Do not bring an end to my name and fame and the purpose for which I am destined to go. The words of the sage are bound to come true. Nobody has the power to nullify it. Why you are going unnecessarily to save the life of the king which is going to be impossible by the curse. It is the innate nature of great persons to think always good of others. I promise to give you more than double of the wealth to be offered by the king".

Hearing these words, the Brahmana pondered over and asked to himself, "by dint of yoga I know that the king has no longevity. He is bound to breathe his last. If this be his fate, why should I deprive myself of so much wealth offered by Takshyaka?". He immediately assured Takshyaka, "I have no intention to bring slur to your name and fame. If you give me wealth as promised I will return from this spot".

On being offered the bonanza of wealth, the brahmana left the place and Takshyaka went to the king seated on meditation on the bank of the holy river Ganges masquerading himself as a brahmana with flowers and fruits. Turning himself immediately into an insect in the fruit Takshyaka bite the feet of the king. The poison of the chameleon like Takshyaka entered into the body of the king and burnt it into ashes to the chagrin of all present there. The celestial beings and gods in the heaven remained stunned at witnessing the scene. During the time of the bite, the king was no more in the body. He was already merged with God. The dead body was only burnt to ashes by Takshyaka's bite. The gods and celestial dancers showered flowers on the king on his ultimate liberation.

Reflections

In the ebb and flow of Time Spirit (kala) the sages, saints and scriptures have located four yugas (a particular time span) on the basis of the attributes of human nature. Kala is devoid of any attribute. It is the nature and type of attributes of human beings in a particular time span that define a yuga. According to them the yugas move in a cyclic way. These are Satya, Tretaya, Dvapar and Kali yugas. The dominant characteristic of Satya yuga is truth. In this yuga people are seekers of truth and are always on the path of truth. Truth is to watch the breath in all actions, and thoughts with wholehearted concentration on the indwelling self. There were no forms and formalities, no cults and no religion. All were in truth. As described in Srimad Bhagavatam in this yuga dharma was having four feet. All divine qualities as described above were inherent in human beings.

This yuga declined with deterioration in these divine propensities. Meditation and sadhana went away with this yuga.

Next yuga is Tretaya. In this yuga truth was prevailing predominantly up to seventy five percent. Purity was lost in this yuga. It was a yuga of activity. One feet of dharma was lost in this era.

In Dvapara yuga truth or dharma prevails fifty percent. This was an era of duality. Two feet of dharma was lost in this age.

In Kali yuga truth or dharma prevails twenty five percent and demoniac forces predominate as described above. Truth or dharma has lost three feet.

Each individual can realise the four yugas depending upon the span of time he is whether under the sway of divine or sway of demoniac forces. If the seeker remains in truth every moment throughout day and night in a thoughtlessness stage, he is very much in the Satya yuga. The self-realised masters belong to this category. If seventy five percent of the span of time is spent in truth without any deviation, he belongs to Tretaya, the second category of seekers who have not yet attained the highest stage of God realisation. If the people remain 50 percent in truth and 50 percent in forgetfulness of the divine, they can be said as madhyama, the third category people. If seventy five percent of one's time span is devoted to enjoying the play of worldly delusion and rest span is towards divinity, then that person is in kali yuga.

The four yugas can be realised by an individual in simultaneity depending on his intensity of love, desire and detachment.

The king Parikshita has the potential and ability like any spiritual seeker to arrest the entry of Kali Yuga into the kingdom. It implies the spiritual seeker needs to subdue or control the demoniac forces in order to realise God. In this body kingdom up to Visuddha chakra from Muladhara chakra man is controlled by the demoniac or evil forces. In *Bhagavad Gita* it is described that human kingdom has nine gates (two eyes, two ears, two nostrils, mouth, anus, and generating organ) through which man enjoys sense derived pleasures. These senses make man extrovert and drive him into the snare of worldly delusion, illusion, error and ignorance. It is declared in *Katha Upanishad*:

paranci khani vyatrnat svayambhus tasmat paran pasyati nantaratman

kascid dhirah pratyag-atmanam aiksad avrtta-caksur amrtat-vam iccchan (II.1.1).

The indwelling Self is not to be sought through the senses. Through the openings of the senses, one goes outward; therefore, one looks outward and not within oneself. Wise men however seeking the eternal, with their eyes turned inward and realise the Self within.

The spiritual seeker is to withdraw his senses inward from the outward sense objects like a tortoise through constant practice and detachment. By the control of the senses through practice of Yoga one is established in the Supreme Self. In *Bhagavad Gita* it is enunciated:

sarvakarmani manasa samnyasya 'ste sukham vasi

navadvare pure dehi nai 'va kurvanna karayan (5:13)

A self-controlled yogi always remains in blissful joy in the physical body likened to a city with nine gates, performing no actions and causing others to act.

In the beautiful words of Paramahamsa Hariharananda, a supreme self-realised master in Kriya Yoga, the mind of each human being remains in the body at three levels. The first level is up to the navel centre starting from the base of the spine covering Muladhara (coccygeal) and Svadhisthan (sacral) and Manipur (lumbar).

The second level is between the navel and the pituitary covering the dorsal (Anahata chakra) cervical (Visuddha chakra) and the soul centre (pituitary).

The third level of the mind is between the soul centre and the fontanel (Sahasrara chakra). The minds of those who ascend above the third level are completely transformed into cosmic consciousness. Their minds merged in brahmananda, the divine bliss, are beyond pleasure and pain. In soul consciousness the devotee though performs all actions through nine gates, he remains detached to the pleasure and pain. A self-realised yogi remaining constantly at the third level of mind feels the soul is the sole doer and remains detached from everything mundane. In a similar vein *Katha Upanishad* pronounces:

puram ekadasa-dvaram ajasyavakra-cetasah anusthaya na socati vimuktasch vimucyate: etad vai tat (II.2.1)

Here two more gates are added, one is navel and the second is Sahasrara (saggital suture, the opening at the top of the skull). By controlling these gates, the embodied soul gets jivan mukta while living in divine bliss and after the death it reaches videha mukta (complete liberation).

Man has long been associated with senses and sense derived pleasures during his previous births. Though these desires like passion, anger, jealousy, greed, ego and self-conceit are the arch foes of human beings, they misconstrue that they are permanent and friends to them. King Parikshita raised his sword to kill Kali yuga but being moved by its supplication he put the sword back into the sheath. It implies every human being has been endowed with the sword of wisdom to decimate these demoniac forces remaining within in the lower chakras of human beings. Unless and until the seeker has thorough control over these fleeting senses, the door to attainment of the highest stage of God realisation will not open. Lord Sri Krishna admonished Arjuna in *Bhagavad Gita*, even one sense organ left uncontrolled despite his thorough control over all other senses will beguile the seeker into worldly delusion:

indriyanam hi caratam yan mano 'nuvidhiyate

tad asya harati prajnam vayur navam iva 'mbhasi
(2:67)

Just as a storm overpowers a boat at sea, even one of the biological forces and the sense organs beguiling the mind makes it devoid of wisdom.

Mind can make a person a thief, a philosopher, a saint, a poet, a scientist and whatever his/her mind thinks him/her to be. Mind is the cause of liberation and bondage as well. Mind with the instrumentalities of senses has put a person into a series of births. It is very difficult to control and discipline the mind. Swami Vivekananda said "if I were to take a human birth in my next life, I will first try to discipline my mind. By controlling mind, I will achieve everything even the impossible". Nothing is more difficult than controlling the mind. Mind flows in many directions being propelled by the fleeting senses. Arjuna asked this question to Lord Sri Krishna: "My mind is very unstable, agitating, and I feel it uncontrollable like wind in the sky". Unless one is strongly established in Truth and wisdom one's mind is likely to fall prey to the play of senses. One incident excerpted from the Mahabharat is illustrative of sometimes the men of knowledge being swayed by the beguiling senses. One day sage Vyasa dictated Jamini his disciple to write that the mind and senses are so powerful that even a person of wisdom is likely to fall down from the righteous path. Jamini did not agree with this, and added a point saying a person of wisdom can remain invincible in the face of powerful senses and mind. Guru dictated one thing and the disciple wrote a different version. Being omniscient sage Vyasa could know within no time what Jamini did. That day in the afternoon, Maharshi Vyasadeva called Jamini near him saying "I am going outside and I may not come back tonight. Take care that the holy fire that is burning in the fireplace is not extinguished to perform the daily ritual". Giving these instructions Vyasadev left the ashram and Jamini began meditating. Unexpectedly, torrential rain started with storm and thunder. Jamini closed the door from inside not to allow storm and water gushing into the room. A little time after he heard a knock on the door with a woman's soft voice entreating, "I lost the way to my village and in this terrible storm I have no other way than to seek shelter here tonight and in the next morning I will leave to my place". Jamini replied, "I am a monk how can I allow you to stay with me in the same room"? After these words he began to think it is the primary duty of a monk to help others who are in distress. Being caught in these two lines of thinking he opened the door and invited the lady inside and he himself came outside. But while coming outside he could able to see the very beautiful face of the lady glowing in the fire. After his exit the woman bolted the door from inside. The exquisite beauty of the woman came rolling in his mind repeatedly propelling a desire that stirred up the quietness of his mind. Even one desire can vacillate a mind to the point of beyond control. He began to think, "it is too cold outside and I can go inside and sit near the fire. Since I am a monk, I am in control nothing will happen". Overpowered by this thinking he knocked at the door requesting her to open the door as it is severe cold outside and he is being drenched by the rain outside. "I am a monk named Jamini and it is my duty to keep the fire burning. The woman remained adamant saying it is not good to open the door to let you in since I am a woman staying inside alone. In spite of his persistence with this kind of solicitous supplications, the woman did not open the door. However, uncontrollable by the incestuous impulse, he managed to go inside. Like fire burning brighter and brighter his desire ignited to the point of suggesting her, "we can stay together as I love you very much". She protested saying it was forbidden and unethical on his part to say so as he is a monk. With finding the monk insistent on with this kind of request, she relented and agreed to go along with his plan but only with one condition. The condition was, "you will be like a horse on all fours and I will sit on your back and move around the fire seven times. Then, I will accept your proposal". Being overeaten by passion a person behaves like a blind person. Jamini agreed to the proposal and did exactly what she put as condition. Sitting on his back the young lady revolved around the fire. While this was going on, she struck the head of Jamini and chanted the same verse he heard from his Guru Vyasadeva: The mind and senses are so powerful that even a person of knowledge might commit a mistake. Hearing this he immediately stood up and asked who are you and your voice resembles like that of my Guru. When he looked at her, he was astounded to see that she is none else than his Gurudeva standing in her place.

Lord Krishna has given the allegory of a tortoise to Arjuna to control the senses. As a tortoise withdraws all his senses from the objects and does not show any reaction to the outside objects, similarly a person in order to establish him in wisdom has to withdraw completely from the senses and sense attached objects (*Gita* 2:58). A person remains completely anchored in wisdom and remains calm and quiet only when he withdrawing himself from the senses controls them.

A person finding no peace in the materialistic world and leaving aside everything he led an ascetic life. His only belongings were his loin ochre cloth and a tortoise. He lives on the alms he used to get by begging every day from householders. After taking his food he feeds the tortoise. Seeing this unusual scene, a visitor one day asked him, "why you have kept such an ugly animal. It is better you leave this in a pond". The saint answered, "to you this is ugly and unnecessary but to me this is the source of my inspiration and I have considered it my guru. With a little touch and likely danger from outside it immediately withdraws all its sense organs into its shell and shows no reactions and responses to the outside world even if it is thrown a little. Similarly, a person has to withdraw himself from all sense organs and sense attached objects outside without any reaction. He has to withdraw always from the internal enemies like anger, avarice, jealousy, violence and enmity which are created by attachment to senses and objects. One has to remain detached like the tortoise. By seeing it every day I practice the way the tortoise withdraws its senses into its shell. The eternal truth it conveys every moment to me inspires me in my spiritual path and attainment of Godhood".

Senses are the path towards the sense objects to which mind is easily distracted. Man loses the power of discrimination to judge what is right and what is wrong. He gets bewildered as he has lost thorough control over his senses and mind. In the Yogic texts (Hatha Yoga Pradipika IV:29) it is said, indriyanam mano natho manonathastu marutah. "The mind is the king of the five senses, but the breath is the king of the mind". By controlling the breath, one can control the wild mind. By the practice of Yoga, the spine of the seeker will be magnetised and breath will be regulated through pranayama. The seeker will be established in the indwelling Self having achieved success in subduing the evil forces, wild mind, wavering thoughts, erratic intellect, flaunted ego and attachment to senses.

The king being thirsty and hungry in the forest reached the ashram of rishi Shamika and asked for water, Since the rishi was in deep contemplation and merged in cosmic consciousness, the king was not shown due honour and regal treatment. In the scripture 'Panchatantra' it is said bhubhukshitam kim na karoti papam. The hunger and thirst when stretched to their tether's end, a man cannot hesitate to do any crime without thinking over it a moment. King's being incensed at this attitude of indifference represents metaphorically a man put in such a condition of doing anything. The king being righteous and embodiment of dharma behaved like an ordinary angry man ready to commit any crime.

When one is in a fury his memory is lost, intelligence acts in a negative way and he ultimately perishes. Anger is considered as one of the six foes to man (sada ripu) and one of the eight nooses (asta pasa) that fetters a man to worldly delusion. The king should have asked his conscience and thought over the other side. A yogi in samadhi stage is not aware of what is happening around him. He even could not be able to know that the king has put a dead snake around his neck out of anger. The king lost his memory that he is the grandson of king Yudhishthira who remains calm, still and unperturbed in every situation. Being descendant of Pandavas, he should have acted like Yudhishthira. Rather, the consequences of his anger resulted in being cursed by Shringi, the son of the rishi to be bitten by Takshyaka to death on seventh day. But the king Yudhishthira behaved differently when he was thirsty during their exile. It is beautifully described in the Vana Parva of the great epic Mahabharata:

During the second exile, while the Pandavas were walking in the forest, Yudhishthira was parched and wanted to drink water. So, he asked his brothers to bring water for him. Climbing to the top of a tree the youngest Sahadeva noticed a pond not far away from the place. Coming down he went straight to fetch water from the pond. Time passed on but there was no sign of his returning. Then, Nakul followed him. In this way all four brothers left Yudhishthira one after another to fetch water but nobody was returning. In great anxiety and curiosity, Yudhishthira himself rushed to the place to see what was happening. He was very much shocked and saddened to see that all his four brothers were lying dead on the bank of the pond. He thought, it was not due to any attack from outside as there was nobody on the earth who would defeat Arjuna. How was that he could be defeated? Perhaps, the water was poisonous. Being thirsty, he went to the pond to drink water. While he was bringing water through his palms to drink, he heard suddenly a voice admonishing him against drinking water without answering his questions. Otherwise, you will meet the same fate as your brothers have. Putting the water back into the pond, Yudhishthira asked him, "first tell me who are you talking?". The voice replied, "I am a yakshya (a celestial). If you want to drink water, first answer all my questions". This is famously known as Yakshya-Yudhishthira dialogue. A person of calmness and stillness, Yudhishthira replied all questions one after another very wisely to the great contentment of Yaxha. Highly pleased with Yudhishthira, he brought life back to all his brothers.

Being in the same situation of thirsty for water, both Parikshita and Yudhishthira behaved differently, one got the boon and the other got the curse of death. Parikshita acted out of anger and egoism and Yudhishthira with calmness of mind and humbleness without show of ego behaved. In *Bhagavad Gita*, Lord Krishna has narrated about the evil propensities like anger, ego, passion, and jealousy and desires which stand in the way of attainment of divinity. In *Bhagavad Gita* it is averred:

duhkhesu anudvignamanah sukhesu vigatasprhah

vitaragabhayakrodhah sthitadhir munir ucyate (2:56)

He whose mind remains unperturbed in sorrows and does not remain buoyant with pleasure and who is free from passion, fear and anger, is called a sthitaprajna (sage) fully established in wisdom.

King Parikshita's mind was disturbed by hunger and anger. He could not remain calm and quiet in an untoward situation when no response was coming forth in spite of his requests. A truly spiritual person maintains an attitude of equanimity in all situations whether adverse or pleasant. He is not to crush his biological or psychological force but to feel the unity in diversity. The soul is both pleasure and pain. He has to realise the soul in all dispositions and moods. Out of hunger or thirst the soul cannot die or perish because it is immortal and imperishable. The person established in wisdom remains in the soul but not attached to the body. Duality disappears. The distinction between subject and objects vanishes, he becomes one and feels unity with the imperishable soul. He is no longer moved by sense perceptions or by pleasure or pain and is always filled with calmness. He can attain the blissful stage of immortality (*Bhagavad Gita* 2:15).

Life is a continuum in which birth and death are at the two ends. As birth entails pangs to come out of the mother's womb, death in order to get out of the pangs of worldly delusion provides the opportunity to fly into immortality. Life is a long journey through many ordeals of hazards, obstacles, difficulties, challenges and pitfalls of which no one knows the beginning and end. In the process of evolution of human life, death is an important and inevitable aspect. It is not to be dreaded or feared. If there is birth, there is also death. Sri Krishna said to Arjuna in *Bhagavad Gita*:

jatasya hi dhruvo mrtyur dhruvam janama mrtasya ca
tasmad apariharye 'rthe na tvam socitum arhasi (2:27)

Birth is followed by death. It is certain and ineluctable. After death, birth is bound to occur. You should not lament over what is inevitable.

It may come to anybody at any time. Like sun rising in the east and setting in the west, death is certain to happen. As we are rejoicing in birth, we should also rejoice in death. It is the natural companion of every living being. It is not a foe but a friend, a teacher and guide. Like a snake sloughing its old skin off to put on a new one, a person (Jivatma) caged in and bound by three bodies – gross, astral and causal and deluded and steeped in material attachment puts on a new garb of another life in the cycle of birth and death for his evolution. Death provides him the opportunity for fulfilment of his desires. On the other hand, death opens the door of immortality to a person who is detached, free from worldly delusion and anchored in the divine. In the *Bhagavad Gita* (2:22), Lord Krishna says, "As a person shirking the worn-out clothes puts on new ones, likewise the embodied soul, shedding the worn-out bodies, enters into new ones". In the long journey of human life from darkness to light, from ignorance to wisdom and from delusion to truth, and from consciousness to super consciousness death has been the trusted companion to help in transformation of life.

God is death. In *Bhagavad Gita* Lord Krishna said to Arjuna:

aham eva 'ksayah kalo dhata 'ham visvatomukhah (10: 33)

I alone am the imperishable and infinite kala. I am the sustainer of everything, having my face on all sides.

Similarly, in next verse Lord Krishna said:

mrtyuh sarvaharas ca ham

udbhavas ca bhavisyatam (10:34)

I am the all-destroying death and the origin of everything that shall yet be born.

I am immortality as well as death (amrutam cai 'va mrtyus ca, 9:19).

In verse 32 Lord Krishna said:

kalo smi lokaksayakrt pravrddho

lokan samahartum iha pravrttah (*Gita* 11:32)

I am Kala, the eternal time spirit, the mighty cause of the world's destruction. I am out to annihilate the worlds.

Death is not to be feared. It is the gateway to liberation if the seeker so earnestly desires. Death opens the door to the unending chain of birth and death to those who are deluded and overpowered by demonic qualities like passion, anger, avarice, pride, conceit and attachment. It also opens the door to the Divine to those who are detached and well established in God with love and devotion with an unwavering mind and above all dualities of gratification of senses like pain and pleasure, sorrows and happiness, gain or loss, victory or defeat. It is through struggle and constant efforts a seeker can enter the stage of attainment of the divine. Within us reside both the devil and divine. It is at your hand to seek. Jesus said, "The kingdom of God is within you". Man is to fight with the inner demonic and evil forces within in order to reach the highest stage of God realisation. In *Bhagavad Gita* Lord Krishna addressed Arjuna:

> tasmat sarvesu kalesu mam anusmar yudhya ca
> mayy arpitamanobuddhir mam evai syasy asamsayh
> (8:7)

Therefore, O Arjuna! Remember Me at all times and fight. When your mind and understanding are directed towards Me, you will come to Me, there is no doubt.

Lord Krishna is the indwelling self in every human being. Arjuna represents every human being, a spiritual seeker. The human beings must fight against their evil and demonic propensities and subdue the wicked biological forces and heighten their spiritual consciousness to the pituitary, the soul centre to realise the conception of God. Uttistha means to rise up to the soul centre and remain there with strong resolve and determination. If a seeker dies before he or she reaches the divine goal, Lord assures that there is nothing to lose, the seeker will attain divinity nonetheless. If the seeker succeeds in getting nirvikalpa samadhi, he will be continuously liberated though staying in the world. In the material world he will perceive the living presence of God. Human life is a constant fight between the biological forces and the spiritual forces within. The enemies are not outside. The real enemies are anger, ego, pride, hypocrisy, avarice, lust and passion. These negative and evil forces keep man always away from his sojourn in the divinity. Without making one's mind captive to these evil tendencies man should direct his mind and intellect towards God. One must remember God at every moment and in every breath, every action and every state of life. So, the Lord is saying, *"O Arjuna! Constantly fight all your negative propensities while remembering Me. I am always with you never lost to you. I am inseparable from you"*.

Parikshita being the grandson of Arjuna has the finest conception of God while he was in mother's womb. There he was privileged to perceive the living presence of Lord Krishna. Being cursed he was sure that his life would come to an end on 7th day from then. He was not fearful of death. Rather, he welcomed it like Naciketa who was sacrificed by his father rishi Vajasraba to god Yama (god of death). He was able to get liberation and returned to earth in his physical form by the grace and teachings of Lord Yama (Death). Similarly, king Parikshita was determined to leave the world and cut asunder all his attachment to the material world. Handing over the responsibility of the kingdom to his son he went to the bank of the holy river mother Ganges and started thinking and contemplating on the Lord without food and water.

When death will come nobody knows. It may come at any time. But king Parikshita was fortunate to know that he had had at least seven days within his hand to think of God. People generally shudder at the news of death. But he was very joyful to face death as he was a spiritual and divine being having the knowledge and awareness of the perishability of human body and immortality of the abiding soul merging with whom is the real identity of every human being not identity with the mortal body. This knowledge he experienced from mother's womb while he was facing imminent death and saved by the Lord. His association with Pandavas, his grand fathers and sages and saints awakened in him the divinity to be attained to.

During the time of death, if one is in the presence of sages and saints, he is considered as divinely fortunate. On getting the news of king Parikshita being cursed to death, all sages and saints including the great Mahamuni Shukadeva along with his followers reached the bank of the river and provided the king the rarely available divine company. It is declared in scriptures:

> sadhunam darsanam punyam tirthabhuta hi sadhavah
> tirtham phalati kalen sadyah sadhu samagamah

"The fruits of pilgrimages are obtained after a long time. The very beholding of saints and sages is like visiting a holy place and the effects of this company with sadhus yield immediate result".

This happened immediately in the case of the king. Within seven days he was able to get liberation by attaining nirvikalpa samadhi by the teachings of Mahamuni Shukadeva. He taught the art of attaining Godhood by narrating the entire Bhagavatam. All the assembled sages and saints were the illustrious witness to the attainment of the stage of complete liberation of the king Parikshita. On seeing him fully merged with the Ultimate, all sages and saints along with Shukadeva left the place. Takshyaka only bite his mortal and dead body in which he was no longer present. Mahamuni Shukadeva taught him the ways by which all senses were to be controlled. As said by Lord Krishna in *Bhagavad Gita*:

sarvadvarani samyamya mano hrdi nirudhya ca
murdhny adhaya 'tmanah pranam asthito
yogadharanam

"All the doors of the body are closed. The mind is firmly confined to the cavity of the soul. One's life is fixed in the head (cranium or fontanel). Then one is established in yoga" (8:12).

Our Gurudeva Paramahamsa Hariharananda, a great God realised Kriya yogi of modern India explains in very lucid words:

"Human body is likened to a city with nine doors presided over by the soul dwelling within. These nine doors are two eyes, two ears, two nostrils, the mouth, the anus and the

genital. Since these doors are open man has become extrovert, restless and indulgent in sense derived pleasures.

In meditation we have to close all the nine doors of the body. That means, the senses are to be regulated and controlled. Since man is ignorant of how to control, regulate or close the doors he becomes restless and extrovert. The Bible says in a similar way: And when you pray, you shall not be like hypocrites... When you pray, enter into your closest, and when you have shut the door, pray to your Father, which is in secret..." (Matthew 6:5-6).

By controlling the breath mind is controlled. Once mind is controlled, the senses are controlled and mind is withdrawn from the senses to be fixed in the cavity. The seeker hears the divine sound, sees divine light and feels divine vibration throughout the body. When mind is fixed in cavity or fontanel, the atom soul or state of anor aniyam is perceived.

In the next verse (8:13) the Lord explains: When the seeker remains fixed for ever in the cavity or fontanel by withdrawing from the senses and mind with constant remembrance of God through divine sound om, he attains to the stage of nirvikalpa samadhi. This is the state of complete liberation. The seeds of rebirth are burnt forever. Lord Krishna reiterated this:

> tatah padam tat parimargitavyam
> yasmin gata na nivartanti bhuyah
> (*Bhagavad Gita* 15:4)

Thereafter, the goal must be sought from which, having gone, no one returns.

The same has been reiterated by Lord Krishna in *Bhagavad Gita* (8:15, 15:5)

Great souls, who have attained the state of highest perfection, having come to Me, are not reborn to the abode of sorrows and impermanence.

Those men of wisdom who are free from arrogance and delusion, who have overcome the evils of attachment, who are in eternal union with God with desires and ambitions extinguished, who are released from the dualities such as pleasure and pain, these undeluded people reach that supreme immortal state.

Under the direct teaching and tutelage of Shukadeva, his Guru to whom he surrendered himself and in the presence of all sages and saints, king Parikshita attained that state of complete union with the Supreme Self.

The teachings of Mahamuni Shukadeva learnt from his father Vyasadeva are the contents of Srimad Bhagavatam.

6

Jaya and Vijaya cursed to born as demons on the earth

The gods beholding the ominous signs looming over the universe assembled together at the feet of the Lord Brahma and asked Him entreatingly to unravel the reasons thereof. Drawing their attention, the Lord Brahma said, Diti, the daughter of Dakshya was married to the rishi Kashyapa. One evening, while the rishi was engrossed in meditation and evening prayers, Diti entered into his prayer room seething with incestuous passion for physical union with her husband rishi Kashyapa and sat adjacent to him. With folded hands she supplicated:

"O my lord, I am seriously simmering within by the fire of sensual union with you. My condition is like that of an elephant smashing the banana trees with its tusks being tormented by the sexual turpitude. Seeing the prosperity and luxurious life style of my sisters my heart is smitten with jealously. You are the lord of the Prajapati. If you wish you can change it into a home of prosperity and luxury to satisfy me. If husband gives joy to his wife by giving birth to father like sons the name and fame of her will spread. All our sons born to us will be righteous and will act according to the nuances of Dharma. Thinking this, my father Dakshya Prajapati with our consent got us married. We the thirteen sisters are always at your feet having unbreakable trust in

you. You are fully appreciative of our beauty, virtues and good conduct. I pray you to have physical union with me now by which I shall be privileged to bear children".

Pained by these words of the agitated Diti being pierced severely by the arrow of passion of sexual urge, rishi Kashyapa addressed her:

"O my dear, I know your mind. That you came this evening for union with me is the general nature of human beings. Nobody can deny this. Out of all, household life is best if it is lived with Dharma. It is like a boat in the sea of life. With wife and children, he lives happily and overcomes all difficulties. Wife is the half of his soul. Shouldering on her the responsibility of the home, he remains happy. With wife on his side, he is able to control senses. I cannot forget your yeoman service to me. I am indebted to you. Nobody has the power to do away with God's wish. I request you to make your mind calm and quiet. This is not an auspicious moment. Wait a moment. In this ominous and dangerous moment, the ghosts and nymphs are busy mating with their partners with much hue and cry. Lord Shiva, your father-in-law smeared with ashes of the burial ground throughout His body amidst His retinues like ghosts is moving around the world on an ox back to behold what the worldly people are doing. The sustainer, creator and destroyer of the entire cosmos, Lord Shiva is fathomless and incomprehensible to gods, sages and saints and what to speak of the common people. He is no dear or averse to anybody He is above calumny and praises. All sages, saints, yogis and gods remain always at His Feet. It is considered a divine privilege to have the last part of the oblations consecrated to Him. Those who are deluded and whose eyes are covered with sheaths of illusion and ignorance see His body smeared with

ashes and Him moving with ghosts and nymphs. Those sages, saints and yogis who are pure contemplate and meditate on Him as embodiment of Infinitute beauty, joy and bliss. By merging with Him following the path of Yoga, the sages and devotees earn unspeakable divine wealth. Those who are ignorant, deluded and unfortunate deride Him".

Since Diti was overpowered by the passion of sex, she did not pay heed to what Kashyapa was advising her. Without waiting she immediately caught hold of her husband's hand and in her left hand removed his cloth. Without finding any way and in the face of his wife's adamant attitude, the rishi with obeisance to God entered into the room and got himself united physically with Diti.

After the union, the rishi came out and got himself purified with water by washing his hands and legs. Then, he sat for contemplation and meditation on God. Engrossing his mind in the divine light he remained silent. Getting herself afresh, Diti came to the front of the rishi with her head lowered out of shame prayed to Lord Shiva, "*O Lord, protect my pregnancy. In grave disobedience to You I committed what is unrighteous and contrary to Dharma. Consort of Uma, you move among the ghosts and if You are kind, the maya of Lord Vishnu will not touch anybody. Your compassion will enable me to disabuse myself of my sin. I bow down at Your Lotus Feet. I am simply a woman. You know the nature of women. I pray You to withdraw your ferocity and be kind to me and protect my child in the womb".*

With these words of prayer to Lord Shiva, she looked at the face of the rishi and trembled with fear. Getting up from meditation the rishi Kashyapa said to Diti:

"O my dear, the sin you committed was under your control. Waiting for a moment would have avoided a great havoc that is going to befall the earth. The sin perpetrated in an ominous moment has ill forebodings. Because of your grave mistake, you will soon give birth to twins as most ferocious and dreaded demons. They will forcibly take away the property and wealth of others. They will wreak havoc on the life of the people. All kings and gods of the three lokas will remain subdued before them. They will take away women of others. The sages and saints will hide themselves in the forests. People will be out of fear and oppression wailing for emancipation. Being enraged by their unrighteous deeds, God will take incarnations on the earth to annihilate them".

On hearing these premonitions, Diti said, *"all my fears vanished with your words that God Vishnu will take incarnations to kill my sons. Those who die by the curse of Brahmins go to hell and pass through the ordeal of excruciating travails and sufferings. They take many births. Now I feel assured that my sons will get liberation by nobody else than God Himself".*

Rishi Kashyapa said:

"You committed a sin for which you deeply repented. It is because of your sorrowful repentance you now come to understand the difference between good and bad. The veil of ignorance over your eyes has been removed and you have obtained the knowledge of discrimination. Your heart-rending contrition made you think of God. Your sons will

get liberation by the hand of the Lord. One of their sons will be a great devotee of God. His name and fame will spread all over because of his deep love and devotion for God. Hearing his deeds of love to the Lord people will be able to cross the worldly ocean. He will behold the presence of God everywhere inside and outside. Everyone will be dear to him. He will be happy with others' joy and feel sorrow for others' suffering. Like moon bestowing coolness to the people in the night during scorching summer, your grandson will wipe out the pains and sufferings of the deluded people. Many yogis will follow his path to get a drop of his fathomless ocean of love for God. After his worldly sojourn he will enter into the eternal abode of Lord Vishnu".

Hearing these predictions from the rishi Kashyapa, Diti regaled herself with immense joy and fell at his feet. It was almost nearing hundred years since Diti became pregnant. The two sons as predicted were yet to be born. She was thinking within, without heeding to rishi "I became easily a prey to passion. Because of this uncontrollable passion for physical union with rishi I lost the power of discrimination and failed to do what was right. God is omnipotent. What this hapless man or demon can do?". With the twins growing within the womb and time becoming imminent for their birth, the people started looking gloomy and morose and darkness clamped all over the earth. Beholding the grisly signs, the gods assembled at the feet of Lord Brahma and prayed:

"Those who take refuge in You, nothing ominous will occur to them. You are above dualities such as truth and falsehood. Those yogis who practice yoga and meditation by controlling breath remaining in the cranium of the head

(fontanel or Sahasrara chakra) are graced by you and become dear to you. They are immune to the seething flames of worldly delusion. With time nearing for the birth of two sons from the womb of Diti, we look saturnine. Our joys started vanishing. We entreat you to reveal us the truth". Pleased with their prayer, Lord Brahma spoke to them:

"When I was in deep contemplation on God for creation with a pure mind and heart four sons headed by Sanaka were born from the infinite space. Men are generally born of flesh and blood. So, they move after blood and flesh. But Sanat Kumar and his brothers being born from space are always in the Infinite God. Devoid of any cravings (vigatspruha), fear and anger (vitaragabhayakrodha), detached and resolved to be with God, taking refuge in Him, purified by the fire of wisdom, they are always in Him. Fully naked and smeared with dusts they are constantly in euphoric state of bliss and joy and roaming throughout in the space".

One day, Sanatakumar and his brothers while roaming reached the abode of Lord Vishnu, known as all adored and all sought after Vaikuntha. Those who are always with God and reached the highest stage of God realisation get access to this abode where always reign peace, bliss and joy and sit in front of Lord Vishnu. Everything looks as Lord Vishnu nothing else. This is eternal, imperishable and above kala (Time spirit). The primordial Purusha standing for undivided truth of unity and the embodiment of Dharma is the Lord from Whom the entire cosmos is seen manifesting within a moment if He so wishes. Unlike the variable climates and seasons of the earth here an even temperature of an eternal spring prevails. Vaikuntha is surrounded by a garden known as Kaivalya where eternal wish-fulfiling trees increase the beauty of the abode. Divine angels in groups seated in palanquins sing the glory of Lord Vishnu. In the pond are blossomed many beautiful flowers matching the beauty of millions of moons with sweet fragrance wafting to all directions. Without being tempted by their beguiling beauty, the divine angels go on singing Thy glory in great ecstasy. Varieties of birds like peacock, swans, doves, cuckoos and parrots also sing the glory of the Lord that enraptures many in the thought of His beatific divinity that will mellow their simmering deluded hearts. The garden filled with flowers of elegant beauty and fragrance like lotus, lily, jasmine feels dancing with the rhythm of the cool breeze that blows constantly. Hundred and thousand chariots studded with gold, pearls and diamonds get down carrying devotees to the feet of the Lord. With blue lotus flower in Her hands Mother Laxmi surrounded by Her retinues in her gold studded abode worships the feet of the Lord to His great joy with fragranced Tulsi leaves and magnifies the abode of Lord Vishnu. This Loka is not accessible to the sinners who deluded by passion, wealth and sensual pleasure forget the Lord in all their deeds, thinking and dispositions. Born on this earth as human beings if they forget the Lord, they are the most deluded and ignorant to lead a very pitiable life. If one is not enraptured by the thought of the Lord every moment with tears of joy in eyes and hairs standing at their roots and every word that comes out of the mouth is only paeans in Thy glory and beauty, the doors to the abode of the Lord are shut against him. Without this God-soaked love and devotion to the Lord if one meditates, contemplates and does yoga very staunchly, he cannot reach this divine abode.

This is the unique and extraordinary abode of the Lord, the Guru of all gurus, the universe and all Lokas. Emblematic of purity, divinity, serenity and sacredness and shorn of any attribute and all dualities representing the indivisible unity this abode is resplendent with divine light making millions of suns, moons and stars look faded. All scriptures, puranas, yoga sutras and other manuscripts get dissolved, revealed and manifested in the Lord and lose their individuality and sing the glory of the Lord. The liberated souls, divine beings and gods are seen busy singing hymns and paeans in Thy glory.

The four sons of Lord Brahma always merged in ecstasy of the thought of the Lord and singing Thy glory reached the eternal Abode crossing through the six doors. The seventh doorway is covered with two doors bedecked with effulgent gems and jewels diffusing light widely in all directions beguilingly attractive to the eyes of others. The two doormen, Jaya and Vijaya standing on both sides of the door were regulating the entry into the Abode of the Lord. Donned exquisitely and adorned with ornaments in various parts of the body and golden canes in their hands, the two with widened chest and covered with beautiful flowers of fragrance elongating from the neck were resembling the beauty and glory of the Lord.

Lord Brahma said to the gods:

"*The moment my four sons tried to enter through the door without asking, the two doormen in anger stopped their entry. My four sons born before gods, are very old but look young lads of five years of age, completely naked. Beholding them without clothes on the body the two doormen laughed derisively at them and forbade them from entering by hurling canes in their faces*".

Thus, forbidden to behold the visage of the Lord even for a moment the four brothers bereaved in their hearts looking at each other said, "*this is strange to find here the sense of duality, self-versus others and friend versus foes and afflicted by the senses of passion, anger, conceit and egoism. Unless and until one is having the realisation of unity with the Lord standing on the graveyard of the demonic attributes and senses, one cannot have a place in this divine Abode. How is that the two brothers get a place here? They might be devils masquerading as divine beings. The Lord is abiding in all beings and pervading the entire space. Where there is death of the sense of duality how is that, the two brothers acted deceitfully with self-conceit, anger and egoistic arrogance? They are not fit to stay in this Abode of the Lord. Let them fast descend to the earth to be born as demons. After three births they will again come back to this Abode.*"

Hearing thus being cursed by the four rishi brothers to be born in the womb of demons on the earth for three lives the two doormen brothers benumbed with fear and sorrows prostrated themselves at their feet in great repentance and remorse. With folded hands touching their heads they prayed:

"O Supreme ones, the curse you all meted out to us is our due. It is our misdeeds that dishonour you for which we are bound to be inflicted severely with punishment. This is not your fault. We have no fear for rebirths in the womb of demons. As we have sown so we are to reap. We entreat you very fervently to shower your kindness on us that we will be in remembrance of the Lord amidst our scornful and demonic life".

With a compassionate and mellowing heart, the four sons of Lord Brahma said, "in your cursed demonic life on the earth you will be having only one sixteenth part of the remembrance of the Lord".

Nothing remains unknown to and happens without the will of the Lord. Knowing the misdemeanour shown to the four rishi brothers by the two doormen Lord Vishnu stepped out with mother Mahalaxmi straight to the four enraged rishi brothers. Sages, saints, yogis and devotees take ages and uncountable years together to mingle with Him. He has Himself came out with His retinues in a procession that begs no description. Lord Brahma has described how the very coming of the Lord in a procession undertaken by His retinues and members of the Abode was the yonder, a spectacle of unparalleled grandeur. Attired in a yellow apparel fastened with a golden lace around the waist ornamented with dazzling jewels, diamonds, sapphires and emeralds, the Almighty Father was embellished with necklaces, bangs, ear rings in artistic splendours which were shimmering with the brilliant glow that was diffusing out of His body and making the multicoloured jewels and gems more effulgent. Splendid was the all-radiant crown on His head with a Kousthuva gem in the middle of a necklace touching His chest. Moving very slowly seated on Garuda with His two hands on his shoulder under the golden canopy fanned by one of the divine countenance with a white umbrella bedecked with lines of jewels of luminescence in his hand, the Almighty Lord Krishna with smiling on His lips resembling that of the half blossomed blue lotus, created a wonderful and majestic scene surpassing the bounds of human imagination even beguilingly kept Lord Brahma, Lord Shiva, sages and saints captive to His magnificent beauty.

What eludes the yogis to realise and comprehend in meditation has been manifested directly in a form resplendent with enthralling beauty before the eyes of the four sons of Lord Brahma. Bowing down at His Holy Feet, the four brothers prayed with folded hands touching their heads:

"Who can bound Thy majestic beauty and greatness to mere words? Thee resides in every being whether saints or demons, good or bad. Our father Lord Brahma immersed in deepening ecstatic joy has revealed before us your incomprehensible and indescribable mysterious deeds, majestic attributes and enraptured divinity which remains imprinted in our hearts. We are privileged to behold you directly in our eyes. You are the supreme and mysterious Truth which yogis, saints and sages do constant sadhana to realise. Conceiving You in their hearts flooded with love and devotion they get liberation from the simmering worldly delusion. Those who think of, and surrender to and take refuge in You, and remain in divine euphoria listening to words about You, get liberation from this world. By cursing

Your two devotees – Jay and Vijaya we committed a great sin, the result of which will be that they take births in the world. We are ignorant and ignoble. By listening to words, praises and hymns in Your glorification and by reciting Your majestic highness in the tip of the tongue, we pray you to let our deluded mind be ever engrossed at Your Lotus Feet. You are Infinite without beginning and end. You are the Supreme Cause of all causes. By showing Your divine form in all its splendour and glory You gratified us and sanctified our eyes. By seeing Thee our heart remains ever in earnestness to behold You again and again. Your form is inconceivable to those who have not conquered their senses".

Invocating thus, the four brothers laid themselves down at the Feet of the Lord.

Content with the entreatingly invoked prayers of the four brothers, the Lord assuaged them with words full of compassion, joy and bliss:

"The two brothers Jaya and Vijay being members of my abode are always at my gate constantly discharging their duties. In disobedience to Me they misbehaved you and as fruits of their misdeeds they were cursed by you. I condescend to your act of inflicting due punishment on them which cannot be negated by anybody even Me. As brahmans are my presiding deities you be kind and be happy and for their sin you pardon Me. Like a disease defiles the beauty of a person, the unrighteous deeds committed by persons denigrate the fame, glory and reputation of his masters or Lord in the world. Being the Lord of the Universe and the Eternal Abode, hearing my nectar like words the devotees get liberation from the bondage of the mundane life. Feeling the pain of your heart caused by these two brothers I came

to meet you all. In a similar vein, realizing that my heart always throbs for the Brahmanas you both shined by the brilliant sheen of divinity in a fury of anger cursed the two gate keepers. The dusts at My Feet have been holy and sanctified by serving the Brahmanas, the constant remembrance and touch of which remove the delusive dirt from human mind and for which My consort Goddess Mahalaxmi never gives up a moment even serving My Feet with love and devotion and sages and saints including lord Brahma are very eager and do sadhana for ages together to get a slight vision. The Brahmanas worship Me by following the nuances of the Vedas and offer oblations in fire ceremony in My name. I am not satisfied with their ways of worshipping Me. I am residing in them. When they are fed rice with yoghurt, ghee and honey to their hearts' content, I feel I am fed. I am gratified to have the dusts from the holy feet of Brahmanas by virtue of which I am enjoying the glories, majesties and everything of the illusive world abiding in all beings. Lord Shiva bears the water secreted from My Feet and the people in three lokas get sanctified by taking this holy water as the grace of Me. On My crown I bear the dusts from the holy Feet of Brahmanas. My body is the body of Brahmanas. The anger of the Brahmanas is unbearable. He who worships and thinking of Me as different from them is committing a sin against Me and never gets liberation from the world. His path to liberation is hamstrung by the god Yama. Those who do not have devotion and love for Brahmanas are ever thrown into the whirlpool of birth and death. One who calms down the fire of anger in Brahmanas with love, devotion and service, easily crosses the worldly ocean and enters into the abode of divinity. Once the Brahmanas are satisfied, I am also satisfied. The person *who hearing the bitter and enraged words of Brahmanas feel happy and serve them joyfully with love and devotion like a father to a son, remains endeared to Me. Because of your curse, the two brothers taking three births on the earth as demons will come back to Me. When their misdeeds reach the unbearable apogee, I will incarnate on the earth and liberate them".*

The Sanatakumars prayed the Lord in deep gratitude:

"Thy will is known to Thee only and to none beyond the comprehension of sages, saints and even gods. You are the primordial Purusha. You are the Dharma and Truth itself. Your incarnations on the earth are for the protection of Dharma and decimation of those wicked who destroy Dharma. Those who take complete refuge in Thee cross the worldly ocean and conquer death".

Praying with their hearts inundated with love and devotion to the overwhelming joy of the Lord, Lord Brahma said, my four sons moved around the Lord and bowing down left the place.

Turning towards the two doormen Lord Krishna said:

"You both will take birth as demons on the earth. I will liberate you on your third birth. Though I am able to negate the curse of the Brahmanas, I cannot do this as I have given consent to this. I also promised goddess Laxmi in a previous Yuga that you both will be cursed to take birth as demons as you did not allow her to meet Me when I was alone. For your liberation I will embody Myself on the earth. Who will adorably hear My incarnation on the earth for your cause, will be devoid of all sins. My glorious deeds and words of

nectar are like the holy river flowing down on the earth. Those who will take dips in this holy water and hear, remember and remain merged in the thought of Me, will be liberated from the mundane life".

Assuaging thus the two cursed brothers with a mellowing heart and compassionate gaze, The Lord returned to His abode with His entourage along with Goddess Laxmi.

The divine illumination that was shining in them soon vanished and with lost glory and fame and in great despondency the two brothers fell down from the Abode of the Lord to enter into the womb of Diti on the earth.

Reflection

Human mind stretches forth like fairy tales and fables to fancy about where God resides, whether it is in a sequestered place far away from and above the cosmos wherein lies a splendidly bedecked and ornamented throne resplendent with light sitting on which God embodied to an imagined figure rules the entire universe and sits on judgment over human deeds on the earth. Many people think that the place of God is in the heaven or in the Garden of Eden as people in the west believes. In the *Bible* (Genesis 1:27; 2:7) it is written: "He made man and woman in His own image, and He breathed into their nostrils the breath of His life, becoming the living soul in the whole universe". Human mind never thinks that the creation and God, the Creator are one. God is omnipresent all-pervading and encompasses the entire cosmos. He cannot be conceived of as separate from His creation. Like cream in the milk and fire in the wood He resides in the universe. Our limbs, organs, plants, trees, insects, animals and everything in the cosmos are pervaded by God. Where is He not and what He is not. In the *Shwetashwatara Upanishad* (3:11) it is pronounced:

> sarvanana-siro-grivah sarva-bhuta-guhasayah
> sarvabyapi sa bhagavan tasmat sarva gatas sivah

He who is in the faces, heads and necks of all who dwells in the cave (of the heart) of all beings, who is all pervading, He is the Lord and therefore, the omnipresent Siva.

In *Bhagavad Gita* (13:13) it is described:

> sarvatahpanipadam tat sarvatoksisiromukham
> sarvatahsrutimal loke sarvam avrtya tisthati

With hands and feet everywhere, eyes, head and faces everywhere, ears everywhere, He dwells in the whole universe, covering everything.

Human body is the temple of God. Thus, the real kingdom of Heaven and hell lies within every living being. It depends on human beings to enter either into the heaven or into the hell. Shri Shyamacharan Lahiri Mahasaya, a supreme God realised householder Kriya Yoga master said:

> *ke bolere svarga naraka ke bolere bahu dur*
> *manusher majhe svarga narak manusher majhe sur asur*

"Who says that heaven and hell are far away? In every human being the abode of heaven and hell exist as the devil and the divine" (quoted from Paramahamsa Prajnanananda, Dancing with Death:150).

Heaven represents a highest stage of God realisation where individual human being merges with the supreme Self. It is a stage of indivisible unity with the Infinite and ultimate liberation from the fetters of the worldly delusion. Hell is a stage where human beings remain engrossed in delusive materialistic world in total forgetfulness of the indwelling all doer Self. This stage plunges human beings back into the unsnapped chain of birth and death. Being in the dungeon of darkness of ignorance, illusion and error human beings overpowered by demonic tendencies never try to see the light of the Divine. The unquenched thirst for materialistic desires and fulfilment of sense derived pleasures is never burnt in the simmering fire of worldly delusion rather becomes the seed for further births after births without bringing an end to this untold misery and human suffering.

What is in the universe is in the human body. Pinda and brahmanda are one. Jesus said, "the kingdom of God is within you". The divine kingdom is in the Sahasrara, the top of the cranium in the human brain. In yogic scriptures it is hundred and thousands petalled lotus. Within it God abides hidden. Inside of the spine of human body there are seven centres or chakras. The top most is Sahasrara (fontanel), the divine passage to the Infinite. In descending order below, it, is Ajna chakra (medulla oblongata) just four inches deep in the mid brain from the midpoint of the two eye brows. Next is Visuddha (neck centre) or cervical. Then is Anahata (Heart centre). Down it is

Manipur (navel centre). Then is Swadhisthan (sex centre) and at the end of the spine is Muladhara chakra. The five centres from Muladhara to Visuddha drag human beings to the worldly delusion. In the Muladhara chakra man is after lucre of wealth. In Swadhisthan man is after endless sex and sensual pleasures. In Manipur man is having inordinate desire for food without having the discrimination to choose what is salubrious or injurious to health. In heart centre man is replete with emotions, ego, arrogance, pride, honour, love, hatred, jealousy, hypocrisy and greed. In Visuddha man remains busy with religious and philosophical pursuits. Human mind engrossed in these centres is deeply embedded in delusion, illusion and error. These centres are wide, broad and spacious open wildly to the extrovert world. They open up the floodgates of doors to human beings for degradation and destruction. These centres are wide enough leading human beings because of their demonic propensities, to excruciating suffering, misery and sorrows. This is the road to hell. In *Bhagavad Gita* it is said (16:16):

Those who are befuddled and bewildered by the fleeting fancies and desires, fettered in the net of delusions and attached to the gratifications of sense and material derived pleasures, slip into the dungeon of hell.

The road to heaven starts from inside of the midpoint of the two eye brows i.e., the Ajna chakra. The nose starts from the midpoint of the eye brows. Sri Gurudeva Paramahamsa Hariharananda said, nose is the door to heaven. It means the nose is the organ that helps us breathe. It is through the practice of breath control and watching in each breath who breathes through us. It is the indwelling God. In each thought, thinking and actions to constantly and calmly watch the indwelling Self through every breath is liberation.

Lord Brahma's four sons Sanatkumaras passed from Muladhara chakra to Ajna Chakra through the wide gates without having gone astray by the delusive world. But on the narrow gate Jay and Vijaya two door men obstructed their passage into Vaikuntha, the abode of the Lord. Sanatkumar is venerated in Indian tradition as eternal child. *Brahma-vaivarta Purana* holds that he is eternally a child of five years, who did not undergo the usual samskaras, a pupil of the very God, Narayana:

vayasa panca-hayanah, acudo anupavitas ca veda-sandhya-vihinakah yasya narayano guruh.

Harivamsa confirms this view, "Know me only to be a child just as I was born and so the name Sanatkumara was given to me."

They failed to understand Sanatkumara as the child of God who have had no sense of duality free from the grip of the senses and worldly delusion. The two door men were cursed by them to be born as demons on the earth for three times. To feel duality not unity with God in all deeds and thoughts is demonic. Persons with demonic tendencies cannot reach the stage of highest stage of God realisation. All negative and animalistic desires and propensities which distract humans in all lower chakras are to be sacrificed and burnt in the fire of wisdom obtained through attainment of breathlessness stage in order to enter the narrow gate. Until the sadhaka attains Nirvikalpa samadhi there is every fear of falling down as Jay and Vijaya were cursed to fall down to the earth. People having demonic tendencies are not eligible to enter the narrow gate. When consciousness remains confined to the lower chakras such as Muladhara, Swadhisthan, Manipur, Anahata and Visuddha, the demonic propensities overpower and rule the conduct of the person. This is the meaning of being cursed to take births as demons. Jaya and Vijaya are cursed to take three births consecutively as demons. That means, every human being has three bodies – gross, astral and causal. In the gross body man moves after money and wealth, physical and sexual pleasure; in the astral body man is guided by egoism, pride, vanity, emotions, jealousy, hatred and passion and the causal body is both knowledge and ignorant body. Here, man poses like a religious person but in reality, he is not. He knows what is Truth but does not sincerely practice to attain the Truth. He remains busy showing religious vanity and pomp. These devilish persons look saintly outside but inside wolfish. In order to enter the narrow gate to Vaikuntha the human beings are to transform themselves by eliminating the attachment of the gross body, delusion of the astral body, and ignorance and duality of the causal body through the practice of prana kriya under the guidance of realised masters.

With a compassionate heart Lord Krishna assured to Jay and Vijaya, "I will incarnate on earth each time and liberate you both from three demonic births". Jay and Vijaya were fortunate that they were assured of liberation after three births. But deluded ones take millions of births for reaching the goal. It means, God is with us in all our births, in all our activities, deeds, thoughts bad or good. When we are earning money, God is with us. Unless He takes breath through our nostrils, we are dead. A dead man cannot earn money. Without His presence in us we cannot enjoy sensual pleasures. He is in our vanity, ego and ignorance. Breath is in our both attachment and detachment, ignorance and knowledge, delusion and illusion, sorrows and happiness, demonic and divinity. It is through breath control we have to come up from the lower centres to the pituitary and fontanel. Moving upward from the Muladhara to Sahasrara and beyond through watching the living presence of the indwelling Self in each breath is end of all sorrows and advent of liberation from the delusive world. Thus, God has been with us in each breath in great compassion and detachment from the million births we have been taking on earth providing us the opportunity to learn from our delusion, attachment and ignorance, and transform accordingly, from darkness to light, falsehood to truth, ignorance to wisdom and from mortality to immortality. Taking complete refuge in God with unswerving devotion and love will dawn in us the opening up the narrow gate to ultimate liberation.

The move in the direction world goes is bondage and against the direction is liberation. Saint Kabir said:

> je jake saran lije take rakhi laj
> ulti jal me machili chale baha gaye gajraj

One who takes shelter in God is protected in every situation. A small fish in the gushing flow of water swims upward against the current, whereas an elephant is swept away by the same flow of water.

Life is like a river flowing down ward from Fontanel to Muladhara in the spine. A small fish symbolizing a sadhaka having complete refuge in God when swims upward against the deluded worldly current of the flow inside the spine through sushumna path from Muladhara to Sahasrara is rescued and liberated. Whereas an elephant symbolizing ego, vanity, jealousy, passion of a person sweeping in the direction of the current of the worldly flow is deluded and destroyed.

> Lord Sri Krishna said to Arjuna
> (Bhagavad Gita 16:20):
> asurim yonim apanna mudha janmani-janmani
> mam aprapyai 'va kaunteya tato yanty adhamam
> gatim

Those who are deluded and not attaining Me O son of Kunti! fall into the wombs of demons birth after birth and from where they sink further into a condition lower still.

The Lord abiding in the body breathes from the very moment of birth. That is why the people are active and alive. Spiritual people seek the soul by ascending to the pituitary – the seat of soul, four inches deep into the brain from the midpoint of two eye brows. People with demonic tendencies are enmeshed in the delusive world and are distracted from the divine path. They do not seek God. They are averse to directing their consciousness upward from Muladhara to pituitary and fontanel. They rather prefer to move downward to lower centres to be engaged in vanity, ego, passion, sex, money and so on sliding into a cesspool of misery, suffering and frustration. Attachment, detachment, woes, sorrows and joys all binary tendencies both demonic and divine come from breath. God is compassionately in negative tendencies with the purpose that the demonic people will transform themselves from devilish to divine. People who are constantly merged in downward pulling demonic propensities in all their activities and thinking forgetting the indwelling soul will never achieve God realisation. They will be ever swirling in the whirlpool of birth after birth in the demonic wombs.

The spiritual life is one of struggle and fight. Life is always caught in a battle between the demonic forces and the divine forces stationed in human beings. Success in spiritual life lies in attainment of the Ultimate Reality by decimating the evil and wicked forces standing in the way. Liberation lies in one's hand. One has to struggle hard every moment as time is very swiftly passing away to reach the goal. One's battle cannot be fought by another. Struggle means practice of dispensing with the evil forces by meditation on watching breath in all activities and thoughts with devotion and love to the inner soul under the guidance of a self-realised Guru. In other words, battle means an inner journey, a pilgrimage to the Infinitude on a path that passes over the graves of the inner demonic forces. In the epochal Mahabharata war, Lord Krishna presided over the battle between Pandavas representing the divine forces and Kauravas – the demonic forces. Within human body the inner soul presides over these two forces watching very compassionately the rise up of the spiritual person to the fontanel and beyond from the lower chakras in the spinal canal. God will never fight for you for your spiritual evolution. Man is the maker of his destiny.

For this reason, Lord Krishna said to Jaya and Vijaya, "I have the power the negate the curse meted out to you both. But I cannot act against the words of the self-realised masters – the Brahmanas, the knower of Brahma. Their words reflect the eternal laws of karma". A teacher can promote the most ignorant student to the next class, but it will not be in the greater interests of the student. The student himself has to work hard for his own evolution of course under the guidance of the teacher with love and surrender to the teacher. As Jaya and Vijaya both have committed the sin of disrespecting the four sons of Lord Brahma out of egoism and vanity, they are to bear the fruits of their own misdeeds. A moment's good company enables one to cross the worldly ocean. Instead of having divine company with these God realised masters they tried to be their masters by restricting their entry. Their vanity, ego and pride became the cause of their own downfall. They are to work out these evil and demonic forces. God assured them that He will incarnate in their three births on the earth to liberate them. To watch in every breath the living presence of the indwelling self is incarnation of God. God remains as the witness to all our deeds, thoughts and dispositions. Being compassionate and detached like water on the lotus leaf in all our evil and divine forces, He guides us for our transformation and evolution. The battle is ours. The success and failure belong to us. Success lies in achieving liberation by subduing and eliminating the devilish tendencies by stationing oneself firmly in the ramparts of the fontanel, and failure means to engross in the mundane world by being servile to the demonic forces. Lord Krishna became the charioteer of Arjuna but the latter has to fight out the inner battle by remaining watchful of every breath with gratitude and love to God for He is inhaling and exhaling His breath of life through his nostril.

A spiritual person in order to achieve success has to fight out his inner enemies like jealousy, pride, ego, anger, greed, passion by remembering God every moment and in every breath. Gurudeva Paramahamsa Hariharananda said, breath control is self-control. One has to be a strong fighter and a brave soldier to vanquish the evil forces. Thankfulness to God at all times and in all deeds, dispositions good or evil, pain or pleasure and thoughts and in each breath edges one towards God. Sarva means in Sanskrit the senses. There are five karmendriyas and five jnanendriyas. Through these instruments man remains engrossed beguilingly in the material world. In order to attain Godhood, the spiritual person should realise in these the living presence of God. Without breath these are impotent. It is the indwelling self that activates these to functioning through breath. In each and every breath one should feel the all-pervading compassionate indwelling soul. Through meditation and breath control all these senses should be tamed into introvert stage to realise the Supreme Self.

Had Lord Krishna wished, He would have finished the war within a moment. This was Pandavas' war. Similarly, it is everyone's war to fight out with the internal wicked demonic propensities in order to transform one's life to divinity. In *Bhagavad Gita* Lord Krishna inspired Arjuna to suppress and subdue the evil biological forces and remain in pituitary to have the finest conception of God in every breath in all deeds and thoughts (2:37):

hato va prapsyasi svargam jitva va bhokshyase mahim

tasmad uttistha kaunteya yuddhaya krtaniscayah

O Arjuna! If you are annihilated in the battle you will go to heaven and if you win the war, you will enjoy the world. Therefore, joyfully arise and fight the war with unshaking determination.

If one dies before God realisation, he will attain divinity nonetheless. If one attains nirvikalpa samadhi or formless and pulseless stage, he will realise in the material world that God abides in everything. He will be constantly liberated remaining in the material world. One should be awakened to this highest stage of God consciousness by his own efforts. In *Upanishads* it is pronounced

nayamatma balahinen labhyo

The soul cannot be realised by the weak. Those who remain easily captive to the material world and do not think of moving upward to the pituitary and fontanel from the lower chakras are weak people. They are swayed delusively by the demonic forces. But a person in order to realise God is to be strong and determined with spiritual valour and strength. One must be unswervingly determined to bear the brunt of spiritual journey in order to achieve the highest goal of life by triumphing over the demonic tendencies. A strong determination and will power will enable one to be God realised. Ratnakar, a hardcore dacoit could transform himself into a great sage Maharshi Valmik, it is because of his will and determination.

Jaya and Vijaya born as demons were Hiranakshya and Hiranyakasyapu, Ravana, and Kumbhakarna, Sisupala and Dantabakra in their three births on earth. They were very ferocious and wicked to the hilt. They wanted to replace God by themselves. When unrighteousness reached the apogee, Lord took incarnations to liberate them as promised to Jaya and Vijaya. They represent the demonic forces within human beings. Demonic and animalistic desires and proclivities are always against the Divine. These wicked forces try to overpower the divine. As depicted in *Bhagavad Gita* (16:14):

"That enemy has been killed by me, and I shall slay others too. I am the lord of all, the enjoyer of all powers; I am endowed with all supernatural powers, I am God and successful and happy".

These demons wicked to the core harbour deep animosity and enmity towards God. In a negative way they thought of God whom they think that He is the greatest enemy to be killed. By having the sense of enmity (Vairi Bhava) towards God they ultimately got liberation.

7

Discourses by Kapil Muni to Devahuti

In the beginning of creation Svayambhuba Manu, the son of Lord Brahma was given the responsibility to increase progenies. His wife was Shatarupa, an emblem of unparallel beauty. Out of them were born two sons – Uttanpada and Priyabrata and a beautiful daughter named Devahuti.

One day, Lord Brahma calling to his side his son, rishi Karddama born out of his shadow asked him to continue creation of progenies. Taking Lord Brahma's words as commands, he went to the bank of the holy river Sarasvati where he started meditating on God following all the techniques of Kriya Yoga. Practicing for a long period of time he attained the stage of samadhi, complete union with God.

God appeared before rishi Karddama

Content with his unwavering devotion and indivisible love God appeared before him in all His divine splendour, grandeur and majestic beauty belittling the beauty of millions and millions of Kandarapas (celestial beings representing the epitome of beauty). Seated on His carrier Garuda, four hands adorned with conch, mace, chakra (disc) and lotus flower, necklaced with Kousthuva gem and heart magnified by the imprints of Sribatsa's feet and bedecked with glittering gems, diamonds and other jewels, the Lord shined resplendently defeating the illumination of millions of suns and stars. A moment's sight of the eternal blissful joy that was coming out through His soft smiling lips was enough to dissipate the darkness of worldly delusion. Beholding Him thus in the space the rishi with tears of love rolling down his face and hairs standing erect on his body and hands folded he got himself prostrated. Merged in euphoric joy and ultimate wish fulfilled at the very sight of the divine majestic presence of the Lord, the rishi implored the Lord with words of inexpressible gratitude:

"O my Lord! My eyes were ingratiated with darshan (seeing) of what the seers, sages, saints and yogis have sought for ages after ages through meditation, penance, austerity and meditation. Thy lotus feet are the cause of people's liberation and are like fleets to cross the worldly ocean. Anyone who discards this divine dispense falls into the hell. In a similar way my mind is engrossed in worldly disposition. As commanded by You, I have embarked upon a journey of a household life. Household life is like a wish fulfilling cow beguiles the mind of the family members. Your lotus feet are the eternal tree taking refuge wherein all my cherished objectives will be fulfilled. By Your command, the people are fettered with household ashram. I will follow their footsteps. To a man simmering in the ordeal of the gross body, astral body and causal body (tri tapa) your lotus feet are like the ultimate divine umbrella providing the shelter. Those whose minds are covetous for drinking the

divine nectar streaming out of your divine majesties, never fall into the wheel of innumerable births and deaths. Who can describe perfectly the mystery of the wheel of time spirit? The Supreme Brahma is its pivot (akshya) on which the wheel of time spirit rests. The twelve months and the leap month are its bars connecting the pivot with the circumference. Three hundred sixty days are the pieces making the circumference. Six seasons are the round iron plate keeping the pieces bound with the circumference. The infinite moments are the edge of the iron plate and three 'four months' (caturmasya) are its three navels. This wheel of time spirit moves on very fast reducing every moment the longevity of human beings which the deluded beings do not know and understand. Those who have taken refuge in Your holy Feet with unflinching love, dedication and detachment can be able to know and realise it. You are undivided and cleave less unity above the wheel of time spirit. Your power of illusion has beguiled the entire universe. You are like a spider creating out of its own saliva the worldly net, sustaining it with insects falling into it and finally, devours it. Your holy Feet are like the eternal tree fulfilling the desires of all who desire and those who do not have any desire. I bow down at Thy holy feet with assiduity of love and devotion for fulfilment of one desire that is solely implanted in me by Thy command. Your glorifying greatness is beyond any body's depiction".

Upon hearing prayers of the rishi, the Lord embodied in the form of resplendent light and seated on the back of Garuda in the space thus spoke:

O son of Lord Brahma! I know what is stored in your mind. As you worshipped me with all love and devotion for the cause of creation, I will certainly fulfil your wish. Whole hearted prayer never goes in vain. Svayambhuba Manu created out of the body of Lord Brahma is now reigning the seven-island clustered universe. Along with his wife Shatarupa leaving behind even Mahalaxmi in beauty he is coming in a chariot after two days from now to see you. Their daughter Devahuti can defeat the celestial Rati, the epitome of beauty. Her virtues and personality are unimpeachable. You are the befitting bridegroom for her. They are coming to offer their daughter in marriage to you. Following the techniques of Kriya Yoga, you became God realised and fully established in Me. You will live on this earth in detachment and My illusive forces will not touch you. You will no longer be snared by the delusive forces of Mine. Making Me as the sole pilgrimage of your internal journey of life you will be blessed with ultimate liberation from this mundane world. After finishing your worldly responsibility, you will come back to Me. Through you from the womb of Devahuti will be born nine daughters who will get married to rishis and from them gradually the creation will perpetuate. In these worldly deeds you will realise Me through your Self. Finally, I will enter into you as energy and will take incarnation from the womb of Devahuti and will be the author of Tattwa Samhita".

With these words of bliss and predictions the Lord returned to His abode from the bank of the river Sarasvati.

Marriage of rishi Karddama and Devahuti

As foreseen just after two days, Svayambhuba Manu along with his wife Shatarupa and daughter Devahuti reached the ashram of rishi Karddama in a chariot studded with gold and gems.

The holy river Sarasvati is also known as Bindusara with the drops of tears of the Lord falling on its water from the His eyes being touchingly moved by the sweep of love that has inundated the heart, mind and soul of rishi Karddama for the Lord. The forest around the river and ashram was not ordinary where the Lord privileged the rishi to meet Him. The river has been the holiest one with tears from the eyes of the Lord falling on it. The forest looked enthralling and captivating the attention of all with its bounties of fruits and flowers of divergent colours, sweetness, fragrance and enchanting beauties, and varieties of birds of different hues chirping and singing to the tune of the Divine and further magnified by the very presence of the Lord a few days back. In this holy shrine the king Manu, his wife and daughter alighted from the chariot.

Beholding the illuminating face and body of the rishi Karddama effulgent with divine light and burning like a fire they remained awestruck and enraptured with exhilarating joy. What beauty more to him whom the Lord had privileged him with a much coveted and earnestly yearned darshan of His divine being! Emaciated body smeared with dust and dirt like a gem not cleansed, matted hair on the head and clad in a loin cloth, the rishi looked immersed deep in the divine euphoria with tears of joy and bliss dropping in and nectar words of the Lord resonating through his ears.

Beholding him thus, the king, his wife and daughter with folded hands prostrated at his feet. Getting up the rishi with Vedic mantras blessed and asked them to sit. With honorific and honeyed words, he addressed them as follows:

O adorable king! This ashram is highly gratified by your august presence. Your divine ordained itinerary is meant for protection and promotion of Dharma and eradication of the evil. The gods such as Sun, Moon, Fire, Yama, Indra, Varuna, Air and Dharma are the presiding deities of eight directions and are like the eight arms of a kshyatriya. The dharma of a kshyatriya is to vanquish the enemies and root out the unrighteous forces from the earth with its military forces. Not performing these duties if a kshytriya sleeps and lives luxuriously, the rise of unrighteous forces will destroy the earth. O king! I ask you the reason for which you have descended in our ashram?"

Reminiscing the nectar words of the Lord the rishi remained more and more in ecstatic joy and became more loving to the king.

The king, on the other hand being eulogised by the great rishi in loftiest words felt ashamed and humbled. He entreated him in a very humble and praying way:

"O supreme venerable one! You are the son of the Lord Brahma born from his mouth. You are the lord of the people. You are pure and immaculate in sadhana of Kriya Yoga. By the practice you have attained the ultimate stage of God realisation. Lord Brahma for the creation has bestowed on you the divine work of procreation and protection of dharma. For the protection of dharma and elimination of evil and demonic forces Lord Brahma has created the warrior class (kshyatriya). By having darshan of you all my doubts vanished. It is due to my good destiny I

met you and beholding your beautiful divine body which is beyond the knowledge of others, I feel gratified. The dust under your feet and water from your holy feet made my body sacred. The sonority of your solemn words still vibrant in my mind has made me highly gratified. Being in worldly delusion I have two sons, Uttanpada and Priyabrata and one daughter Devahuti. It is natural and not unexpected of a householder to be worried about her marriage. Devarshi Narada has spoken to her in details about your divine majesties and glories. Since that day she has been dreaming of getting married to you. If a strong desire in a sannyasi for household life remains winking in his mind then he will be subject to calumny not only in this life but also after life. You are embodiment of dharma and wisdom. Since you are God realised and detached there is no harm in adopting a household life for the cause of creation as commanded by the Lord. Your celibacy has now come to an end and as per the rites prescribed by the Vedas you tie the nuptial knot with my daughter Devahuti".

The rishi Karddama replied:

"O great king! Accepting your words as directions of the Divine I will surely get married to Devahuti for the cause of creation and spread of dharma. No doubt, she is second to none in terms of beauty, virtues and purity since she is the sister of Uttanpada, the great. As my karma is destined, I am bound by her. Nobody can defy this being in this delusive world. I will be highly gratified at her being offered to me but with one condition. Till she begets a son from me I will be in the household life. Then, I will tread the path of a sannyasi life leaving this world behind as directed and wished by the Lord".

The king Manu and queen Shatarupa being overwhelmed with unspeakable joy by the condescending words of the rishi, following the Vedic ritual and rites got their daughter married to the rishi. On the completion of the marriage ceremony the king and queen filled the ashram with all kinds of wealth, precious jewels, gems, jewels and other necessary things in abundance as gifts and presentations for the day-to-day comfort living of the rishi and Devahuti.

A melancholic note seemed to have resonated in the cool breeze that was blowing over the serene water of the holy river Saraswati, through the leaves of various trees, flowers and fruits and in the sweet chirping and melodious singing of birds on the very moment, the time of departure of the king and queen arrived. With their hearts inflamed with agony and pain, and at the same time moistened with the remembrance of their buoyant love and tears falling on the head of their endeared daughter while embracing, both paid homage to the rishi and bade adieu. While returning in the chariot they hastened their eyes back to the ashram of rishi Karddama and other rishis situated on the bank of the holy river and beholding their ineffable joy and beauty in a blissful environment under the canopy of the divine, they became highly gratified for having successfully fulfilled the wish of the Lord and returned to Brahmavartta to the grand ovation of their people.

Conjugal life of rishi Karddama and Devahuti

Devahuti finding her husband rishi Karddama engrossed in sadhana tried to serve him in all possible ways. Beautiful and replete with all divine attributes she knew well what rishi wanted to have. Like mother Parvati serving Lord Shiva with all assiduity and care she was always at his beck and call. A simple gesture from her husband was enough to draw her to his service. Purity of heart and soul, trust and faith in the divine, calm and quiet, peaceful and self-control, serving, compassion, kindness, sweet words, humbleness, soft spoken, detachment, non-violent, no passion, no ego, no falsehood, no laziness and procrastination and obsequious to husband's joy and happiness were her divine propensities with which she served the rishi. In adoration of her husband as God she was always serving the rishi with dedication, devotion and love. Perceiving her dedication, love and devotion, whole hearted serving attitude and unquenched thirst for getting his blessings, the rishi felt buoyant with joy and happiness and thought she was the epitome of chastity, dedication and obeisance. She stood preeminent among the women being well cultured and adorned with all divine and virtuous qualities.

One day, while remembering her divine and virtuous qualities, out of compassion in love-soaked words he called on her and said:

"O the beautiful one! Beholding your mind completely engrossed in me I am highly elated and enthralled. Having

devotedly served me you have become my endeared one. With your mind fully engaged in me, you have no care for your body. By the grace of the Lord Krishna, I practiced Kriya Yoga and attained the highest stage of God realisation for the liberation of mankind. I am proffering you divine vision by which you see the splendid majesties and glories of God. This sadhana is within your grasp. By taking refuge at the feet of the Lord you practice meditation and all your sorrows, suffering, woes and fear even the fear of death will vanish. Because of your dedicated and devoted loyalty and service to me, you are endowed with this divine vision to see the glories and majestic beauties of the Lord by which you will be merged in ecstatic joy which is precious and not easily available to human beings. Before this euphoric union with God all other joys are meaningless. To realise the undivided unity with the Lord is the most priceless bounty of life. With pure heart, mind and soul remain fixated in the Lord in all your thoughts, deeds and dispositions for liberation".

Endowed with the divine vision to behold the splendid majesties and glories in paeans of the beauty of the Lord, Devahuti felt gratified and enthralled with bliss and joy spoke these words very humbly full of sweetness and gratitude:

"O my venerable Lord! By your grace let me be always at your feet to serve you wholeheartedly and ceaselessly. By your kind consent let us together perform the dharma of a household life. This dharma is like an eternal wish fulfilling cow performing which we will enjoy the bliss and joy of divinity".

Perfectly understanding what was being fancied about in her mind, the rishi very joyfully invoked Visvakarma, the god of architecture to build a very unique chariot made of gold and gems luminescent with light. The pillars were made of gold and studded with gems, jewels and diamonds. A garden beautifully landscaped amid the chariot was laden with fruits of all seasons amenable only to gods and celestials found in bounties in trees. Where the gods and divine beings are happy, the time spirit also bestows joys and happiness on all. The exquisitely ornamented chariot resembled a multi storied palace betraying a beguiling spectacle of unparalleled grandeur. The towering archways, pillars and doors and gateways were bedecked with dazzling diamonds, sapphires, pearls and emeralds with blue gem at the top of the chariot emitting light that would make suns blush. The sweet fragrance of flowers in different hues strewn into garlands in golden strings adorning the chariot wafted through the air. The water filled pitchers made of gold and placed at doorsteps and corners added to the magnificent beauty of the chariot. Provision of various bed rooms abutting the golden yard attracted everybody including the gods. The melodious sound of the bees and exalted sound of the white swans and doves in the garden sent a sweet note into the rooms and attic of the chariot. The peerless picturesque beauty of the chariot in the resplendent glow of a magnificent palace in all its splendour and grandeur stood to shower encomiums on Visvakarma's architectural dexterity and artistic skill.

In contrast to the chariot glowing with gems, gold, diamonds and various stones Devahuti looked fading and unglazing. She was not content with that. Rishi Karddama having attained the highest stage of God realisation was able to read everybody's mind. He asked Devahuti to take a dip in the holy river Sarasvati to her heart's content remembering the Lord. This was the holy pilgrimage made by the Lord taking dip wherein everybody's desires are fulfilled. In obeisance to rishi's words, she entered into the river and remained awestruck to see hundred and thousand young celestial girls emerging out of water in divine forms with their bodies wafting fragrance of lotus flowers. Divinely exalted these celestials singing hymns in the praise of Devahuti with their hands touching their heads bowed down at her feet and implored to remain at her beck and call. Saying these sweet words, they smeared her body with fragrant things and making her bath in the holy river they adorned her body with new clothes and ornaments made of gold, gems and diamonds gleaming with light of the moon. Feeding her with varieties of delicious dishes they washed her mouth with scented water. Making her seated on the bed they kept before her a mirror to see her divinely purified elegant beauty. They locked her hair in the back with flowers strewn around it. Her body exuded a sweet smell by application of fragrant things. They ornamented her with a necklace of gems touching her breasts, waist chain, anklet and head chain to the magnification of her beauty to the captivation of many in lust and passion. With eyes like a lotus bud, beautifully chiselled teeth and smiling within her lips she looked majestic and remembered her husband rishi Karddama. By his yogic power the rishi could know the mind of Devahuti. Highly elated glancing her incomparable beauty he caught hold of her hand and amid all celestial beings moved the chariot in ten different directions in various Lokas (planes in the infinite space). While flying over, the chariot entered into the abode of Lord Vishnu where the devas (gods) eulogised their beauty illuminating like moon amidst the stars. In this way he moved from plane to plane from the domain of the masters of eight directions to the domain of siddha and celestial dancers and musicians where they were merged in merry making. Then, they moved into dense forests, divine gardens, the mountain Meru and into the Manasarovar. Like air entering everywhere they amidst celestial women itinerated in the chariot very speedily like Kuber in all ten directions. On whom Lord is pleased, nothing remains unfulfilled. Fatigued by long journey the rishi and Devahuti returned to the ashram and lived according to the nuances of household life. The rishi who had already reached the acme of God realisation took no time in materializing his soul into nine forms and started sensually enjoying Devahuti for hundred years of Devas (gods). The result was the birth of very beautiful smelling like lotus flower, nine daughters from the womb of Devahuti. On finding the rishi on his heels to adopt a sannyas life, Devahuti became perplexed and disturbed. With tears welling her eyes she approached the rishi and prayed with soft and plaintive voice:

"O my Lord! By your bliss and compassion, I got all joys and happiness remaining at your feet. I have no other thinking than about the marriage of our nine daughters. If you leave the world and lead a sannyasi life, how can I give marriage to them selecting the proper bridegrooms? My mind will not be joyful in your absence. To keep me joyful and happy I pray you to bless me with a son. For a long period of time, I rejoiced with you pandering to our senses. Born in a divine family and having company with you my life was wasted with sense derived pleasures. I did not know what was the ultimate goal of my life? I did not think about the liberation of my soul. I remained busy with dualities like pain and pleasure in total forgetfulness of God. I entreat you very fervently to be kind to me and liberate me from the delusive world. Where is the liberation of the one who remains submerged under the waves of the worldly delusion? Bounded by the fetters of karma he or she remains trapped in the snares of delusion, illusion and error and falls inexorably into the cycle of births after births. Knowing this who diverts his/her mind towards and remains engrossed in the Lord, he/she never drowns in the worldly ocean. Being deluded who shuns the dharma of resting in the Lord, he is considered dead while living. For gratifying my senses and bewitched by simmering worldly delusion I forgot to realise God in all my deeds and thoughts. Even serving devotedly at your feet with love I could not seek and earnestly earn for liberation. I pray you to show me the path following which I will cross the worldly ocean"

Birth of Kapil as God incarnate

Keeping his mind fully rested in God, the rishi Karddama listened carefully to the supplication of

Devahuti. Recollecting the words of the Lord on the day of his attainment of the highest stage of God realisation, he said:

"You are impeccably the epitome of beauty. Very soon you are going to give birth to the Lord in a new incarnation. Keeping the feet of the Lord in your heart you meditate on Him very devotedly with all your thoughts and actions directed at Him, all the worldly knots will be cut asunder to release you into the infinite realm of the Divine like a bird liberated from the cage into the infinite sky of absolute freedom by His words of wisdom".

Reposing unshakable faith in her husband rishi Kardddama's words she surrendered herself at the feet of the Lord. At the propitious moment of their union, Lord Krishna entered into the vigour and energy of rishi Karddama and took birth from the womb of Devahuti as an incarnation for the liberation of humanity. A great festivity of music, songs and dances took place among the celestials in heaven in great laudation of His all compassionate and merciful heart always moistening with love for the liberation of humankind. The gods started showering bunches of varieties of flowers in great adoration of His splendour and splendid majesties. The ten directions all around looked hilarious, serene and pure. The waves in the ocean rose in great heights in an eagerness to touch His holy Feet. The nature around the ashram of rishi Karddam and the water of the holy river Sarasvati seemed to be enthralled with joy at the news of God's coming to the earth. The seven rishis like Marichi and Lord Brahma himself disembarked in the ashram in great veneration of the love and devotion of the rishi Karddama that brought Lord Govinda down to the earth in incarnation for the spiritual awakening of the people through His words of wisdom. In great praises of the rishi, Lord Brahma said:

"O my son! in obeisance to my words you accepted the worldly life and amid many travails and trials you steadfastly got engrossed in the path of Yoga and meditation and by which you got ultimately the much sought after by rishis, yogis and seers, privilege of being united with Him. It is said, if the son thinks it is his sole duty to do everything as wished by the parents in a heart full of joy, he makes the Lord happy and in this and after life he earns the divine dividends. Your nine daughters are superb in beauty and virtues. You listen to my words and give them marriage to the Marichi and others. For they will be the cause of furthering the creation. For the liberation of mankind God has taken incarnation and will be widely known as Kapil".

With these words Lord Brahma turned his attention towards Devahuti and said:

"O venerable mother! Your life has been gratified by the birth of Lord Krishna from your womb. Your son is not ordinary. He is God incarnated to crack the knots of your delusive heart. He will teach you the path of karma, jnana and bhakti integrated in Kriya Yoga. He will be adored as the epitome of unparalleled beauty and wisdom with matted hair on the head and lotus eyes and feet. Bestowing on you the supreme knowledge he will itinerate the entire world as a sannyasi. He is the master and God of all siddhas, sankhya yogis, realised saints and sages. Your name and

fame will spread far and wide by the wisdom of Kapil, the God".

In company with His sons like Narada and other sages Lord Brahma returned to his abode in his divine chariot beatified by swans. Keeping the words of Lord Brahma, the rishi Karddama on an auspicious occasion invoked the rishis and gave them marriage of his nine daughters. He proffered Kala to rishi Marichi resembling Lord Shiva and mother Parvati; the second daughter Anasuya to rishi Atri; the third daughter Shraddha to rishi Angirasa; Havi to rishi Pulyastha; Kriya sati to Kratu; Kshyati to rishi Bhrugu; Arundhati to rishi Vasistha and the ninth daughter Shanti to rishi Atharvana. On completion of the sacred marriage in his ashram, rishi Karddama with plenty of wealth bade adieu to the rishis with daughters to their respective ashrams.

As foretold by the Lord on the day of his attainment of the highest stage of God realisation, Kapil took birth in his ashram as an incarnation. Reaching near him, the rishi said:

"O my adorable Lord! It is because of my demoniac nature I did not serve and take refuge at Thy Lotus Feet. The household life is like moving in a blind alley. It is by virtue of doing Kriya for many births in the past, I am able to shun the worldly life and retiring to the forest to remain engrossed in Thee. To behold Thy Holy Feet, I continue practicing Kriya Yoga for many years. To liberate me from the worldly delusion You have incarnated in this world. To keep Your words as told to me You have taken birth in my ashram. Residing in everybody you enhance the fame of Thy devotees.

For protection and liberation of Your devotees You have been embodied in many wombs. The very divine fragrance flirting from Your Lotus Feet attracts the seeker towards Thee leaving the worldly life burnt in the fire of detachment. With their love and dedicated surrender at Thy Feet, they ultimately mingle in You. You are the supreme Brahma manifested in the form of efflorescent light and epitome of infinite energy, splendid majesties, detachment and wisdom. I took refuge in You and implore You fervently to pardon me for being indulged in worldly delusion. You are the supreme Purusha. Earth, water, fire, air, ether (vacuum), mind, intellect and ego are the eightfold divisions of Your nature. Your para sakti (supreme nature) has been the cause of all activities in nature (prakriti). You are the indwelling self in everybody. You have taken birth in this world for awakening the knowledge of the self in all. I have taken refuge at Your lotus Feet. Let my mind be fixed in You. You are the adorable Lord of Brahma, my father. You have gratified me by taking birth as my son. The moment you took birth, I was released of my three debts – indebtedness to my father (pitru runa), indebtedness to sages and saints (rishi runa) and indebtedness to gods (deva runa). I pray earnestly to permit me to accept the sannyasi life with my heart and mind ever in thought and love and singing paeons of Your glory and supreme nature".

Moved by his heart rending and earnest prayer Lord Bhagavan (Kapil) said:

"It is because of your highest attainment of God realisation, intensity of love and perpetuating sadhana and assiduous meditation I have taken birth keeping the words I promised you then. For what you have been gratified with my darshan for your love is not easily available to yogis. For the spiritual

wellness of the people of the world I will remain ever in this embodiment for enlightening the world with the light of wisdom so long as sun, moon, stars and earth are here. The knowledge of self (tattwa jnana) was before but it was lost and buried in oblivion under the sway of Kala (Time Spirit). What is endeared to you, surrender to Me and remain merged at My Feet. Leaving behind the family you follow the path of a sannyasi and with determination, dedication, and detachment retire into fathomless solitude devoid of any thought where you realize unshakably that you and Me are indivisibly one and eternally in unity. You will soon conquer the invincible death and cross the worldly ocean. I am sojourning in everybody as divine light ever in bliss and joy. Behold and realise in your own self my Self. Knowledge of the self is the supreme knowledge. Get liberation from the delusive world by realizing this truth. Devahuti will also attain the Godhood by this supreme knowledge".

As directed by the Lord rishi Karddama left the home and remained engrossed in mediation following the techniques of Kriya Yoga in the solitude of the forest. Completely detached and surrendered at the feet of the Lord and the entirety of mind centred in Him in each and every breath he was able to unfetter the shackles of Kala (Time Spirit). He rejoiced and exalted in seeing the presence of God in all beings, in all leaves, trees, flowers and fruits, rivers, seas, and all creation. Realizing the wholeness of spirit (Supreme Self) pervading the entire creation, he ultimately climbed the summit of God realisation. By the practice of Kriya yoga, he attained ultimately the much sought-after liberation forever from the seething worldly life.

Inner significance

In Odia language kardam means kara dama. Kara denotes to do and dama means self- control or control over the senses. It means to control over senses.The key to self- realization is the mastery or through control over the senses and mind. To control the mind and senses is not that easy. This difficulty in keeping under control the senses was raised by Arjuna before Lord Krishna as mentioned in Srimad Bhagavad Gita (6:34). The senses are very difficult to control like the boat disturbed in the sea by the storm. The senses headed by mind are like unbridled horses which drag the seekers into dangers. The senses are like the invincible enemies which need to be controlled by the seekers in order to have self-realization.

Condescending to this fact Lord Krishna replied, there is no doubt about it, it is to be mastered and subdued by constant practice of breath control and detachment. Breath control is self- control as precepted by a great world-renowned Kriya Yoga master Paramahamsa Hariharananda precepted. Lord Krishna said to Arjuna:

> tani sarvani samyamya yukta asita matparah
> base hi yasya indriyani tasya prajna pratisthita (2:61)

Having through control over the extrovert senses if one is completely ensconced in God surrendering his heart and soul and his senses he is established in wisdom because his senses are completely subdued.

The rishi Kardam was a great realized master who had through control over his senses. He was established in wisdom. He assumed a married household life by the direction of God for procreation. He simply carried out what he was divinely ordained to do. After the birth of Maharshi Kapil, the incarnation of God he renounced the world and retired into deep forest for practicing Kriya Yoga for ultimate liberation.

If the word dama is reversed, it means mada. Mada means wine. Those who are addicted to drinking wine are lost in the wilderness of life. They remain under the control of wine. They are mentally deranged and gone astray. In a similar way, the people lost in wilderness of delusion, attachment and ignorance have no control over senses and mind and are thrown into the unending chain of birth and death remaining away from the path of God realization.

Another meaning of mada is madya which means intoxication. It has an underlying spiritual connotation. The Kaivalya Tantra, a renowned tantric scripture says,

> yaduktam parama brahma nirvikalpam niranjanam
> tasmin pramadana jnanam tanmadyam parikirtiam

Being completely absorbed in parabrahman, which is described as a state free from all modification and description gives a divine intoxication known as wine.

If one is completely united with God through yoga and meditation, it gives a divine intoxication full of joy and euphoria. Like a drunkard remaining always unaware of his existence and steps, the realized sadhakas remain always in divine intoxication. It was the state of realization which Kardam rishi attended.

The meaning of the word karddam is mud. From mud is born lotus flower. Lotus flower is a divine flower and the feet and eyes of the Lord are described padapadma (lotus feet) and lotus eyes respectively. In one of the hands of God lies the lotus flower. One of the sons of lord Brahma, rishi Karddama was able to merge with God by his sadhana. We are all deluded and merged in the mud (karddam) of worldly life without being able to remain at the lotus feet of the Lord, the Ultimate.

It is pronounced very candidly in Srimad Bhagavatam that rishi Karddam was practicing Kriya Yoga. The word yoga has multiple meanings in Sanskrit. In yogic language yoga means to be united, union or merge. The union of the individual self with the Supreme Self is the meaning of yoga. Yoga itself is the union or the process by which this ultimate union takes place like the rivers completely dissolved in the ocean without any individualised identity. This union is already there in each person, otherwise our body, senses and mind cannot be able to do any work. But out of ignorance and delusion we do feel or realise this constant union in us. Just as a thread is the link in a garland keeping flowers together, the thread of the breath keeps the body and soul together. If we have any virtuous deeds and spiritual earnings in our past life, we can be able to obtain the grace of masters and the blessings of God in order to practice yoga –

the science of soul culture by which all the mud of impurities will be cleansed from our mind and we can be able to realise this constant inner union in us. In Yoga Sutra of sage Patanjali, it is pronounced:

yogas-citta-vrti-nirodhah (Sutra 2 of Samadhi Pada)

Yoga is the elimination of mind stuff or memory and all thought waves.

Mind (manas), intelligence (buddhi), ego (ahamkara) and mind stuff or memory (chitta) are the four inner instruments (antahkarana chatushtaya) lying in each human being. The scriptures say, samshayatmika manah. It means, the mind always doubts. Mind is the doubting faculty. It always remains in confusion thinking in terms of duality and never arrives at a decisive conclusion. It fails to differentiate between what is good and bad, right and wrong. Mind is always blind like Dhritarashtra failing to judge what is right and what is bad.

Buddhi (intelligence) is the faculty of knowing the distinction between what is good and what is bad and then deciding to do what should be done. The scriptures say, nishchayatmika buddhi, meaning it is deciding faculty.

Ego (ahamkara) arrogates to itself the doership. It does like to take credit for and boasts of all things done successfully. Thus, scriptures say: abhimanatmika ahamkara. This faculty of egoism claims, I am the doer, I am the doer.

The fourth faculty is chitta (memory). It is also called anusandhanatmika or smaranatmika, the investigating or memory faculty. The mid brain in human being is the reservoir of all human experiences kept as memory. The memory is the cause and breeding ground of all thoughts. Whenever any thought comes to mind, be sure that it comes out of a specific memory. Without memory there cannot be any thought. The chitta is born out of human experiences through the mind which in turn, is activated by memory. Mind is a miniature of chitta. If ocean is to waves, thoughts are to the mind. The flow of thoughts one after another like waves rippling in the ocean one after another is chiita vritti. Thoughts self-generated from the memory reservoir one after another make the mind restless, bewildered, undeciding and confusing.

Human beings embedded in delusive world run after material things, persons and objects thinking that these will give them permanent happiness and joy in life. But in reality, these are very transitory and illusory. Their frantic search turns out to be a nightmare for them. The experiences, impressions and dispositions that humans earn in their search for joy in persons, material things and objects of the world gather in them as memory. These material memories are the source of chitta vrittis. Assuming these perishable and transient as eternal and permanent is ignorance. This inability to distinguish between what is apparent and what is truth is born out of ignorance which in turn, gives rise to *chitta vrittis*. Humans forget to search within the real happiness. They do not get themselves merged in the changeless and imperishable indwelling self. This process of searching within and ultimately being united with the indwelling self in all actions, deeds and thoughts is known as yoga. Yoga is both the means and the end. The ultimate union is known as yoga and the process of being united is also yoga. It is the process of preparing and cultivating the body land by removing the weeds and pebbles of negative attributes and evil propensities and planting the seed of divinity into it and nourishing it with love, knowledge and constant deeds by the practice of yoga and meditation to see that it grows into a divine tree bearing fruits of union with the Divine.

The process of wiping out the chitta vrittis from the mind is hastened by yoga. These are like flow of waves in the water bodies. When there is no wind, the water remains tranquil and still. With the blowing of wind water shows ripples of waves agitating the ocean. Here, wind is the cause of waves in the ocean. Similarly, the breath is the cause of thought waves in the ocean of chitta. The *Hatha Yoga Pradipika* (2:2) says:

> *cale vate calam cittam niscalam bhavet*
> *yogi sthanutvam apnoti tato vayum nirodhayet*

"When the breath is restless, the mind is restless. When the breath is calm and quiet, the mind is no longer restless. So, by controlling the breath, the yogis attain the state of inner tranquillity".

The turbulent, agitated and restless mind can be made calm, quiet and still by the practice of yoga as said by sage Patanjali.

Yoga is the union of the two - the jivatma with the paramatma or the union of the individual self with the Supreme Self like the river merging in the ocean. When the mind is well poised, calm, quiet, tranquil and still, the union takes place. Kriya Yoga is the royal and master science of achieving this union in a rocket speed. It is most scientific, shortcut, simplest and easiest path to God realisation. It quickens, hastens and accelerates human evolution in the path of God realisation. It ensures simultaneous development of body, mind, intellect and soul. It is the integration of karma, jnana and bhakti.

The secrets of Kriya Yoga were revealed by Lord Krishna to Arjuna. It is said by our Sri Gurudeva, God gifted the royal techniques of Kriya Yoga to humankind with its creation. In *Bhagavad Gita* (4:1) Sri Bhagavan said:

> imam vivasvate yogam proktavan aham avyam
> vivasvan manave praha manur iksvakave bravit

"I revealed this indestructible science of yoga to Vivasvan. Vivasvan told it to Manu, and Manu taught it to Ikshwaku".

In the solar dynasty king Vivasvan and after him it spread to the successors. Sri Ramachandra, the incarnation of God was also practicing. It gradually passed on to the lunar dynasty. The king Yudhishthira of this dynasty was also practicing. The secret knowledge of Kriya yoga did not escape the corrosive power of Kala (Time Spirit). It was lost to humankind in the passage of time due to secrecy. In the modern age, the mysterious and deathless Kalpa

Yogi Babaji Maharaj living in seclusion far away from the knowledge of the common people in the caverns of the Himalayas even at present, taught the techniques of Kriya Yoga to his disciple Shyama Charan Lahiri, a self-realized and highly advanced Kriya Yogi and householder in 1861 who later on, played a pioneering role in spreading Kriya Yoga throughout India and abroad.

The word Kri means to do any work. All works and thoughts refer to Kri. Ya means in Sanskrit the indwelling soul who does the work in human body. A dead man cannot walk, cannot talk, cannot listen, cannot see, cannot think, cannot do any work in hands, cannot speak, and cannot taste etc. It means the indwelling soul is the sole doer in man. The soul does the work through breath. It is the inhalation and exhalation that enlivens a man. Without breath man is dead. The breath is the witness to the living presence of God within man. Thus, kriya means to feel the union between the doer – the indwelling soul and the work done. The doer and done are one. The seer and seen are one. To realise this in each and every breath is kriya. Yoga as discussed above, is the union between the indwelling soul (Ya) and the deeds (Kri). In the ultimate union, the 'Kri' is dissolved in the 'Ya' like a river dissolved in the ocean. This is the release of the embodied self from the prison of body and mind consciousness into the Infinite Essence.

In Patanjali Yoga Sutra is found the mention of Kriya Yoga only and no other yogas. It is pronounced:

tapah svadhyayesvara pranidhanani kriya yogah
(Sadhanapada 2:1)

Tapas carries different and wide varieties of meanings. As elucidated by our Guruji Paramahamsa Prajnanananda, it is derived from the root verb tap, which means, to shine, to blaze, to be hot, to suffer, to mortify the body, or to burn. To burn all impurities stored in the body, mind and heart and make the mind ablaze with purity, knowledge and love. Burnt in the fire of worldly life of dualities such as pain and pleasure, heat and cold, happiness and unhappiness, joys and sorrows and honour and dishonour, the mind is perturbed, affected, agitated and bewildered. Tapas makes this agitated and unbalanced mind free form these gnawing dualities and makes it calm, quiet, still and pacified. With such a purified and pacified mind through tapas one can easily attain the state of union with the Almighty.

In *Bhagavad Gita* (17:14-19) there has been description of the three kinds of tapas - sattvik, rajasik and tamasik. The tapas meant for purification of body, speech and mind remaining wholeheartedly in God and detached to the fruits of action is sattvik. The tapas are the methods by which yogis and seekers of the Divine engaged in discipling, purifying and tuning the body, speech and mind to the Divine.

If a dead man is touched, one feels cold and everything is inactive and functionless. But a living person feels heat and temperature in his/her body. Everything is active and functioning. From where this heat is coming? Wherein it is generated? In human body within the spine there are seven chakras representing seven Lokas - bhuh, bhuvah, svah, maha, janah, tapah and satya. The Ajna chakra represents the tapah loka. It is the soul centre where fire is burning every moment. Each and every breath is the oblation (ghee) offered to the soul. Because of this inner fire the heat is maintained in the body, all senses and limbs, body, mind, intelligence and ego are active and all functions within the body are carried on. To remain in each breath conscious and absorbed in the indwelling soul is said as tapas. This is also karma performed remaining absorbed and merged in soul through every breath. This is transformed into pranakarma. The seeker is no longer bound by the fruits of the karma. He remains in a state of akarma as the soul is the sole doer in him. Tapas is pranakarma.

Svadhyaya

It connotes multiple meanings. The study of *Vedas*, scriptures and chanting mantras such as Gayatri mantra in a prescribed manner comes under svadhyaya. Another subtle meaning of it is sva means self adhyaya means to study. The study of self is svadhyaya. To know Thyself is also svadhyaya. The proper place to know thy self is the Ajna chakra. From pranakarma proceeds the knowledge of the self or divine. To know means to remain conscious of every breath touching the soul centre in all actions and thoughts. Without establishing oneself in the soul centre any kind of study of scriptures endows one only with theoretical understanding nothing else, it does not lead one to liberation. Fully absorbed in soul centre (tapa loka) in every breath is svadhyaya. Both svadhyaya and tapas are closely connected. In the *Bhagavad Gita* (17:15) Lord Krishna while elaborating upon vocal tapas (austerity in speech), spoke of svadhyaya abhyasanam, the practice of svadhyaya as an essential part of speech tapas.

Ishwar Pranidhana

Ishwar means God, the Supreme Lord of the entire creation. Without Him nothing can be conceived of. He is omnipotent, omnipresent and omniscient. Pranidhana means complete surrender or subordination to Him. Taking ultimate refuge in Him is pranidhana. Without any ego or pride when one surrenders to Him means in true sense pranidhana. Love and devotion enable one to dedicate or surrender to Him without any second thinking.

Kriya Yoga integrates these three practices simultaneously: tapas, the path of karma, svadhyaya, the path of knowledge, and ishwar pranidhana, the path of love and devotion. It is a superb synthesis of karma. Jnana and bhakti.

Rishi Karddam through the practice of Kriya Yoga attained the ultimate union with God. Highly pleased with this heightened attainment of divinity God appeared before him and instructed him what to do and predicted how He will take birth from them as Kapil. This has been discussed elaborately above.

Discourses by Maharshi Kapil

After renouncing the worldly life rishi Karddama entered into deep forest for sadhana to get ultimate liberation, God incarnate Kapil stayed put in the ashram near the bank of the river Sarasvati for the liberation of his mother Devahuti. Devoid of any birth and death he is Supreme Purusha and lord of all yogis and he is the wisdom and truth himself. Mother Devahuti prayed him with a heart full of love, devotion and humbleness:

"You are immortal and without any attribute and beyond anybody's reach. You are primordial Purusha and God. You manifest for the cause of your devotees. You are incarnated as the saviour and liberator of those ignorant and worldly deluded people. I am a woman and because of my devilish nature I do not know what is good and what is bad. Being young and ignorant I do not know how to unfetter myself from the worldly bondage. You are my Lord and endowing me with the eye of wisdom you liberate me from the illusion and ignorance of the worldly life. Being your mother, you be kind and blissful to me by which I can delve deeply into your fathomless nature".

God speaks thus moved by the prayer of his mother:

"O mother! In reply to your earnest question, I can say, in those who adore my feet and remain merged therein with inalienable love and devotion, detachment to the delusive world is found grooming because of their virtuous past deeds in previous births. Thus, to be fully established in the indwelling soul is yoga, the cause of liberation. In my previous incarnations, I have already taught the sages and saints about what is yoga. In this world of deep and dense

delusion, for liberation is required unconditional bhakti (love without any attributes) about which I am instructing you. In this delusive world one cannot be well accomplished in yoga and attain the ultimate without control over senses. As self-realised yogis condescend, mind is the cause of both bondage and liberation. If mind is attached to and engrossed in worldly delusion, it becomes the cause of bondage and mind is transfixed in God, it turns out to be the cause of liberation. Man is created out of his own mind stuff (chitta), the seed of his innumerable births. If chitta is cleansed of all desires and passions, it becomes pure. Mind takes both pleasure and pain and all dualities with equanimity. To a pure and God intoxicated mind there is no difference between Jiva (embodied self) and the Supreme Self (God). All are one and this mind fixed in God sees God as different from Prakriti. From this is created knowledge, bhakti (love) and detachment. If one remains merged completely in the Supreme Self with all love and devotion, he/she attains Him. There is no other path than this".

Significance of divine company

Continuing His discourses Lord Kapil says:

"One can cross the worldly ocean rippled with waves of delusion in company with sages and saints. It is because of their divine company one gets union with the Ultimate, mind never wavers anywhere. It remains fixed ever in God. O Mother! Listen to me carefully the characteristics of sadhus. They look others as the reflection of their own indwelling soul. They view the whole world not their enemies but the prototype of their own souls. They remain ever content and enthralled in joy being merged in their indwelling souls. Not a single moment is lost without

remembering, singing and reciting in paeans of the divine majesties and glories of God remaining merged at His feet. Renouncing their homes, wives, children, relatives and everything, they live in the deep forest for undeviating meditation and ultimately merge in Me. In each and every breath they feel the presence of the Divine. In His thought they remain enraptured and intoxicated. In such a state the sadhus get liberation from the delusive world. Leaving aside your association with the world, you seek good company with such realised sadhus which will enable you to cross the worldly ocean. All your ignorance and warped view of the delusive life will disappear".

Elaborating on love and devotion Lord Kapil says:

"In remembrance, recitation and invocation of my fathomless divinity, splendid glories and magnified true nature and revealing the same before others, your body will be enthralled with untold joys and tears welling your eyes. By this, your love and devotion towards Me will day by day increase and the worldly shackles will be pulverised to pieces. It is because of the good fortune of previous births one gets rise of love and devotion towards Me. In the thought of my divine play and glories detachment is born in one's heart. With elimination of his devilish nature and by virtue of his love, detachment and knowledge of the self, he takes ultimate refuge in Me. Upon taking Me as the boat you can cross the worldly ocean by the oar of your deepest love and devotion".

Highly gratified at these nectar-like words of God incarnate Kapil and overwhelmed with joy, Devahuti falling at His feet entreated to enlighten her on the characteristics of bhakti and how could one know that he/she had bhakti. What is this yoga of bhakti? How it is to be practiced? "O all compassionate Lord! Since I am quite ignorant of this difficult and incomprehensible yoga, I pray you to elaborate on this".

Lord Kapil in reply said:

"O mother! Listen to Me the saliences of bhakti. The senses in human body are activated by the gods (devas) and do the works according to their nature as directed by the Vedas. In whatever position (varna) man is placed according to his/her nature, the senses perform the work accordingly. Those who surrendering all these works at My Feet with wholehearted devotion and love with a concentrated and unwavering mind on Me, remain detached in this delusive world, are the supreme and endeared bhaktas to Me. They ultimately attain Me without fail. From the fetters of bondage of desires and passion they are released for ever not to fall again into the deep ocean of worldly delusion. They remain always immersed in waters of love for Me enthralled in divine joy while remembering and singing in paeans of My glory and majesties. Eternally united with Me and liberated forever from the chain of worldly delusion, they are privileged to behold My true nature manifested in My inexpressible beautiful blue coloured body, beguiling face beaming with ineffable joy and glistening eyes blossomed like lotus flower in all their divinity and splendour. While remembering and revealing before others My divine form, they remain ecstatic and the hairs on their bodies stand on their heads. At the very beholding of My splendid divinity, their chitta and mind get dissolved in Me. They are endowed with eight divine majesties (astha aisvarya). Whatever they wish all come to their feet. There is nothing in three Lokas

which is not attainable by them. Infinite majesties remain within their reach. They remain immune to the all-engulfing power of kala (Time Spirit). I am their Guru, closest and dearest friend and everything. All these great yogis and endeared bhaktas remain always at My feet. While living in this world with their mind fixed on Me, they serve the poor and work for the liberation of the worldly people".

Knowledge of the Supreme Self

Maharshi Kapil said:

"O mother! I am revealing before you the secret knowledge of the Supreme Self by which the knot of the heart centre will be opened and the soul imprisoned in the cage of body and mind will be liberated. The indwelling soul is like the sun in the body that reflects the light of the knowledge of the soul. The soul abides inside the body and also outside. It is all pervading, and encompasses the whole universe. It is above prakriti and without any attributes. It is manifested everywhere as divine light. The entire universe and everything of it are always active, dynamic and in motion and in the process of change, it is because of the omnipresent, omniscient and omnipotent soul. He was alone and wanted to be many. So, by creating everything He entered into creation and sojourned in them very subtly and hidden as the indwelling soul. On creating the three attributes (Gunas) – rajasik, sattvik, tamasik, He remains detached to them. With rajasik attributes He created the universe and everything living and non-living. By sattvik attributes He sustains and maintains them and by tamasic attributes He destroys them. In His cosmic play He has given birth to beings in various forms as animals, plants and trees and human beings keeping them deluded by Maya

(illusive power) full of attributes. He Himself remains hidden behind the veil of ignorance and illusion. He remains a mere witness to what is done in the body. Those who are swayed away by the delusive propensities (pravritti) never escape from falling again and again into the cycle of birth and death. Those who remain detached to the worldly delusion (nivritti) get liberation. The indwelling soul as the witness sees everything without being affected or deluded by the propensities, whereas the man being deluded by prakriti thinks himself as the sole doer of everything and reaps the fruits of both bad and good deeds".

Discourses on Prakriti and Purusha

Mother Devahuti invoking Kapil as the Supreme Purusha sought to know, how the universe has been expressed in gross and subtle forms and how prakriti and Purusha have been manifested. To this Kapil, the God incarnate replied:

"The soul abiding in everybody in the form of light has been manifested in the world. Everything is performed through Prakriti being the sole instrument of doing. There are twenty-five tattvas such as five elements (bhutas) – earth, water, fire, air and vacuum (space); five jnanendriyas such as form (rupa), rasa, smell, sound and touch; ten indriyas (senses) such as tongue, ears, nose, eyes, skin, hands, feet, words, genital and anus; and mana, buddhi, chitta and ego. The twenty fifth element is kala (Time spirit). The prakriti in these forms does everything. God in the form of kala manifests all. Out of egoism the jiva (manifested form of the detached indwelling self) does and enjoys everything as the sole doer yet remains fearful of the kala. Prakriti creates and destroys all on the earth. God by His own power of

illusion (maya) deludes all into the unending circuit of birth and death".

Continuing His discourse, Bhagavan Kapil further elaborates to Devahuti:

"Like moon reflected in water, God – the Supreme Purusha is all pervading and abides in everybody and everything in the living as well in non-living. Prakriti born out of Him assumes the form of a golden plate as a veil between God and the human beings. God is the manifested soul of the entire cosmos in the subtle form. Being the indwelling soul, He removes the darkness of all demoniac propensities like anger, enmity, jealousy, ego, pride, passion etc. With attainment to this haven of divinity everything is nothing but the manifested all effulgent light known as Vasudeva, a state of super consciousness, immortal, detached, pure, devoid of any attribute and gunas. He is kshetrajna. He is the supreme tattva. He is the infinite and invisible power within us. This power in association with ego creates three gunas – sattvik, rajasik and tamasik. All the senses, mind and five elements are created according to these three gunas. The presiding deity of all these is Sankarshana with hundred and thousand feet and hands pervading infinitely all and everything. The five elements, body, mind and senses are the instrument through which all works are done and the real doer in the body is the indwelling soul. The human beings are deluded by the three gunas (attributes). The presiding deity of intelligence is Brahma and its adored form is Pradyumna. Moon is the presiding god of mind and its manifested form is Aniruddha to be worshipped

Intelligence (buddhi) is attached to rajasik attributes. It is also attached to material things, senses and knowledge.

Doubt, wrong understanding, determining, memory and sleep are the five features of intelligence. From ego which is rajasik are created senses. These senses perform the functions as determined by their tendencies. By the power of prana (breath) these senses do all and accordingly, the humans enjoy being attached to these. When buddhi becomes determined and has the knowledge to conceive the indwelling soul as the sole doer and activates these senses through breath, mind becomes still and makes the humans detached. Intelligence without the knowledge of the soul is destructive and deludes the man.

The five elements (pancha tanmatra) are tamasik and created out of Lord Vishnu. From the attributes of sound (tanmatra) vacuum is created. This expresses the infiniteness of the soul, all pervading and abiding in all both inside and outside yet remains invisible. It carries the infiniteness, invisibility and detachment characteristics of the vacuum (space).

From touch (tanmatra) is created air by which the sensations of heat, cold, softness and hardness are felt. Coming in contact with senses air enables us to smell and hear. Air is breath within the body as witness to the presence of soul in every living being. All forms, beauty and lustre of the body are due to the air element (tanmatra).

From air element is created fire. From this teja (fire) eyes are created which see things in forms in their finite shapes and give the knowledge of matter and material things and their attributes. Cooking, hunger, thirst, drinking, eating, sucking and chewing, digestion and protection of body from cold and winter are the characteristics of fire.

When fire is degraded rasa (juice) is created. Man is attracted towards outward beauty and passion is created for physical union or meeting. This passion gives rise to anger which is expressed in fire of words. That's why it is said a person is burning with anger. Without juice there cannot be expression of words from mouth. From rasa is created water in gross form. For this reason, the tongue being attached to rasa relishes all kinds of taste such as pungent, astringent, bitter, sweet, saline and sour. Though rasa is in all, one tastes different savours being attached outwardly to rasa or water. This body is like an earthen lump. Water keeps it cool. When a person is angry, by drinking water anger vanishes. When something catches fire, by spraying water on it the fire is extinguished. The extreme hot weather is made cool by application of water through various mechanisms. When soil is dried water makes it wet and plants and trees on it survive. Water always flows from high to low.

When water is degraded or deviated smell is born. From smell earth is born. To smell the nose is created. Smell is one but it becomes different such as sweet, soft, fragrant, pungent and stale or stench depending on attachment to various elements and things of matter. When one is not attached to soul from which smell or ability to smell is coming but to objects and things, difference in smelling is created. God is all pervading and abiding in all places, objects and things but to see the differences not unity among beings, things and objects is the characteristic of the earth.

The characteristic of vacuum (space) is sound. The object of ears is to hear. The attribute of air is touch sensation. The object of skin is touch. The attribute of teja (fire) is form or shape. The object of eyes is sight. The characteristic of water is juice or rasa. The object of tongue is juice. Smell is the attribute of earth. The object of nose is smell. Having been pre-coded into these attributes in their previous births and born with these imprints in this life, the human beings are deluded by these attributes and see the differences among them, objects and things in terms of sound, touch, forms, rasa, and smell. Without introverting their senses into the immanent and indwelling soul – the creator of all these they are extroverted and beguiled by the senses and their attached objects and things. Without getting themselves engrossed in the invisible and all-pervading, all-powerful soul, the sole doer in them, they prefer to see the differences not the unity in all and waver outside like a deer in search of the fragrance of kasthuri without knowing that the smell is coming from within. When the man gets himself fully dissolved in the indwelling soul, all attributes like sound, touch, form, smell and taste cease to exist. All becomes one and lose their inherent characteristics.

During the great eternal deluge, all beings, all things and all creation get dissolved in God. There is nothing. God remains alone enraptured in the euphoric ecstasy of eternal yoga sleep unbounded in a timeless web of infinitude. When He awakes and wishes to be many, creation begins. By creating He enters into every creation. In the vast mass of water, He floats like a great golden sheath out of which gradually evolves a form of His with hundred and thousand heads. From His navel centre Lord Brahma was born to start the process of creation. He is the Lord of creation and carries the primordial form of God. From His mouth fire, from nose prana, from eyes fire, from ears directions, from His senses ten devas (gods), the hair on His skin, the medicinal plants are created. Water is His serum. His anus is the abode of death. Indra resides in His hands. All nerves and arteries joined together in His navel centre are the rivers and streams. In his stomach are oceans carrying the fire of hunger and thirst. Mind is created out of heart and makes objectified differences. Then, is created buddhi (intelligence) from Mahat. Thus, the fourteen lokas (planes) reside in Him. He has entered into human body as kshetrajna. Getting consciousness, He awakens from water and enters into the creation and resides in human beings as the indwelling soul. The mind and senses being activated by the indwelling soul delude the humans."

"O mother! Knowing all these, those who remain wholeheartedly at My feet and adore Me are able to cross the worldly ocean", said Kapil Maharshi.

Discourses on Prakriti and Purusha

Maharshi Kapil said to Devahuti, the daughter of Manu:

"God is immortal, formless, imperishable, undeluded and detached and resides in all beings. Detached and dissociated from Prakriti He lives like sun rays reflected in the water. Attached to the body, mind and senses humans betake the soul as the egoistic self and experiences joy and sorrows as that of the soul. Activated by the light of the indwelling soul the senses and mind do perform all deeds with an egoistic sense of doership and enjoy the fruits thereof but the indwelling soul remains unaffected by the fruits of these deeds. Without having the knowledge that the soul is the real doer and by the light of the soul the body, mind and senses are shined and activated, the human beings are deluded and fall easily into the cycle of birth and death. The *seeds of the karma (deeds) done by the beings are the cause of tortuous cycle of birth and death. Death is like drowning one's head inside water and then raising up the head above water is birth. The image of the sun reflected inside water is not real. Similarly, life in this deluded world is like a dream. All dualities like pain and pleasure, sorrows and happiness, failure and success, friend and enemy and self-versus the other are mere delusions. In deep sleep, all waking and dream experiences disappear. There is no sense of any existence. Attachment to body, mind, senses, intelligence and ego disappears. There is no knowledge of where one is sleeping. But the soul abiding in the body remains witness to all these. After awakening from deep sleep, he only feels that he has got a good sleep and could not know anything. If mind remains like this without the consciousness of the abiding soul in deep sleep, he cannot have the knowledge of the soul as the sole doer. Without the soul where is the knowledge?"*

On listening to these solemn words, Devahuti asked Kapil Muni, "O God! *As earth and its smell, water and liquidity are inseparable, the supreme Purusha (Param brahma) and prakriti never leave one another. How can Prakriti without the Brahma manifest? The creation is done by Purusha with the instrumentality of Prakriti laden with three attributes-sattva, raja and tamas. Being attached to the worldly delusion because of these three attributes, when one leaves the world, the knowledge of the delusive world remains with him. How he is liberated?".*

Maharshi Kapil said:

"*O mother! If one remaining fixed in the indwelling soul and practices meditation, the science of yoga with a purity of mind, love, detachment, consciousness and constant hearing of the name of Lord Krishna, he/she will attain the samadhi stage. His worldly fetters will be torn apart. The prakriti will gradually leave the association with Purusha like fire taking birth from the wooden sticks, burns the sticks first. With the end of prakriti, the liberated one unfetters himself from the bondage and revels in the eternal union with Purusha. The worldly life looks like a dream in sleep coming untrue after one awakens. He is no longer snared by my delusive power. Because of the virtuous deeds in the past lives, one gets the knowledge of the Self. With the attainment of samadhi my devotees remain merged in the euphoric bliss, joy and peace and attain the ultimate liberation (Kaivalaya mukti) burning forever the seeds of being fallen into the chain of birth and death into ashes. This is the stage where the fear of death ceases".*

Reflection

In *Bhagavad Gita* Lord Sri Krishna clarified the doubts raised by Arjuna the same way Bhagavan Kapil dispelled the doubts of mother Devahuti:

adhibhutam ksaro bhavah purusas ca dhidaivatam
adhiyajna ham eva 'tra dehe dehabhrtam vara (8:4)

All created beings are perishable. The basis of all divine elements is the shining self or cosmic spirit. O best of all those in human form (Arjuna)! The basis of all sacrifices (fire ceremony) is I, Myself, in this body.

What is the meaning of adhibhuta? In the *Upanishad* it is said that from the imperishable Supreme Self, the five gross elements such as first vacuum, then air, fire, water and earth are created. From earth and all other elements emerged life such as fungus, insects, weeds, plants, trees, animals, and human beings. Bhuta means the five elements as well as all living beings. All living beings have a body made of the five elements. All these are the living presence of God.

All these being material nature are perishable (kshara). Nothing in this material world is permanent. Everything is subject to change. In every moment changes are taking place to body and all other constituent elements. These changes are coming from the changeless and imperishable soul (akshra). This is remaining at the top – the fontanel. Without the living soul (Purusha), where is the creation and where are the living beings and the elements?

The word 'adhidaiva' comes from Purusha, the indwelling soul. As interpreted by Paramahamsa Hariharananda, Purusha means *puryam shete it, the one who is hiding in the city of the body*. Every human body is the abode of God. The living power of God hiding in the body shines all the centres and sense organs like the sun illuminating everywhere. God is Purusha (adhidaiva), the sole doer and cause of all action and light.

Aham adhiyajna: God said to Arjuna I am adhiyajna. I am the perishable body and also the imperishable spirit. I am in everything, and beyond everything. I am the sole conductor of all living beings and the twenty-four elements.

Aham atra dehe: I am residing in the body from the pituitary to fontanel. Those who practice Kriya Yoga may attain the true stage of adhiyajna, the fire ceremony or divine sacrifice in the soul fire. Indwelling soul is the fire always illuminating. The breath is the oblation offered to the soul fire in all actions and thoughts done in the perishable and imperishable body. Thus, every action is yajna, sacrifice and worship of God. If one by practice of Kriya Yoga goes beyond the perishable nature and the imperishable kutastha, one enters into the state of the supreme self.

God further revealed (*Bhagavad Gita*, 9:4)
maya tatamidam sarvam jagad avyaktamurtina
matsthani sarvabhutani na ca 'ham tesv avasthitah

I have pervaded the entire universe as the unmanifest divine form. All beings are within Me, but speaking the truth, I am not abiding in them.

Lord Krishna said to Arjuna:

Maya tatami dam sarvam jagat means God is omnipresent. He pervades the entire universe. In all directions and in all spaces outside and inside He is abiding, But He is avyakta, unmanifest, and beyond the perception and comprehension of the senses and intelligence. The physical eye cannot be able to see Him though His presence is everywhere. He transcends the boundaries of our senses, mind and perception.

I am abiding everywhere; I am in all the senses but beyond the senses. I can see without eyes and hear without ears. I need no legs. I can be at all places and at all times. I am infinite. I am compassionate and detached. I am the soul in all living beings. I am giving life force, vitality and activity to all living beings. I illuminate all and I am beyond illumination. I am self-effulgent. I have no form and name. I am neither male or female. I am unaffected by the triple qualities of nature. I am the cause of breath. I am therefore, everyone and everything that is alive. I am both inside and outside. In this way, all living beings are born in Me, living in Me and are merging in Me.

In next verse (*Bhagavad Gita*, 9:5) God said, it is true that I am abiding in all. Though I am the sustainer and creator of all beings and all elements, My Self, in reality, dwells not in those beings and elements.

This verse looks contradictory to the previous verse. God said, I am in all and all are in Me. Now He says, all are in Me but I am not in them. The reality is that when a sadhaka or spiritual seeker remains in pure consciousness and in between pituitary and fontanel and also goes beyond by the practice of Kriya Yoga, he/she remains merged with Supreme Self and realises that he is detached and remains above the senses and triple qualities of nature and also the gross elements.

In what came to be known as the subtle explanation of final dissolution and creation given by Kapil muni to mother Devahuti, was reiterated by Lord Krishna to Arjuna in a different situation:

sarvabhutani kaunteya prakritim yanti mamikam

kalpaksaye punas tani kalpadau visrjamy aham
(*Bhagavad Gita*, 9:7)

"O Arjuna! With the final dissolution of one cycle or kalpa all beings enter into my divine being. Then, in the beginning of new creation I send them forth".

Creation and dissolution occur at all times and everywhere in the form of God's divine nature. This divine nature is eightfold (five gross elements, mind, intelligence and ego). In each human being the dominance of eightfold nature can be discerned in the spine. In a very beautiful interpretation Paramahamsa Hariharananda says, though kalpa has many meanings; one is calculation of time, another is cycle of creation. But the real meaning in this verse is kalpana, the modifications of mind, thoughts, or desires. When a desire (kalpana) is born in a person, the entire system marks a change, the physical body as well the breath pattern changes. The desires are both good or bad, material or spiritual. Kalpana means the dissolution of all desires. During deep sleep or during deep meditation the person feels no desires or activity. This is a temporary state because with the waking from the sleep the desires again enter into the mind. In deep meditation the person remains conscious of the indwelling soul. Deep sleep is meditation without consciousness and meditation is deep sleep with consciousness. When a person wakes up from deep sleep (kalpadau - creation) he looks afresh and energetic but he remains the same old person without evolution. After deep meditation (kalpadau) the seeker looks different, a changed and better person. Meditation accelerates human evolution towards attainment of divinity and realisation of God.

Lord Krishan says to Arjuna on Prakriti and Purusha (*Bhagavad Gita*):

> prakrtim purusam cai 'va viddhy anadi ubhav api
> vikarams ca gunams cai 'va viddhi
> prakritsambhavan (13:19)

While describing the body nature and the indwelling soul, Lord says, Prakriti (nature) has no beginning and no middle but it has an end. Kshetra is the body and the kshetrajna is Purusha, the indwelling soul which has no beginning, no middle and no end being formless. The Purusha residing in every human being is beyond the triple qualities of maya. The soul is breathing for everyone and accordingly changing the dispositions of individuals. When a person remains in the pituitary and fontanel, he does not fall prey to maya. When he goes below the pituitary, he remains engrossed in the body nature – in money, sex, appetite, anger, pride, cruelty and many types of religious activities. People do all these things from body nature, but it is because of the soul (kshetrajna) abiding in human body. Through the practice of Kriya Yoga if the spiritual seeker remains in the pituitary in between the two eye brows, he remains above the body nature and attains the state of freedom from all worldly ties and transcends the triple qualities of maya. When one goes beyond the fontanel to the all-pervading state, he perceives complete freedom and no sense of world exists.

Discourses on Yoga

Lord Kapil instructed mother Devahuti on Yoga and its eight limbs. If mind is calm and quiet, still, unperturbed and unagitated it moves on the right path. Withdrawing one's mind from the lower centres one has to follow the path of detachment. The attributes of the lower chakras such as Muladhara, Swadhisthan, Manipur, Anahata, and Visuddha within human spine tend a person to run after money, sex, appetite, ego, self-conceit and religious ostentations. Thus, being confined to these attributes and lower chakras is gramya dharma as Kapil muni said. Not elevating one's mind from the lower chakras to the top of the head i.e., pituitary and fontanel has been the common attitude of many deeply engrossed in material and worldly life. To be swayed away by the beguiling delusion of the mundane life is what Kapil said as gramya dharma. This gramya dharma is the path of pravritti (attachment) and detachment is the path of nivritti. In order to have detachment one has to practice the eight limbs of Yoga. Kapil Maharshi said:

"O mother! One has to do meditation in a place of solitude and silence. The food one has to take must be simple and not excessive or too little. It must be balanced. The seeker must follow the principles of truth and non-violence without a sense of possession. With purity, tapa, sex continence and self-study, surrender at the feet of the Lord. Sitting motionless on a seat made of kusha (a kind of grass used for

worship in Hindu tradition) covered with deer skin and blanket, and maintaining complete silence, meditate by doing pranayama".

The techniques as taught by Kapil Maharshi are nothing but the techniques of Kriya Yoga.

Maharshi Patanjali in his Yoga Sutra (Sadhana Pada Sutra 29) has enunciated exactly what was taught by God incarnate Kapil to mother Devahuti:

yama-niyamasana-pranayama-pratyahara-dharana-dhyana-samadhayo' stavangani

Self-discipline, vows of observances, physical postures, regulation of breath, self-withdrawal, concentration, meditation, and realisation (samadhi) are the eight constituent limbs.

Yama (self-discipline), the first limb consists of five aspects as defined by sage Patanjali:

tatra ahimsa-satyasteya-brahmacaryaparigraha yamah (Sutra 30)

The practice of self-discipline (Yama) consists of non-violence, truthfulness, non-stealing, continence and non-possessiveness or non-acquisitiveness.

Kapil muni advised mother Devahuti to sit in a purified place on a mat of kusa (a kind of grass) covered with the skin of a deer or tiger and silk cloth upon it and practice pranayama.

In *Bhagavad Gita* Lord Sri Krishna told Arjuna where to sit, how to sit and what should be the nature of the seat for meditation (6:11,12):

sucau dese pratisthapya sthiram asanam atmanah
na 'tyucchritaam na 'tinicam cailajinakusottaram
tatrai 'kagram manah krtva yatacittendriyakriyah
upavisya 'sane yunjyad yogam atmavisuddhaye

The place for meditation should be a purified and clean spot that is not too high or low. Upon it is put a grass mat covered with skin of a tiger or deer and spreading on it a silk cloth.

Making the mind concentrated one may practice meditation by mastering the mind and senses.

These verses have metaphorical meaning. As Gurudeva Paramahamsa Hariharananda says, "the real place of meditation is the cranium. This is mentioned in John where Jesus says, "Ye are from beneath, I am from above". In the *Prashana Upanishad* the same thing is reiterated, atha-akshaya urdhvam, which means that you must sit in the north (top) of your body, inside the pituitary. In the *Katha Upanishad* (1:3:8) it says, yas tu vijnana van bhavati sa manaskas sada suchih, which means that people keep their attention inside the pituitary, in the soul, are pure. The cranium is the real place for meditation, the real place of solitude and purity".

Bhagavan Kapil further taught her the techniques of pranayama as practiced in Kriya Yoga.

This is well described in *Bhagavad Gita* (4:29):

apane juhvati pranam prane 'panam tatha 'pare
pranapanagati ruddhva pranayamaparayanah

Others offer their exhalation (prana) as an oblation of the external air. Still others offer apana (inhalation) as an oblation to prana, and in this way, they stop the flow of inhalation and exhalation. They practice in this way pranayama.

Its metaphorical meaning as delineated by Gurudeva Paramahamsa Hariharananda is that inhalation is apana, oxygen. Apana refers to the oxygen outside of the body (a means na or not). The soul must inhale this oxygen into the body so it can be transformed into usable energy. So apana is pure oxygen outside that is inhaled and offered as an oblation to the soul. Therefore, soul remains in the body. Sa is inhalation and sa is the soul. When apana, oxygen is inhaled and offered to the soul, it is immediately burned, like oil that touches the flame in the lamp. As the soul flame burns the apana, it gives off life force, prana, to energise the body. We experience prana as body heat (tapa) and as the ordinary consciousness of experiencing the world through the five senses. If the ham (body nature), constantly watches this normal breath and perceives the living power of God entering it in the form of oxygen (sa), that body will experience God realisation. This is continuous oblation to God.

Prana is the outgoing breath of the soul, which provides the life force that animates the twenty-four gross elements of the body and mind. The soul's exhalation includes the carbon dioxide that is offered to the external air. When one is not watchful of the breath constantly, his/her spirituality and Godhood is lost. Continuous alertness of the breath produces continuous God realisation.

It is pronounced in Gheranda Samhitha (5:84): hamkarena bahiryati sakarena viseta punah, which means that "the breath entering into every person makes the sound of sa and when exiting it makes the sound ham". This is ham-sa sadhana, watching the inhalation and exhalation with so-ham. The outgoing breath is prana, ham, and the incoming breath is apana, sa. In same vein it is mentioned in Shiva Sarvoday (51), hakaro nirgame proktah sakarena pravesanam, which means "the process of exhalation contains the letter ham, and the inhalation contains the letter sa".

Lord Kapil said to mother, "If you do practice Kriya pranayama with stillness and quietness of mind, your heart, mind and soul will be purified free from the dirt of worldly delusion like an iron piece heated by fire becoming pure without any dirt. With pinpointed attention between the two eyebrows remain fixed on Me without being diverted towards the extrovert world".

This is exemplified in *Bhagavad Gita* (6:13) by Lord Krishna to Arjuna:

samam kayasirogrivam dharayann acalam sthirah
sampreksya nasikagram svam disas ca 'navalokayan

With body, head, and neck held firmly straight, erect, still, motionless and with unswaying attention fixed between the two eyebrows, not looking about hither and thither.

Kapil Muni taught the mother how to sit in meditation and with what correct posture and where to keep the attention and on whom. Practicing Kriya Yoga this way with entirety of attention ensconced on the Lord between the two eyebrows i.e., in the pituitary and fontanel, He said, O adorable mother! "You will be able to behold the Lord in all His majestic beauty and splendour. When the sadhaka's heart is dissolved with the thought of God and nothing else, tears of love will flow down making his body, mind and soul united with Him overwhelmed with joy and ecstasy. In this way he becomes detached to the world without any desires and attains *turiya* **samadhi**. Everywhere he beholds the living presence of soul in the form of light. Devoid of any attributes he ascends to the highest stage of God realisation where there exist no dualities like sorrows or happiness, birth or death. As a drunkard has no sense of body being intoxicated the realised one similarly remains always oblivious of body and mind consciousness. He feels the body is doing the work without any attachment. Without attainment of this stage of perfection in God realisation, man's mind gets engrossed in worldly affairs with attachment to son, wife, family and wealth. As fire cannot be seen clearly in its effulgence by the smoke, the indwelling soul is not perceived by the worldly delusion in its true splendour and nature. Fire and smoke both are within the wood. But when fire comes out of it, it first burns the wood to ashes. Similarly, by sadhana of Kriya Yoga, knowledge created out of the ignorance and worldly delusion destroy these. God is one but He has become manifold and assumed many forms abiding in beings. In this way He enacts the worldly drama. All those who are merged in Him behold the entire universe as the manifestation of God, and perceive in all both living and non-living His effulgent presence. Though all are looking different according to their different attributes, but Light of God pervades them all. Sun is one but when it shines the entire universe looks in diverse forms because of the difference in their attributes (Gunas). There is no other way than to seek refuge in Him. With all your mind and thoughts remain merged in the abiding soul. To remain dissolved in Him is the real love and devotion to God. By the constant practice of Kriya Yoga, you will get liberation from the deluding worldly life".

Characteristics of Love

Mother Devahuti entreated Bhagavan Kapil to highlight on the nature of the knowledge of the Supreme Self by which darkness of ignorance would be dispelled and love would surge for Lord Krishna.

Lord Kapil said, *"O mother! Listen attentively what I am expatiating on bhakti (love). It is of three types: sattvk, rajasik and tamasik. Worshipping Me with a mind and heart full of jealousy, greed, ego, conceit, anger, passion and violence is tamasic bhakti. Those who worship Me with desires for name and fame, wealth, position, status and attachment to the worldly matters are said to have rajasic bhakti. Others who take complete refuge in Me with detachment to the worldly delusion are known to have sattvic bhakti. Each is of nine types and in this way, it becomes of twenty-seven types. As these twenty-seven are of three types each like higher, middle and lower, it becomes ultimately eighty-one types of bhakti with attributes (Saguna)".*

Kapil Muni said, *"Mother! Now you listen to nirguna (without attributes) bhakti. Those who are imbued with nirguna bhakti they revel every moment in listening to my divine majesties and glories with esoteric joy and exuberance; they behold My indivisible self in every being and realise My inseparable unity with them and like rivers and streams joining the ocean, they always get united with Me. With attainment of this knowledge of my Supreme Self by nirguna bhakti they get ultimate liberation unfastening forever the snares of worldly attachment. There are five types of liberation in the path of nirguna bhakti: samipya, sarupya, sajujya, salokya and aiswarya (divine majesties). Samipya means to live near God. Sarupya means to get always the image of God. Sajujya means to get dissolved in God. God and bhakta becomes one like the rivers and ocean. Salokya means to abide in the abode of the Lord. Aiswarya means to be entitled to all divine majesties like those of the Lord. One who loves Me unconditionally remaining invincible before the temptations and enticements of the three attributes, is dear to Me. This is surely attainable by following the path of Kriya Yoga as I have instructed you".*

Kapil Maharshi instructed the following to be pursued to purify one's chitta (mind stuff):

Always follow the path of non-violence

With an equanimity attitude behold all as the reflection of your own Self

Think and treat all as your friends and kith and kin and with honour to the great persons

Sing always in paeans of My glories and beauties

Seek always company with sages and saints and listen to their discourses on Me".

Lord Kapil continued:

"If you practice all these your chitta will be purified like the fragrance sweeps away the bad smells under the force of strong wind. In meditation realise the all-pervading soul which is pure, detached and short of any attributes. Leaving all the above aside and without perceiving Me as the indwelling soul and I am the Lord of all if anybody pursuits the other path and worships Me in the form of an image, it is like doing yajna with ashes not with fire. He will not attain Me and will not be able to break the knot of worldly delusion. Without realizing Me in all and everywhere he remains engrossed in duality by creating differences between and among all. He fails to cross the worldly ocean and falls back into the dungeon of mortality".

Continuing His discourses Lord Kapil said to mother Devahuti:

"The living beings are superior to the non-living in that prana is supreme in the former. Superior to prana is consciousness which is not in non-living. In living non-human beings, senses are supreme. The trees and plants are sensitive to touch. The fish like beings are sensitive to taste. The bees like insects are sensitive to smell. The serpentines are sensitive to sound. The others are sensitive to forms. Among the living the humans are superior. Among the humans, brahmins are superior. Among the brahmins is the

vedajna (mastery over vedas) *and among the vedajnas superior is the knower of the hidden meaning. Superior to them are those who are above doubts and dualities. Superior to them are those who are engrossed in their own dharma. Above all are those who are detached free from the worldly delusion and have completely surrendered, engrossed and taken refuge in Me. Bethinking Me as the sole doer they are fully merged in Me and revel in perceiving Me everywhere and in everything. To them God is kind to bless with His majestic darshan (sight). There is nothing above God. He is the beginning and end of the creation. He is kala (time spirit) and beyond kala. All in the entire creation are subject to the all-devouring nature of kala. I am abiding hidden in all as adhiyajna (indwelling soul). He is the all-devouring Mahakala (Supreme Time Spirit). Nobody is dear or abhorrent to Him. All are bound to the gnawing jaws of death by the inexorable laws of the Kala. It is the because of the fear of the Mahakala, the wind blows, the sun emits light, the gods give rain to the world, the moon and stars emit light in the night, the trees and plants bear flowers and fruits and provide medicine to the people, the rivers flow with water, the oceans never cross the shores, the fire burns and gives heat, the sky has been all pervading giving space to the seven lokas. By His command the body has been covered with seven sheaths with prana (life giving power) within. It is the fear of Him that the process of creation, sustenance and destruction continues with everybody including gods take births very often. He is imperishable, infinite, unmanifest and indescribable adored as Ananta. Those who are devoted to and have taken ultimate refuge in Me are not bound by the Kala and can cross easily the worldly ocean".*

The same exhortation by Kapil Maharshi is echoed in *Katha Upanishad* (II.3. 2):

yad idam kin ca jagat sarvam prana ejati nihsrtam
mahad bhayam vajram udyatam, ya etad vidur amrtas te bhavanti

The whole world, whatever here exists, springs from and moves in life. It is the great fear like the upraised thunderbolt. They that know that become immortal.

Adi Shankar said, the whole world trembles in Brahman. parasmin brahmani saty ejati kampate.

In verse (II.3.4) *Katha Upanishad* pronounces:

bhayad asyagnis tapati, bhayat tapati suryah

bhayad indras ca vayus ca, mrtyur dhavati pancamah

Through fear of Him, fire burns; through fear of Him the sun gives heat; through fear both Indra (the lord of gods) and wind and Death. The fifth, speed on their way.

Man is in delusive, perishable and impermanent world

Furthering his exhortations God incarnate Kapil Muni continued:

"Man is deeply involved in and attached to the delusive world. Knowing not that he is speeding towards the death he is craving insatiably for fulfilment of desires, passions, and pandering to the egoistic propensities. Overpowered by the rajasik and tamasik tendencies he is after materialistic aggrandisement, wealth, wife, sons and daughters without understanding these are all temporal. Lost in the wilderness

of illusion, ignorance and error he tends to forget the permanent, changeless and eternal and gets tormented by bewilderment, sorrows, suffering and woes. He thinks the mundane ties and bondage as eternal and truth. Revolving around the world of mine and thine with glued attachment he falls into the trap of millions of births and deaths without attempting to ponder over the means by which he can get liberation from this agonizing worldly delusion. He amasses wealth after wealth by unfair means for the comfort and enjoyment of his family members. He covets others' property and remains busy earning day and night without thinking that all these one day will perish. His entire life is spent away meaninglessly for the cause of bodily comfort and merry making of his family members. The time for death arrives when nobody is ready to share the pain of separation and severance of bondage to the world. Since the person has never attempted even for a moment at realizing the duality of body and soul and taking sojourn in the latter consciously, during time of death the separation of the soul from the perishable body involves excruciating pain. The deceased one with astral and causal bodies leaving the lifeless gross body behind is forcibly carried away by the attendants of Yama (lord of death) to the abode of hell. All kinds of unbearable punishment are meted out to him for his sins committed on the earth. He is given to animals such as dogs and wolves for eating. He is thrown at the feet of elephant to be trampled upon. He is left among scorpions, snakes and other poisonous creatures to be bitten to the marrow. He is put inside the burning cauldron".

Kapil Maharshi said:

"Mother! Nobody accompanies him and shares the fruits of his own deeds (karma) done on the earth. He is solely

entitled to the fruits thereof. He enjoys the fruits of his bad and good deeds. At the end, with the seeds of his karma not completely burnt out he is again allowed to enter into the wombs of animals or humans according to the fruits of his deeds. In this way he frequents into the unbreakable chain of birth and death until he is liberated by dint of detachment with love and devotion to God".

The mystery of human birth

Sri Bhagavan Kapil said to mother Devahuti:

"According to the very nature of the past deeds, God puts him into the womb. During the copulation of male and female, God puts him into the semen of male to be united with that of the female. In the ovary of the female the united potency gives rise to a foetus. In the first day it is simply fluid. Within five days it is formed into a lump. After ten days it is hardened into a lump of flesh and assumes the form of an egg. To form head resting on shoulder takes one month. Within two months feet and hands are shaped. By the end of third month fingers with nails, bones, heart, nerves genital, sense organs and hairs on the body are formed. At the end of fourth month, fluid, blood, flesh, fat, bone, marrow and semen are formed. On fifth month sense of hunger and thirst appears. By sixth month the pangs of thirst and hunger affects the foetus very much being within the confines of the womb. It solely lives on what mother eats. By taking in the essence of what mother intakes as food, the foetus within grows in energy, potency and strength. Within the ovary it urinates, leaves excrement and remains amidst blood, puss, fluid and saliva, insects, bacteria and other organisms. Every moment it is drawn into spasm being bitten by insects. It wriggles out from one side to another in *pain. It often becomes senseless. Very much suffering from eating sour, salty, excessively hot, sharp, harsh, dry, pungent and burning food and milk of the mother it gets much grief and pain. Confined to the narrow and limited space within the womb it lacks the space to move. By the time of seven months, it gets knowledge and consciousness; the scenes of past lives flit through the screen of its memory. The scenes of bad and good, virtuous and sinful deeds unfold one after another pushing into deep repentance and remorse. Despondency of the foetus within the womb caused by harsh pain and pangs of pre-birth along with the repentance for past deeds leads one to seek earnestly the Divine. Within the womb it happens to behold the soul and starts pondering over the means of liberation from this hell. Finding no other way, it starts entreating God with folded hands to be kind to him so that this will be his last sojourn in the womb and bless him not to come back for the second time into the dungeon of the womb".*

Lord Sri Krishna told to Arjuna (*Bhagavad Gita*):

Out of four types of devotees one type is the men of distress who earnestly seek God (7:16). Since the foetus within the womb is troubled with discomforts, difficulties and sufferings, it meditated upon God wholeheartedly to overcome these.

The embodied self (Jiva) prays as told by Bhagavan Kapil to mother:

"I surrender at the feet of the Almighty Father who has put me here with singing paeans in His glory and majesties. He is the supreme and ultimate goal, the maintainer, the great Lord, the witness, abode, the refuge, the compassion, the place of origin as well as dissolution. I am the sinner with

evil mind. I have no other shelter than in Him. I take refuge at His Feet of fearlessness. Anyone who has taken ultimate refuge in Him faces no difficulty. Being tempted by the illusive world I have been here. I have been fettered here by the chain of my own past deeds. The ordeal of unbearable and indescribable suffering and affliction that I am passing through has emboldened me to take refuge at His feet who has abided in me. He is imperishable, indivisible, pure and without any attributes. The body in which I am imprisoned has been constituted of five elements. It is perishable and engrossed in illusion, ignorance and error. He is supreme Purusha standing apart from Prakriti. In forgetfulness of His true nature, I have been moving ceaselessly in the chain of birth and death. It is He who can liberate me from this illusion. Nobody except Him can endow me with such divine knowledge. It is because of His compassion I am getting the knowledge of my previous births. I have been steeped in the well of urine, pus and faeces from which to escape I am counting the days and months. He is the ocean of compassion for which I get the knowledge of my previous births. It is because of His compassion I get the knowledge of the Supreme Self and the illusory nature of the world. I do not know by giving what I will please Him. I have nothing except my deeply felt gratitude with folded hands and surrender at His Feet to offer. Beholding Him in my thirsty eyes in all His effulgence and glories in all grandeur and splendour within the confines of the womb has been possible by His inconceivable compassion. Drowned in the ocean of immortal bliss and joy I prefer to live in the dungeon of the womb to coming to the outside world which is enveloped in darkness of illusion. I do not want to fall further into the worldly trap. The worldly trap is more dangerous than the suffering and sorrows in the womb. I will collect strength and fortitude to forbear the travails and trauma of the womb in order to get liberation here. With my entire mind and attention on the soul making detachment, knowledge and conscience as the charioteer I will try for liberation. Ebullient with divine euphoria and ineffable joy the embodied self (Jivatma) by the perception and beholding of God gets determined not to leave the womb and prayed for that to the Lord".

Kapil muni continuing the discourse said to the mother Devahuti, after ten months of indomitable pain and suffering in the womb, the embodied self comes out through the genital by the force of air within the ovary. By touching the earth and affectionately cuddled by kith and kin as babe, it starts crying. The entire knowledge and perception of the Divine in the womb is wiped out from its mind. No more it is the realm of the Divine. It gradually gets engrossed in the worldly delusion among parents, relatives, and friends. Till the age of five it suffers from the childhood difficulties as nobody understands its suffering and pain. The entire adolescence is lost in acquiring worldly education and knowledge about the material pleasures. The youth period is busy running after women for being tied up with a family and children. Mind fully merged in thought and thinking and association with woman makes his fetters with the evanescent world stronger. Those who are lost in sexual pleasure have gone to hells. Even lord Brahma and Shiva are not exception to this chimerical temptation of body pleasure. It is very difficult to overcome the temptations of the sexual pleasure. Without being engrossed in God nobody can conquer the invincible passion for sex. Too much engrossment with sensual pleasure and material objective world results in according primacy to what is temporal, transient and changing and ignoring the changeless, eternal and permanent. Company with the unrighteous and centrifugal forces withdrawing man from the path of truth, destroys his conscience, purity, and all divine attributes. Worldly attachment is like a fathomless well covered with leaves of illusion attracting human beings to its trap. Men of wisdom guard themselves against being betrayed into the delusion. Like birds being trapped into the net of the hunter by the temptations of various baits, man is trapped easily into the well of worldly Maya by the temptations of wife, children, friends and relatives and material wealth. He is tied closely with the fetters of egoism, conceit, wealth, avarice, sensual pursuits, anger and invincible passions. What looks on the surface as sweet and pleasing is in the end distasteful and ruinous.

In the *Bhagavad Gita* (18:37) Lord Krishna said to Arjuna the same thing:

> yattdagre vismiba pariname amrutopamam
> tatsukham sattvikam proktam
> atmabuddhiprasadjam

The happiness that man gets from indulgence with senses looks like nectar in the beginning but in the end is poisonous. But true happiness obtained from engrossment with the Divine looks like poison in the beginning but in the end, it is nectar. This is sattvik attribute of the devotee.

The pleasure derived from sensual indulgence leads to death and the true joy born of complete merge in God leads to immortality. Man is like a deer easily cajoled into the trap of the hunter being attracted by the melodious songs. The ultimate result is death. The illusion, delusion, ignorance and error associated with the mundane are considered as truth and what is truth is termed as falsehood. Egoism, avarice, jealousy, anger, hatred and passion become his friends and not foes in his dealings and deeds. He gets himself identified with the body and not with the indwelling soul. The entire life is wasted after money, sex and egoism. Thus, caught in the trap of worldly delusion and attachment he breathes his last and as usual continues to move in the chain of innumerable births and deaths in various wombs.

As explained by Kapil Muni:

"Each and every human being is the product of his three types of karmas – sanchita, prarabdha and kriyamana. Sanchita karma is the unfructified karmas whose results are not yet reaped. Prarabdha karma borrowed from past lives are what the man enjoys in this present life. The kriyaman karmas are what the person does at present. Man is thus the product of the fruits of these karmas which remain imprinted in the subtle body as seeds for the next births in various forms. With the death of the gross body made of five elements – earth, water, fire, air and space (ether) the subtle body the store house of all karmas, thoughts, desires carried by the causal body into another plane. The actual title of

the man or any living being is given by the subtle body. What form of life one is to be born into is determined by the subtle body. Death is nothing but the inability of both gross body and subtle body to function. Birth is the other name of beholding the body and birth of death. For example, with the illness a person ceases to see the outside objective world. By this the subtle body also fails to direct the gross body to see what it wants. Thus, the failure of both gross body and subtle body is death. In reality, there is no death or birth. It is the karmas which change from one form to another like change of clothes. With complete love, surrender, refuge and merge in God by practice of Yoga the seeds of all karmas will be burnt bringing an end forever to the cause of birth and death".

In *Bhagavad Gita* Lord Sri Krishna assured to Arjuna the same way as Kapil Muni did to mother Devahuti:

tesam aham samuddharta mrtyusamsarasagarat

bhavami nacirat partha mayy avesitacetasam (12:7)

"I will liberate very quickly from the ocean of death and the world those whose minds are fixed on Me, O Partha (Arjuna)".

The world is nothing but the world of death. It is likened to an ocean. Everything in this world including the human body is evanescent and subject to change, grow, decay and death. Attachment to this transitory world gives one pain and sorrows. The ocean of the world is always dangerous, vacillating and restless and binds the man to the body, senses and mind. As in the ocean there are pebbles, rocks and small hills along with storms, hurricanes and tempests obstructing the smooth sailing of the ships, similarly human body becomes dangerous and obstructive if the lower centres hidden in the spine are not controlled. If man is to be completely engrossed in the God residing in the fontanel (Sahasrara chakra), then he has to cross the temptations and obstructions of the lower chakras. To identify oneself with the body, and the objectified world is death. But to identify oneself with the soul residing within and the all-pervading God manifested in the whole world is immortality. It is also reiterated in *Katha Upanishad* (2:1:10): mrtyoh sa mrtyum apnoti ya iha naneva pasyati: "To perceive manyness (diversity) is death, and to perceive unity with the indwelling soul is immortality". To be constantly aware of the unity with indwelling self in all deeds, activities and thoughts is liberation and to forget the unity with the divine self is death.

"God is one and formless but manifested in various forms according as the devotee seeks to behold Him. Citing an example, Kapila Muni explained, "There are various types of sweets. But one thing is common in all that is sweetness. The eyes see it as white; the tongue tastes it sweet; the skin feels it either cool or warm. The nose smells it fragrant. The indwelling soul and God are one and same. He is perceived to assume different forms as per the wishes of the devotees. The yogis perceive Him as formless devoid of any attributes and the seekers treading the path of bhakti cherish to behold Him in various forms of their liking. Whether He is formless without any attribute or having forms with attributes, the fact remains is that without Him there is no path for liberation. Shunning the ego of doership the seeker should

perform all deeds with detachment to the fruits thereof and remaining fixed in the Lord. The fruits of the detached karmas will not be binding on him. All ties with the world will be unknot with detachment, perception of sole doer – the indwelling self and with love, devotion, surrender and gratitude to the Lord. Following the path of Yoga with love and devotion, detachment, renunciation and fixing mind on the Lord, one can soon obtain liberation from the worldly ocean. Yoga is nothing but the integration of jnana, karma and bhakti".

Mother Devahuti paid tributes of gratitude and sang hymns in glorification of Bhagavan Kapil muni for having taught and shown her the path of liberation from this worldly ocean:

Mother Devahuti prayed:

"O God! *You are all pervading and creating this universe you remain hidden in all both living and non-living. There is no place where you are not manifested. The entire creation is God manifested. I keep wondering, there are so many universes within you and how could you find place in my womb. You gratified me by being born as my son. The very utterances of Thee and singing Thy glories, even the lowest and degraded gets liberation and becomes the most adorable one in the world. My life is gratified to behold you and listen to the words of wisdom you were kind to reveal before me what yogis, sages and saints have been eagerly doing sadhana to get by renouncing the world for ages to ages. You have been kind to remove the sheaths of ignorance covering my eyes. My false and egoistic I have been replaced by the universal self which is my real and true I. You are the Lord of the universe. I bow down at Thy holy feet knowing nobody except Thee".*

Bhagavan Kapil moved by the prayer of the mother said, "*O adorable one! You follow the path as taught and shown by me with unswerving devotion, love, detachment and keeping yourself merged at the feet of the Lord Krishna, you will soon get liberation from this worldly ocean. I said this for your salvation*".

As directed by her son Bhagavan Kapil, mother Devahuti retired herself into deep forest and engaged in meditation on the bank of the river for final liberation. The place where she attained liberation was widely acclaimed as Siddhipada (the place of liberation). With her attainment of Nirvikalpa samadhi her body got dissolved and flew as a holy and sacred river known to all seekers and devoted ones as the holiest and supreme place of pilgrimage. It was widely adored and worshipped as Siddhida, the touch of which it was believed, liberates many.

8

Extermination of the demon Hiranyaksha

Hearing from Lord Brahma about Jaya and Vijaya, the two gate keepers in Vaikuntha being cursed by Sanatkumars to be born as demons on earth for three births, the devas departed to their respective places with obeisance to Him. Diti gave birth to twin sons as foretold by her husband rishi Kasyapa after hundred years. With their birth in both heaven and earth a dreaded calamity was unleashed. The earth, the moving and unmoving, living and non-living all trembled with this unforeseen havoc. In all directions was found the fire burning with flames rising high. The wind was blowing very harshly like a thunderous tempest with trees uprooted and dusts flying high enveloping all the ten directions. A pall of darkness was clamped on earth preventing the light from stars, moon and sun from falling on earth. The waves in the ocean soared above roaring to the fear of all. The clouds in the sky without rain started thundering and lightening to the horror of all. The rivers dried up with muds coming up. The birds fell from the trees with their nests blown off by the harsh wind. The animals started roaring as if their mouths were burning with fire. The foxes facing the east started crying loudly. The asses in company with foxes looking at the sky started crying. The cows did not give milk but blood. The deities were seen in temples wailing. The clouds started raining not water but pus and blood. In the sky was seen the collision among the stars and planets with balls of fire sparkling out in flames making people shiver. Nobody was in the know of the reasons of sudden rise of catastrophe except the Sanatkumars. The entire universe was seen slipping into a holocaust. It was on the brink of great devastation.

The two sons started growing up like mountains with their gold studded and jewelled crowns touching the sky. When they walked on the earth, it started shaking and roamed in the sky, all looked in awe and eerie. Seeing their movements, rishi Kasyapa named one as Hiranyakasipu for his strong body and the other as Hiranyaksha for efficiency in war. Hiranyakasipu pleased Lord Brahma by tapasya and moved in all directions creating ferocity and horror in all. Even the devas remained obsequious to and served him out of fear. Invincible in mace Hiranyaksha entered into heaven forcibly and all the devas fled into forests in great fear like snakes in sight of Garuda entering into holes. On seeing the heaven filled with all majesties and with none present in his fear he roared in thunderous voice and left for the earth. In quest of an equal competitor to fight with him he entered many sheaths below (patala) under the earth and even to the fathomless part of the ocean. In the relentless quest for someone who would fight with mace against him, he entered into the palace of the king Varuna. With his exhalation and inhalation, the waves in the upper part of the ocean got agitated and rose in great heights. One day, before night arrived, he met the king Varuna and approached him with all humility to fight with him. Hiranyaksha said, "*O king of water (Varuna), you are one of the strong pillars of dharma. Everybody knows your greatness. You please pulverise my pride and ego of being a mighty warrior to pieces and after my being vanquished, you please perform the fire ceremony in honour of your victory*". Enraged but calming down himself, the king replied in a soft tone, "*O greatest among the warriors! I am not your enemy. How can I fight with you? You are the supreme and greatest among the warriors. Paying heed to my words, you please calm down and stay some days more. Your thirst for war with mace can be quenched with the primordial Purusha (Lord Narayan). He will annihilate you in the war. You will sleep among the dogs in the battle field. He is known for vanquishing the demons like you*".

At these words the demon reminisced:

The king Varuna is not the right person to be fought with. Devarshi Narada has also told me; God will take the incarnation in the form of a wild swine and install the earth taking it up on his teeth from the deluge of water. In order to save the devas from the oppression of the demons, God will also kill me".

Thinking thus, he entered into patala, the lowest strata below the earth to confront with the God incarnated in the form of swine. Staring at the glowing and resplendent swine with the earth raised on the tip of its teeth, the demon closed his eyes in great fear and awe. The demon looking at the swine thought and derisively said, *"If Devarshi Narada's words were true, why it is not Lord Krishna but a mud smeared wild and ugly swine?"* Coming near to Him the demon said, *"you immediately put off the earth in Patala loka from the tip of your teeth as it was in the past given to its people by Lord Brahma. If you do not keep off the earth, you will surely die in my hand. I will take revenge on you for having killed my brother. Let the people in three lokas (world, heaven and patala) enjoy the mace war between us. By the heavy blow of my mace your chest will split and fly in the sky like a tree uprooted by the storm"*.

The earth trembled with fear after listening to the words of threats from the demon. Noticing the earth in great fear, God rushed out of water in rage and anger. His body looked like a huge mountain. Like a lion jumping over to the elephant the demon asked, *"you have no shame. You are saying you are the Lord of the devas but you are going away as a swine"*. At these words the Lord became furious and left off the earth in the lap of the ocean; Witnessing His ferocious divine form, the devas singing hymns in His glories showered flowers on Him. Surges of anger and rage started gushing out of Him on hearing the demeaning words of the demon. Staring at the demon the Lord said:

"By nature, I am looking like a wild swine. You are like a fox not fit to fight a mace war with me. Tied strongly with the fetters of death you are swelled with pride and conceit. I have little strength; everybody praises your valour and bravery. You come and fight with me. By killing me you quench your thirst for fight. It is said, who does not fulfil the promise, is unrighteous. All devas seeing the mace in

your hands left the heaven out of fear and approached Me. How I will leave the place? I will kill you in war and liberate the devas from your shackles".

Seething with anger at the very words of the Lord, the demon frowned upon the God incarnate Swine with his mace. Both were engaged in fierce mace war wreaking blows on each other creating a cacophonous sound of thunderbolt. With heavy blows by mace on the thigh of the demon, blood started oozing out. With no sign of decimation of the demon Hiranyaksha despite heavy wreaking by the Lord on him, Lord Brahma in company with sages and devas prayed the Lord:

"O Lord of the devas and all we took refuge at Your Lotus Feet. This demon has been doing havoc to the devas, brahmins and cows. With mace swirling in his hand, he has created shudders in three lokas like a mad elephant moving eluding all kinds of restraints and obstacles. We entreat you not to play with him anymore. He is increasing every day in size and strength. He has enveloped the entire universe with darkness. It is the right moment to kill him as the night is falling on earth. It is for his death he came to your proximity. Let victory dawn on us".

In this way all devas, sages and Lord Brahma supplicated the Lord very fervently and earnestly seeking His compassion to kill the demon.

While fighting with the demon the Lord incarnate Swine wreaked a blow with His mace near its ear. With retaliation from the demon, the mace from the hands of the Lord fell down. Thinking that it was not in accordance with the nuances of Kshyatriya dharma to fight with the enemy who was not having weapon in his hand, the demon deterred himself from attacking the Lord. Seeing the devas shocked at this, the Lord assured them safety and raised His hands above to receive the Sudarshan chakra which came instantly to His hand. With the illuminating light of the chakra the darkness vanished and demon rushed to the Lord and wreaked on His head heavy blow with mace. Broken into several pieces the mace fell down on the earth. God offered the demon a mace which the demon declined to accept. Instead, he came forward with a trident to pierce into the Lord. With His chakra the trident was smashed into pieces. The demon put a heavy blow with his fist on the head of the Lord which was like a flower thrown to the elephant. The Lord remained unperturbed. Then, the demon resorted to a war of illusion. Nobody could be able to see him where he was. Immediately there was a heavy storm like a calamity with wind blowing at high speed. There was heavy shower of stones and pebbles from the sky. The entire earth in all directions were filled with dust and darkness. Thunderous sound filled the people with fear. There was unceasing lightening and rain of blood, pus, urine and stool. With naked body and hair unlocked and weapons in their hands the demons ran amuck. With the light of the chakra the illusive power of the demon disappeared. Beholding the Lord in the light the demon ran to Him and wreaked heavy blows with his two fists on the chest of the Lord. In a similar way, the God incarnate swine beat the demon on his ears with His fists. Like a tree uprooted in a tempest, the demon fell down on the earth dead. It was to the good fortune of the demon that he was liberated from one demonic life as cursed by Sanatkumaras. The devas, the sages and lord Brahma assembled to sing hymns and prayers in laudation of the glories and divine majesties of the Lord:

"It is for the liberation of the devotees you have been taking incarnations on the earth. It is our good and privileged fortune that you killed the demon. It is due to your compassion we remained secured at Thy Feet".

The incarnation of God as wild swine came to an end with the annihilation of the demon Hiranyaksha.

Reflections

Hiranyaksha is hiran+ya+ksha. The word hiran is delineated In *Brhad-aranyaka Upanishad* (V.15.1):

hiranmayena patrena satyasyapihitam mukham;
ta tvam pusan, apavrnu, satya-dharmaya drstaye.

"The face of truth is covered with a golden disc. Unveil it O Pusan, so that who love the truth may see it".

Whose mind is not concentrated on the indwelling soul cannot be able to perceive the truth. Sage Sankara said, a-samahita-cetasam adrsyatvat. That means whose mind is not fully engrossed in the Lord cannot realise the truth. Verily, thou art a god that hidest thyself (Isaiah, XLV.15).

The worldly delusion (maya) is like the golden disc snaring the humans into its dazzling net. Behind the veil of this golden disc of ignorance, delusion and error lies hidden the all-pervading indwelling soul in the cavern of the fontanel. Until human beings rise above the lower chakras within the spine from Muladhara to Sahasrara (fontanel) and remain established there with unwavering concentration and devotion by the special techniques of breath control as taught by self-realised masters, the veil of ignorance hiding the truth cannot be removed.

mukham: face, essential nature. It is said by Kuranarayana:

mukha-sadrsam mana (mind) ity arthah

It means mind is the main obstacle to the realisation and unveiling of the truth.

Mind is the cause of bondage and mind is the cause of liberation. A mind engrossed in the material world is in bondage, and a detached mind is in the state of liberation.

The master of the senses is the mind. The master of the mind is the breath. Breath is witness to the presence of soul in our body temple. By breath control mind is controlled. If mind is fixed constantly in the fontanel (indwelling soul) by incessant practice, love and detachment, God realisation is ensured by penetrating deeply into the veil of ignorance.

Pusan means the sun or god of light, who is the protector of the world. Adi Sankar said, jagatah posanat pusa ravih. Without God there is nothing. The entire creation is His. Nothing can be conceived of without Him. He is the supreme goal, the sustainer, the great and ultimate Lord, the witness, the abode, the refugee, and compassion. He is the place of origin as well as dissolution. I am the treasure-trove and the imperishable soul (*Bhagavad Gita*, 9:18).

Vedanta Desika says, it is the very nature of God to give protection to those who seek refuge in Him (asrita-posana-svabhava). In *Bhagavad Gita* (9:22) it is pronounced:

> ananyas cintayanto mam ye janah paryupasate
> tesam nityabhiyuktanam yogaksemam vahamy aham

Without being enticed by other thoughts who remain concentrated on Me and who sincerely worships and meditates on Me, are constantly united with Me - I entitle to them what they lack and preserve what they possess.

Our Gurudeva Paramahamsa Hariharananda said, those who practice Kriya Yoga they know the techniques of breath control by which mind is kept concentrated in the indwelling soul. Their minds are free from any kind of delusion and bondage. They remain in a stage of complete tranquillity of mind. In deep meditation mind is completely absorbed in God consciousness and merged in God. Neither a single moment nor a single breath is wasted. It is wasted only in God. Every moment is divine and God alone. Nothing else. God endows him with the perception of his own divine nature. The Lord gives him all auspiciousness of liberation through meditation.

apavrnu: darsana-pratibandha-karanam apanayet. The cause of obstruction to union with Lord who is hiding behind the veil of golden disc is to be removed. The mind, senses, worldly delusion and all negative demoniac attributes which impede the union with the Lord are to tamed and controlled by constant practice, love and detachment.

Satya dharmaya: the rendezvous with and complete dissolution in God through meditation is the truth, the unveiling of the delusive cover of the golden disc. This is dharma. The liberation from the worldly delusion is the pursuit and realisation of truth. To seek constant liberation in each and every breath through the attainment of truth is true dharma.

The above analysis is about hiran.

Ya means the indwelling soul in Sanskrit. In our body temple resides the soul compassionately with detachment. He is the sole doer. Without Him there is no thought and no deeds. He breathes the breath of His life through our nostrils. That is why we are living. It is pronounced in *Svetasvatara Upanishad* (III.17) and *Bhagavad Gita* (13:14)

sarvendriya-gunabhasam sarvendriya-vivarjitam sarvasya prabhum isanam sarvasya saranam brhat (*Svetasvatara Upanishad* 111.17)

All the senses with their qualities or attributes are active by Him and yet He is devoid of all the senses. He is detached and free from all their qualities. He is the Lord and ruler; He is the supreme and ultimate refuge of all.

The indwelling soul is like the all-powerful electric current which lights all the sense bulbs of the body. But due to ignorance and delusion, the human beings fail to unveil the sheath of golden disc of worldly attachment. They tend to forget the indwelling soul who is the sole doer. Such humans engrossed deeply in worldly delusion are perished. This is the meaning of ksha. Those who forget the inner self are the slayer of their soul. We are all Hiranakshas ignorant of our indwelling soul.

In *Isa Upanishad* (4.3) it is said:

> asurya nama te loka andhena tamasa vrtah
> tams te pretyabhigacchanti ye ke catmahano janah

Those who are enveloped in the darkness of ignorance are demoniac in nature. They go after death and become slayers of the indwelling soul.

asurya: attributable to asuras, those who are highly engrossed in the material world and addicted to bodily and sense derived pleasures. According to Adi Sankar they are not the knowers of the Self. It includes all men and even gods who lack the knowledge of the Supreme Self. andhena tamasa: deeply embedded in the darkness of ignorance not being able to perceive the indwelling Soul.

Forgetfulness of the inner Self through breath in all our deeds, thoughts and dispositions means to slay the all-pervading soul. atmahano janah:

prakrta avidvamso jana atmahana ucyante, tena hy atma-hanan-dosena samsaranti te.

Enveloped in darkness of ignorance they forget the all-pervading and all doer, the indwelling Self and remain engrossed in material and sensual pleasures. Being the slayer of the soul, they perish.

One who does not realise the essential unity of the soul as God in every being and in everything is proceeding towards death (*Katha Upanishad*, 2:1:10).

> yad eveha tad amutra, yad amutra tad anviha
> mrtyos sa mrtyum apnoti ya iha naneva pasyati

What is here that is there. Whatever is there that too is here. Whoever perceives anything like manyness here goes from death to death.

We are all demoniac in our nature. We remain forgetful of our inner Self, the sole doer in us. We do not realise the real unity between the soul as God in all living beings and in everything. We do not feel that the seer and seen are one. When we are hearing we do not feel that who is hearing through our ears. It is our indwelling Self who is doing everything for us. In our deeds, and thinking we do not feel the unity between God and the work done. Thus, in the oblivion of the essential unity between the inner Soul as God and every being and everything we are heading towards death. It is like killing our inner Soul. That is why, Hiranyaksha, the demon was bent on killing the Varaha, the incarnation of God. That means being forgetful of indwelling soul we are every moment killing God.

The earth centre is represented by Muladhara chakara within our spine. The earth is filled with riches and bonanza of material wealth. When man's mind is immersed in this centre, he is after money, wealth and material pleasures and enjoyment. This centre snares man into the nightmare of delusion and ignorance. The more he enjoys the more he runs after it. There is no end to desires as well no end to pleasures. Those who are demoniac, they think and try to have mastery over the earth and possess everything. By being the master of the earth, they boast of being the Lord of the universe (*Bhagavad Gita*: 16). That was what the demon Hiranyaksha was trying to do submerging the earth under the deluge of water. Varaha, the incarnation of God liberated the earth raising it up in the tip of His teeth and established in the space. That means, everything is God. We have to feel the wealth in the earth centre is also divine. Without God there is no earth, no water, no fire, no air and no space. The entire creation is Divine.

Killing of Hiranyaksha means the complete annihilation, elimination and sublimation of demonic propensities. With this the realisation of God takes place.

9

The King Pruthu and Prithivi (Mother Earth)

In the dynasty of Dhruva, the great devotee of the Lord, was a king known as Anga. He was childless. Once, he did a fire ceremony in the presence of many sages and saints. But to his utter dismay the oblations offered venerably to devas (gods) were not accepted by them. The reason being he was without any son and the result of his deeds in the past life as revealed by the sages. On being advised by the sages, the king Anga performed a fire ceremony offering oblations to gods and to the Lord to get a son. Out of the fire vase appeared a strange divine being with a golden plate filled with porridge (sweet milk) and offered to the king. Tasting it to his heart's content by smelling, the king handed over to his queen Sunitha. Because of this unnuanced act, the queen gave birth to an irreligious and unrighteous son known as Vena. Being born of unrighteous and the son of the daughter of Yama he started behaving rudely and ferociously. He unleashed a reign of terror among the people. Killing animals, children and people was his daily routine. People in the kingdom cried haplessly. The king tried his best to make him spiritual and taught him nuances about dharma. But no change in him was perceived, he remained as cruel as before. A pall of gloom and sorrows overtook the king. In the dead night the king left the kingdom and waded his way into the forest. His ministers and courtiers searched him but failed to locate the king. But for the king, the kingdom will be forged into deep chaos and will be annexed by other kings. Thinking so, on the advice of the sages, Vena was coronated as king. Instead of walking on the path of divine and righteousness as behoving of a king, he preferred the path of demons. He disregarded the sages and saints and paid no heed to their much-adored words. Bethinking himself as the lord of the universe he called all the sages, saints and brahmanas of the kingdom to his court and said:

"You all look to the divine marks on my body parts from which you can know doubtlessly that I am God. Nobody in my kingdom will do any fire ceremony and worship God and offer oblations to the deceased and gods. No charity will be given to brahmins. Nobody will henceforth go on pilgrimage and visit temples. All worldly and religious deeds are to be offered to me. There is none superior to me in this cosmos. The name, fame and my divine attributes are to be hymned by all. Instead of counting beads in the name of God count in my name. I will be the principal presiding deity in all fire ceremonies. Anybody found disobeying my dictates will not be spared".

The commandments of the king were announced throughout the kingdom. Without finding any other respite, the people in great fear started worshipping the king as God. Nobody dared to speak out anything good or righteous that would be considered as disobedience to the king. Without the practice of what was righteous and noble the kingdom looked forlorn, hapless and distressed. There was no rain in the absence of fire ceremony and other spiritual deeds. People started starving without any crops, vegetables and food products. Despondency was noticed everywhere in the kingdom. The entire kingdom was resonant with heart rending sounds of woes and wailings of the people. The sages and saints staring at the doom of horror unleashed by the king Vena started blaming themselves for having enthroned Vena as the king. It was like feeding the snake with milk that would increase only its poison and it would first bite the provider of the milk. They bemoaned saying, *"we gave the throne of the kingdom to a wicked person and who will be affected? It is we. Let us go to him and advise him to do what is righteous on the part of the king. If the king will not listen to us, he will be ultimately ruined."*

Thinking thus, the sages and saints reached the king and started saying,

"O King! we have come here with the ostensible purpose of saying what is righteous and good for you and what will establish your name and fame in this world forever. Those who dedicate themselves for the good of others they conquer not only this world but also the next world. Those who are averse to this they die even though they are living. If the people conduct themselves in a righteous way following the nuances of dharma, the wealth and prosperity of the king increases. Without dharma where is the prosperity of the king? When the people are assured of security of life and property, that king begets not only a joyful life in this life but also in next life after death. The king who worships the

Lord and people who live righteously according the dharma of the stage of life they are placed in, are blessed by the Lord. If God is pleased, your name and fame will be established in this world. God is all pervading. He is abiding in all. All gods are like small hairs on His skin. By surrendering yourself at His feet you will earn bliss and joy in life. Nothing will remain unattainable to you in this mundane world. All bonanza of prosperity and divinity will rain on you. The sages and saints are the embodiment of God. You adore them for your benevolence".

Cruised into a fury of anger at these words, the king blurted out:

"You are all ignorant unable to understand the distinction between what is truly dharma and adharma. All the attributes of adharma you are admonishing me as dharma. Forgetting me the real donor of your food and sustenance you are all worshipping Lord Vishnu like a newly married woman enters into another house ignoring her real husband. You know, I am the incarnation of God. In my body are abiding Lord Vishnu, Lord Shiva, Lord Brahma and all other gods like Sun, Varuna, Indra, Yama and Kubera etc. Thus, the body of this king is inhabited by all gods and divine beings. Without knowing the greatness of this body, you are speaking on dharma and adharma. There is no God other than me who is entitled to receive your oblations offered at the fire ceremony. Go back and worship me adoring me as your God".

All the imploring of the sages and saints went in vain. Day by day, the king became more arrogant, aggressive, wicked and performed things contrary to the Vedic nuanced dharma. He humiliated the sages and saints and showed no respect to their words. When the entire kingdom was burning with oppressive and unrighteous rule of the king, the sages and saints thought to themselves, "a person who denunciates the Lord is not fit to be a king. Enraged over his demonic conduct they all cursed him to death. As a consequence of the fruits of his misdeeds, the king Vena lost his life. Mother Sunitha kept the body of Vena in a big pot of oil with the hope that a son will be obtained from him to ascend the throne.

One day, the sages and saints after having bath in the holy river Saraswati worshipped the Lord in the fire ceremony singing hymns in magnification and exaltation of His divine majesties. While doing this, they saw the people hounded out from their homes in different directions in great horror and fear by the wicked ones with arms and weapons. Pained and shocked at the deplorable plight of the people in the kingdom, the sages and saints discussed among themselves that the people became master less after the death of the king. They said to themselves, *"the life of Brahmans is meant for the welfare of others. They are even minded and equally poised in both sorrows and happiness. They are peaceful, calm and quiet always guided by their untainted conscience. If they delay or neglect to do the right remedy for the afflicted and grief stricken poor, their sadhana is meaningless like putting milk in a porous pot. They prayed together God for the birth of a person embodying the divinity of the Lord whose life will be devoted to the welfare of the people".*

Praying thus, they in Vedic way churned the thigh of the deceased Vena, a black skinned, ugly, and ferocious person with elongated nose, copper coloured hair and red eyes named Bahuka was born. When he fell at the feet of the sages and asked to do what, the sages thinking him to be unfit to be the king ordered him to be Nishad and go to the forests where he would be the king. Gradually, with the passage of time, Nishad dynasty flourished in forests and jungles. All demonic sins swept away with Nishad.

On finding the body of Vena sacred the sages and saints churned his hands with kusha (a type of grass used by Hindu priests in puja) in their hands and with recitation of *Veda* mantras. As a result, two persons one male and another female with all divine attributes were born. The rishis besides themselves with joy exclaimed:

"Newly born male and female seem to be direct embodiment of Narayan and Laxmi and will serve the people of the kingdom on righteous path. The dynasty of king Vena will continue". Since the male was primordial, adored and famous for divinity, he was named Pruthu. The female was named Archi as she earned Pruthu for her elegant beauty, gems like teeth and divinely adorned and shining like sun. Pruthu born as embodiment of Lord Krishna and Archi as Laxmi would be the king and queen of the kingdom. All sages and saints, gods including Lord Brahma, Lord Shiva, Yama, Sun, Moon, Varuna and celestial beings, nymphs arrived on the world to see with great exhilaration the birth of Lord and Laxmi as Pruthu and Archi. Hymns and songs were recited with dance and music. Flowers from heaven were showered on them. Beholding the divine marks like chakra, conch, lotus in the body of Pruthu and knowing him as the embodied self of Lord Krishna all assembled there decided to coronate him as the king. All living beings starting from humans to animals, serpents, birds and others and non-living from the five elements like earth, ocean, etc. brought the essentials required for performing coronation. Lord Kubera offered him a golden seat on which Pruthu was to be coronated. Varuna gave him an umbrella named as Jalasraba (streaming water) unfolding of which gives rains. Lord air gave him the fan. Lord Indra gave him the crown. Lord Yama gave him the stick. Lord Brahma gave him the brahma shield. Mother Saraswati adorned him with a garland. Lord Govinda gave him the chakra in his hand. Mother Laxmi sat in his thigh. Lord Shiva gave him the sword in his hand. Moon gave him the immortal horses in his chariot. Visvakarma adorned his chariot with gems and gold. Fire gave him the bow and sun gave him the arrows. Yogamaya gave him the shoes under his feet. Ocean gave him the conch. With great festivity the coronation of Pruthu was performed.

All sages and saints prayed in his adoration:

O Supreme One! Your limitless divine majesties and splendid attributes are beyond description. Lord Brahma and others have failed to know your omniscience. You have taken incarnation on this earth to eliminate unrighteousness (adharma) and sustain and promote dharma. You are the fountain of kindness and compassion. You are equally abiding in all without discrimination like sun falling on all, siphons off the water drops and give back to the world in form of rain. Like mother earth you bear the brunt of everything without any disposition. You are the embodiment of compassion to wipe out the sorrows from the people. Like rain coming from lord Indra to the earth for cultivation and harvest, your immortal and nectar-soaked words soothes many bereaved and dejected hearts and causes liberation from the delusive world. Beholding your beguiling smile on your lips has removed signs of wail and woes from the heart of the people. Your receptacle of divine majesties is infinite and fathomless. You are outside as well as inside all beings. You are unmoving and moving as well. You are very far and at the same time very near. Like breath inside body, you are detached. You are the ultimate refuge of the people. You are endeared to all, the poor, famished and the mendicant and to the beggars. Your life is meant for the joy, happiness and prosperity of the people. You keep company with the liberated ones and away from the unrighteous and deluded. You are without any attribute and remain hidden in the pituitary. All intellectual aridity and abstruse concepts about truth look meaningless before you. Your incarnation is for the liberation of mankind. You are the supreme warrior. When you will itinerate the entire earth in your chariot with bow and arrows all enemies will be subdued. You will be careful not to move south. Giving life to the people you will maintain and sustain the mother earth".

Praying thus, the sages and saints predicted, "*under you all enemies will be vanquished. You will do hundred asvamedha (consecrating horse in the fire ceremony) yajnas. Indra will steal your horse. In last part of your life in company with Sanatkumars you will get liberation surrendering at the feet of the Lord*".

Mother earth as cow

After coronation in the congregation of all sages and saints, the people met the King Pruthu and with their heads touching his feet expressed their woeful life:

"Like fire inside the tree burns the tree itself the fire of hunger has been burning our body and mind. We pray you to provide us food. Hunger is about to finish our life. Without food there is no life. If there are no subjects, where is the king. We entreat you to provide us a respite to our disastrous and sorrowful life".

The king was shocked to hear the distressed wailing of the people simmering with hunger for food and asked them who was the cause of your suffering and took away your food. The people said, "when your father Vena was the king immorality, wickedness, cruelty and unrighteousness were the order of the day. The earth taking advantage of this ate all crops in the form of a cow in the night and during day time went hiding in the ocean. For this we are suffering and afflicted severely by unsatiated hunger".

Outraged at this, the king proceeded with his bow and arrows to kill the earth hiding in the ocean. On seeing the valour and fierce of the king, the earth came out and stared at ten directions in great trepidation. Like a deer running away in the fear of being shot at by the hunter, the earth was racing away in different directions being followed by the king with his arrow pointed at it. Finding no other way than to save life from the clutches of imminent death, the earth fell down at the feet of the king and started praying him:

"O Supreme one! You are the incarnation of dharma. Your life is meant for the protection of life. My Lord, I entreat you to save and protect me. You are omniscient. Why you are asking me? I am not the sinner in your eyes. If a woman, cow and me (earth) die, how you will sustain the creation and perform your duties. If you kill me, you will commit two sins at same time bringing obloquy to your own self. The wise says, if a woman sins, she is not to be killed. You are the ocean of compassion and friend to the poor and hapless. I am like a broken and weak boat not able to bear the burden anymore. If I die, how and where you will keep the people?"

The king Pruthu replied to the earth:

"If you die, I have no fear. Since you are not obeisant to me, killing you will not be a sin. During my father's reign of terror, you devoured all the crops in the guise of a cow, how the people will survive? Where there is no food, there is no life. The king is there because there are people. Without people king cannot be conceived of. For this I am bent on killing you. To kill a wicked is the nuance of the king. If I will not kill you, how the people will survive. Since the people are mourning and wailing with their hearts rending for respite, I have no other duty than to kill you and wipe out their sorrows. If the king does not punish the one for whom the people are starving painfully, the king is not worth being the king. It is the well accepted and enunciated dharma on the part of the king".

The earth with all heart-rending supplications and tears welled up in eyes prayed:

"O Parama Purusha! Salutations to Thee. You are unmanifest and beyond expression. When you take

incarnations, your attributes are manifested. You have shrouded the entire world in your delusive Maya. You know your own Maya. The entire world is your expression. You create, sustain and dissolve the universe. You are the Guru of the entire universe and definer and sustainer of dharma. Without knowing the truth, why you are in arms to kill me? In your previous incarnation, embodied as a swine you held me up in your teeth and re-established me in my place for the benevolence of all beings. How do you think to annihilate me? Deluded by your Maya I am moving like an innocent child. I do not know your volition. I bow down at your feet entreating you earnestly to protect me. I take refuge in you. Lord Brahma during creation stored in me all food, crops, vegetables, medicinal plants, pulp and cream for the sustenance of living beings. During the reign of your father and after his demise unrighteousness and adharma prevailed. The wicked ones eliminated everything. On beholding everything trees and plants being mowed down, I swallowed all in the form of a cow for future protection. Had I not swallowed, the burglars and thieves would have destroyed all. All crops and vegetables have remained in store within me as milk".

Completely surrendered and prostrated at his feet, the earth said,

"O Supreme One! you now milk me. As a wish fulfilling cow, I will secrete milk to everybody. Keeping aside your weapons make my body plain, nourished, and cultivate nicely. With rains my body will be soft and then from my milk will sprout all plants, trees, crops, vegetables and medicinal plants on which the beings will survive and continue living joyfully".

Dipped in euphoric joy by the assuaging words of earth, the king Pruthu directed Manu to drink in the form of a calf the milk of the earth. The moment Manu did so, the milk in torrents flowed out to fill the entire earth like a sea surfeited with waves. The seeds of all plants, crops and vegetation coming out with the milk started sprouting to the great joy of all people. The earth was filled with crops and vegetation.

The sages, saints and persons of wisdom milked the earth cow making Guru as the calf in symphony with *Vedas* and started drinking in the plate of senses and mind to eliminate their delusion, ignorance, error and confusions.

The devas (gods) making Indra as the calf milked the cow and drank in a golden plate for nectar, divine majesties, strength, lustre and beauty.

The demons making Prahalad as the calf milked the cow and drank in an iron plate.

The celestial beings, musicians and dancers milked the cow making Visvabasu as the calf and drank in a lotus plate for beauty, sweetness and fragrance.

The deceased and forefathers started drinking milk in the form of consecrated cereals one by one in a plate of mango leaves making Aryama as the calf.

The God realised ones and siddhas making Kapil as calf milked the cow in a plate of pledges for the welfare and benevolence of all.

The divine beings of wisdom in their respective plates drank the milk as khechari merged in their divine dispositions.

The beings expert in magic, enchantment and black magic at will making Maya demon as the calf drank the milk in the plate of mind.

The ghosts making Rudra as the calf drank the milk in the plate of skull as blood and wine.

The serpents making Takshyaka as the calf milked the cow and drank the milk as poison making holes as the plate.

The beasts and animals milked the cow making the ox as the calf and drank in form of grass. The carnivores like lion and other animals started drinking the milk of the cow in the form of meat and flesh in the plates of their bodies. The birds making Garuda as the calf drank the milk in the form of fruits.

The plants and trees came forward to milk the cow making the banyan tree as calf and drank in the form of juice percolating to their trunk, branches and leaves. All mountains and hills making Himabanta as the calf milked the cow and drank in the form of metals and ores.

The earth cow remaining obsequious to the king Pruthu thus became the giver and fulfiller of everything and what the animals, plants, trees, mountains, human beings, demons, celestial beings, the sages and saints, the realised masters and devas cherished from her.

Looking at the all-compassionate earth cow the king thought, *"moved by the sorrows and pain for the people she bore patiently everything in the form of a cow. By giving away her milk in various forms as required by all beings starting from plants, trees, animals, human beings, demons, devas to divine and spiritually advanced masters and sages and saints and devas she regenerated life in all. Her body has been divinely gratified at this act of benevolence and sacrifice for the wellbeing of all and sustenance of life on this earth. Hence, she will be my daughter and renamed as Prithivi"*.

Reflections

What is in the macro cosmos is also found immanent in the micro human body. The five elements (earth, water, fire, air and space) exist in gross forms while composing the external universe and are found in subtle forms in human body. Inside the human spine there are seven chakras. At the base of the spine is the Muladhara chakra where the earth element exists in subtle form but manifested throughout the body. Mula means in Sanskrit root or foundation and adhara means support or base. Whether within the body or outside the body there is the need of a foundation represented by the earth. Under the earth is found bonanza of wealth, many precious metals, gold, diamond and natural resources. Earth is the base of existence of both living and non-living. When mind is engrossed in Muladhara chakra it runs after money, wealth and possessions. There is no end to the desires for material aggrandisement. Man, never remains content with what he has. In Muladhara chakra are found both material wealth and divine wealth. If the seeker tries to transcend his mind from the Muladhara to the top of the Sahasrara, he shuns the cravings for material wealth and seeks the divine wealth. The distinction between the matter and divine ceases to exist. Both gold and dust are similar to the eyes of the self-realised ones. An incident in the life of Mira Bai is an illuminating one to buttress this:

Mirabai belonging to the royal dynasty of Mewar was the disciple of Saint Rabi Das. The common talk in the palace was that while the disciple Mirabai was living in the palace with all regal luxury, her guru a poor cobbler steeped in abject poverty was living in a hut. Her guru was earning his livelihood by mending shoes – a very ugly and demeaning work in the eyes of the people. On hearing this Mirabai felt shocked very much and thought to remove the cause for which he was doing the despicable work in the eyes of the people. Her love, devotion and reverence for her guru were immense. She pondered over very deeply what to do for her guru. One day she went to her guru with a piece of diamond. Paying homage at his feet Mirabai entreated with a choking voice you are my guru. You are earning your livelihood by mending shoes which people consider as humiliating whereas I am residing in the palace with all luxury and comfort. I am feeling shame of it. You please take this diamond and make a good house and arrange your livelihood by selling this diamond. You need not do this humiliating work. You can spend your life without financial difficulty and wanting. Without being attracted by the dazzling diamond he went on mending the shoes and said, mother! Whatever I am getting it is out of mending the shoes. It is enough for my sustenance. What I will do with this diamond? It will be of no help to me. If you feel humiliating you need not come to me. You can practice meditation and other spiritual things sitting at home. You said that people are criticizing you for coming to a poverty-stricken cobbler. But I am getting indescribably ineffable joy. Before this immeasurable and fathomless divine joy your diamond though seems to be priceless but is perishable and is nothing but a mere dust.

But Mirabai was hell bent on giving this diamond to her guru by any means. All her imploring and humble prayers to her guru to accept it turned into fiasco. Finding herself defeated and dejected she said to her guru, I am seeking leave of you keeping this diamond with you. If need arises you can use it. With these words she left for her palace.

Meantime, many days elapsed. Mirabai coming again to her guru found him busy mending the shoes as before without any change in his conditions. Perturbed and with a heavy heart she asked her guru humbly why you did not use the diamond I kept for you in your hut. With a face lit with ecstatic joy, he said beamingly mother! What I could have done with this diamond? Completely established in God what divine majesties I am getting have been enough for me. What more I need in comparison to the divine treasure-trove? You can take your thing back. To her surprise, while uncovering she found the diamond in the place as it was before kept. Realizing the greatness and deepening divinity in her guru she fell flat at his feet with tears of love streaming down to mingle with the ocean of his guru's bliss and joy.

The realised masters think the material prosperity and wealth as perishable and akin to dust. Nothing however glittering and priceless to the worldly people could divert their attention from God in whom they are well positioned.

In all forms of matter the seeker perceives the divine. Once the seeker is well established in God, he remains detached to the world and its possessions. He leads a very simply spartan and ordinate life full of continence and self-control with basic human needs fulfilled. He perceives the all-pervading God in all and in everything. He approaches to the material world and its existence with divinity. Money or wealth is essential for meeting the basic needs of man. But one should not remain engrossed in amassing wealth at the expense of realisation of God. Paramartha is not to be sacrificed for material wealth. One should use money judiciously for the sustenance not only of his self but for the wellbeing of others. The entire life and energy should not be wasted for earning money. The cravings should be not for wealth but for God. Human beings' ceaseless cravings for money, wealth, prosperity, luxurious living, fame and exorbitant life style keeps them anchored in this lower centre. In *Bhagavad Gita* it is said (16:13):

idam adya maya labdham imam prapsye manoratham

idam asti 'dam api me bhavisyati punar dhanam

Today I have obtained this by which I shall fulfil this ambition. This is my wealth today and I will earn more in future.

This maddening avarice for money and wealth and egoism born out of this entraps him in the snares of worldly delusion. Mind becomes extrovert and roams outside for wealth and money. The infinite divine energy (kundalini sakti) lying dormant in Muladhara (coccygeal) chakra can be rightly harnessed by the practice of Yoga as taught by self-realised masters. When the divine energy lying latent in the Muladhara will be raised through susumna within the spine by Kriya Yoga techniques to the fontanel (Sahasrara) and beyond into the infinite, the craving for wealth gets transformed into craving for the divine. Establishment in God does not mean material abnegation rather in the enjoyment of all these material goods one feels the living presence of God and thus, remains detached to the material wealth. Without falling prey to the delusive world, one should have complete control over the Muladhara chakra. For this, the mind is to be raised from Muladhara chakra to Sahasrara and remain transfixed in it constantly. By dint of sadhana the mind will be always roaming in the cosmic consciousness. To the realised spiritual person there is no distinction between gold and dust as everything is pervaded by God.

If a person's mind is introvert and remains awakened in super consciousness then, he remains detached to the devilish attributes of Muladhara chakra such as greed and avaricious cravings for material wealth. Even the entire possession of the wealth of the world will not be enough to satiate his ever-increasing desires. One's attainment of detachment to the demoniac attributes of the Muladhara chakra can negate his/her craving for wealth in the earth. In *Isa Upanishad* (I: I) it is pronounced:

isavasyam idam sarvam yat kim ca jagatyam jagat

tena tyaktena bhunjitha, ma gridhah kasyavid dhanam

(Know that) all this, whatever moves in this moving world, is enveloped by God. Therefore, by surrendering to Him enjoy and do not covet what belongs to the other.

Isavasyam: Everything is pervaded by God. The world is not or does not stand separate from or independently of God. The Psalmist says: "the earth is the Lord's and the fullness thereof; the world and they that dwell therein".

Isa: isita paramesvarah, vasyam, nivasaniyam, vyapyam (Kuranarayan). The world is steeped in God. It is the household of God. God dwells in all things. Anandagiri says:

isvaratmakam eva sarvam bhrantya yad anisvar-rupena grhitam.

It means, God is the indwelling soul of everything. Those who do not know this, they deluded by the forms and things.

The word '*jagat*' is derived from the root 'gam' which implies to go or move. Everything in this world is moving and changing. Nothing remains constant. One thing that is constant and changeless is God. God's power has pervaded everything. Anything that you are enjoying belongs to God. While you are enjoying, then remain grateful to God, it is because of Him you are enjoying. In reality, who is enjoying? It is God. If He does not breathe through your nostrils, you are simply dead. A dead man cannot enjoy even though he has all organs. It means, enjoy with detachment by surrendering to and remaining firmly established in God. If everything including your life and breath belong to the Divine, to claim it is mine then you are coveting what belongs to another.

What exists is bound to perish. But who has brought all these to existence is imperishable, eternal and immortal. God having created this universe has entered into His every creation. That means, the very existence is God. The plants, trees, insects, animals and human beings exist because in all these God abides as the indwelling soul. It is He who functions through all of us. A dead man cannot speak even he has mouth, cannot see even if he has eyes, cannot hear even he has ears, hands cannot work even if he has hands and cannot feel touch sensation even if he has skin. That means somebody was functioning within him before he was declared dead. That somebody is the indwelling soul. All organs, senses and mind are defunct and functionless without the indwelling self. If the power house stops supplying current, no machinery, bulbs and fans will work. It is He who really activates our mind, senses, intelligence, body parts and everything of us. Without Him there is nothing. The entire creation is His projected Self. Because of our ignorance we tend to identify ourselves with the body not with the real doer, the abiding soul. Instead of giving doership to God we give to ourselves and are bound by the effects of our doing. It is the current which makes the fan move and bulb to emit light. Like current the soul remains detached. For example, in the electric light a man can read, write, philosophise, help others and the needy, the doctor can operate and a thief can steal from others and a criminal may kill another. But light is not attached and bound by the effects of all these actions done in its presence. Soul like the light silently and detachedly helps in the performance of all these without being bound by the fruits of all these actions. If we identify ourselves with and remain in the soul always in our actions, thoughts and deeds we will feel that the body works and the real I (soul) remain free and detached.

Those who are well established in wisdom, and God realised remain detached, witness and without any attributes always conscious of the inner self doing everything (sakshi, cheetah nirgunasch). They think that their body is doing (jnani deha kritam) not they (jnani kritam). What does not belong to you if you do and possess that it creates egoism in you. Egoism born of ignorance keeps you in bondage. An excerpt from the life of Lord Krishna can illustrate this truth:

In Krishnavatar gopis were one day observing Katyayani Brata by worshipping Mother Katyayani for fulfilment of their cherished wishes. The tradition was that at the end of celebration they were to feed some rishis or realised Brahmins. All they went to Lord Krishna and asked Him whom to feed? Lord

Krishna advised them to feed rishi Durvasa who was living on the other side of the river Yamuna. Accordingly, the Gopis preparing all delicious and sweet food made of milk, butter, ghee and yoghurt went to the bank of the river Yamuna to cross to the other side of the bank. To their utter dismay they found the river flooded with water flowing on both sides of the bank to the brim. They returned to their beloved Lord Krishna with an entreaty for His intervention. Lord Krishna said,

"You go and say to the river Yamuna, if Krishna is the staunch Brahmachari throughout His life, Oh Yamuna provide us a way".

At these words the Gopis first got into a puzzle how Shri Krishna would be a brahmachari when he had had so many Gopis with him because a strict brahmachari would not look at the face of a woman? Was he not playing with them? Since they have had implicit and unflinching faith in Shri Krishna, they followed his words and reaching the river Yamuna, told the same thing as instructed to them by Shri Krishna. To their joy and astonishment, the water parted and a path appeared enabling them to cross the river with ease. On reaching the ashram of rishi Durvasa they fed the rishi to his heart's content all their delicious food with much care and devotion. After serving food it was late afternoon almost evening, in a hurry when they reached the river to return, they found the river inundated as before. Finding no other way, they returned to the rishi with an imploration to bring an end to their dilemma. The sage asked them how they came to him. They narrated what Shri Krishna told them to do. At these words sage Durvasa smiled and said, go and tell the river, "*Oh Yamuna! If sage Durvasa has not taken anything and is ever fasting, give us a way to cross to the other side*".

The gopis were really perplexed over the ways in which they were instructed by Krishna that he was a strict Brahmachari in spite of his association with them and also by Durvas that he was ever fasting and had not taken anything despite his being fed with so many delicious foods.

The answer to their bewilderment lies with the problem of doership. Who in reality does body or soul? In both these cases it is their knowledge that they are not the doer it is the indwelling soul who really does. So, they will not be bound by the fruits of their action. If one is established in wisdom that he/she is not the doer, the real doer is the indwelling soul, he is free from the consequences. Srimad *Bhagavad Gita* declares this (3:27):

"All the works are done by the attributes of nature, but the egoistic and ignorant thinks that he is the doer"

Since the consequences of all deeds, works and thoughts are the seeds of our bondage by taking births after births for the fulfilment of our desires, the wisest comes to this realisation that the real doer is the indwelling spirit and gets liberation. This is the sublime essence of *tena tyaktena bhunjitha*. The very centrality to spiritual life lies in transferring the egoistic doership to God as the real doer. It implies self-denial. "If any one wish to come after me, let him deny himself" (Matthew XVI.24).

kasyasvid dhanam. Wealth belongs to whom? If the entire creation is Lord's, without a bit of doubt wealth belongs to Him. "What hast thou that thou hast not received" (I. Cor.IV.7). A true devotee never craves for wealth and possessions.

paramasuhrdi bandhave kalatre suta-tanaya-pitr-matr-bhrtyavarge

sathamatir upayati yorthatrsnam purusa-pasur na Vasudeva-bhaktah

(Aitareya Aranyaka II.3.2)

For friends, relatives, sons and daughters, father and mother, wife and servants who is governed by hunger and thirst for wealth is purusapasu (human animal) not the devotee of Lord Vasudeva.

In other words, it also implies not to pretend to anything which in reality belongs to God. Everything of the creation is Almighty's. What is beyond your minimum need and very simple way of living is not to be accepted. It is pronounced in Yoga Sutra of sage Patanjali (Sadhana Pada, sutra 39):

aparigraha sthairye janma kathantasambodhah

"If you are well established in aparigraha, you will be able to remember your own past lives clearly".

Aparigraha means non acceptance and non-covetousness. From possession and acquisition of things and wealth is born attachment. A spiritual seeker remains happy with whatever comes to him unsought for. From attachment to possessions comes attachment to body, family and ultimately to the world. If everything including your body, mind and soul belong to God, then attachment to the body, family and world is *parigraha* and covetousness. If one is unshakably perched in aparigraha, he or she can be able to remember his past lives. That means, the knowledge of what was one? how was one? What is the body? How is it? what one will be? Or how will I be, is revealed. This helps one know thy self and tries hard to realise the indwelling self. This will accelerate one's spiritual evolution. Jesus said, "If you want to be perfect, go, sell your possessions and give to the poor, and you will have treasure in heaven, then come, follow me" (Matthew 19:21).

To lay your claims on what does not belong to you is stealing other's property. Your possessions and covetous acquisitions deprive others of fulfilling their most basic human needs. If you do not give to others who are in dire necessity and adversity, in spite of your having a bonanza of wealth, then, you are committing theft. By giving to others without expectation brings in contentment, detachment to your possessions and universal love, fellow feeling, universal brotherhood and compassion for others. This kind of non-possessiveness and giving to others for fulfilment of their basic human needs heightens one's spiritual progress. Sage Patanjali said in Yoga Sutra (Sadhana Pada 37):

asteya pratisthayam sarva-ratnopasthanam

Those who are perfectly established in asteya (non-stealing), are entitled to be rewarded with the most precious things that will come on their own.

This is the reason the common adage is that by giving you take. The seekers who are always engaged in benevolence and wellbeing of others are dear to God (*Bhagavad Gita* 12:4). Mahatma Gandhi in an address at Kottayam (Harijan, 1937) in reference to the above verse in *Isa Upanishad* was eloquent on service and sacrifice for others:

"Since God pervades everything, nothing belongs to you, not even your own body. God is the undisputed and unchallengeable Master of everything you possess. If it is universal brotherhood – not only brotherhood of all human beings, but of all living things–I find it in this mantra. If it is unshakable faith in the Lord and Master – and all the adjectives you can think of – I find it in this mantra. If it is the idea of complete surrender to God and of the faith that he will supply all that I need, then again, I say I find it in this mantra. Since he pervades every fibre of my being and of all of you, I derive from it the doctrine of equality of all creatures on earth and it should satisfy the cravings of all philosophical communists. This mantra tells me that I cannot hold as mine anything that belongs to God and that, if my life and that of all who believe in this mantra has to be a life of perfect dedication, it follows that it will have to be a life of continual service of fellow creatures".

In yogic interpretation the Almighty Father is the sole doer abiding in all beings with compassion and detachment. In all our deeds, thinking and dispositions we should be conscious of the sole doer keeping a watch on each and every breath. The seekers of God always remain conscious of the inner self in all their doings and thoughts. They always remain in that heightened stage of super consciousness from where they perceive that they are mere onlookers and witness to the deeds being performed by God. It has been very candidly explained by Lord Krishna to Arjuna in *Bhagavad Gita* (5:8-9):

> nai 'va kimcit karomi 'iti yukto manyate tattwavit
> paysan srnvan sprsan jighrann asnan gacchan svapan svasan
> pralapan visrjan grhnann unmisan nimisann api
> indriyani 'ndriyarthesu vartanta iti dharayan

The one who is established in God (yukta) knows the truth and thinks, "I do not do anything at all", even while seeing, hearing, touching, smelling, eating. moving, sleeping, breathing...

...speaking, releasing, holding, opening and closing the eyes. The yogi remembers that the body organs function only in relation to the objects of those organs.

When the mind of the seeker goes up from the Muladhara chakra to the Sahasrara (pituitary) and remains fixed there, the seeker becomes detached and through his third eye he feels God working through him. He remains ever grateful to God for perceiving in constant awareness that God is the sole doer.

It shows all those who are not engrossed in God and do not perceive that God is the sole doer in all their activities, they are accused of stealing in the sense that they have wrongly taken unto themselves the role played by God in all their activities. God has been residing in us from the beginning in the form of breath. He has given us life and everything that are required. We have taken from Him everything but have forgotten by delusion and ignorance to pay Him off with our unconditional love and gratitude. Thieves are those who take away everything without giving anything in return. In that sense we are thieves. Out of delusion and ignorance they have claimed what in reality belongs to God. Such deluded persons find their way easily into hell. In *Bhagavad Gita* (16:20) Lord Krishna said to Arjuna the consequences of being deluded and not seeking God:

> asurim yonim apanna mudha janmani janmani
> mam aprapyai 'va kaunteya tato yanty adhamam
> gatim

Those who are deluded not attaining Me, birth after birth will enter the wombs of demons, O son of Kunti (Arjuna)! From there they descend to a condition lower still.

Spiritual persons seek the soul by ascending to the pituitary – the seat of the soul and beyond. People with demoniac propensities are completely deluded. They are not attached to God. They never seek the truth. They never rise up their consciousness from the lower chakras to the pituitary and fontanel, instead they relish in being engrossed in the ever-lower centres maddening after ego, vanity, sex, money and so on. These activities lead them from bad to worse.

These devilish people dwelling in these downward pulling propensities during all their activities and behaviour will never achieve God realisation. These demoniac attributes will sink them into the most despicable lowest state of humanity. They will live like animals not finding the way out. Leading such a miserable, degraded and deluded state of humanity is the real hell.

To the self- realised persons God is the witness to all their activities, thinking and deeds. Their inner self is reflected in the outside world. In all things outside they see the living presence of God. The material world looks divine world to the spiritual persons who remain always in Sahasrara (fontanel). In Indian spiritual tradition all things are adored as divine. The earth is venerated as embodiment of the divine. In *Brhad-dranyaka Upanishad* (III.7.3) it is pronounced by the sage Yajnavalkya:

yah prthivyam tisthan prthivya antarah yam prthivi na veda, yasya prthivi sariram, yah prthivim antaro yamayati, esa ta atmantaryamy amrtah

"He who dwells in the earth, yet is within the earth, whom the earth does not know, whose body the earth is, who controls the earth from within, he is your self, the inner controller, the immortal".

The meaning of this is that God dwells in the earth. The earth is His body. Within the human being the Muladhara chakra represents the earth centre. God abides in that also. It is said in *Bible*, "He was in the world and the world was made by him and the world knew him not" (St John I.10).

In invocations as described in *Vedas* it is pronounced:

Om dyauh santirantariksa, gvam santih prthivi santih apah santih santirosadhayah santih, vanaspatayah santih.

May the brighter regions, the mid way regions between the earth and sun, the waters, herbs, vegetations so on remain in peace.

Let all in the creation starting from earth to the space which encompass all both living and the non-living live in peace and harmony without any harm or suffering. Earth is adored as mother. Like a mother nourishes and provides her child from birth to the old with all care, love and necessary requirements. Mother tolerates, forbears and suffers everything for the peace and development of the child. Similarly, mother earth provides everything to the living beings for their growth, living and development. All beings get everything for their sustenance. It is like a wish fulfilling cow. From it are obtained crops, plants, trees, vegetation, herbs, diamonds, gold and what not. It is a cornucopia of everything. In the *Brhaddranyaka Upanishad* it is invoked:

iyam prithivi sarvesam bhutanam madhu, asyai prthivyai sarvani bhutani madhu; yas cayam asyam prthivyam tejomayo' mrtamayah purusha, yas cayam adhyatmam sariras tejomayo' mrtamayah purusha, ayam eva sa yo'yam atma, idam amrtam idam brahma, idam sarvam

The earth is (like) honey for all creatures, and all creatures are (like) honey for this earth. This shining, immortal person who is in this earth and with reference to oneself, this shining, immortal person who is in the body, he, indeed, is just this self. This is immortal, this is Brahman, this is all.

The earth and all living beings are mutually dependent, even as honey and bees are. The bees make honey and honey supports the bees. Anandagiri said:

parasparam upakaryopakaraka-bhave phalitam aha
Brahma is the self in each, in the earth and in the individual.

Exploitation of Mother earth

With industrial revolution and science and technological innovation in the west the mother earth was portrayed as mere matter and a resource cornucopia to be exploited, maimed and bruised to the hilt to meet the ever increasing and unsatiated wants of the greedy people for inordinate and exorbitant life style. This attitude of destroying the mother earth for sense derived pleasures was called development. This western way of defining development at the expense of the mother earth gradually contaminated all parts of the globe. The eastern way of adoring earth as mother and seeing the entire creation as the embodiment of the divine was replaced by the western portrayal of earth as nothing but a lifeless matter. Mastery over the earth and nature by the application of modern science and technology has become synonymous with development, modernity and civilisation. The result has been deep environmental catastrophe dragging the entire existence to the brink. Entire humankind is now bearing the brunt of scarcity of drinking water, pure air, pure and unpolluted vegetation and the consequences of climate change in the form of global warming, sea level rise, floods, cyclones, intensified drought, lack of rain, drying out of rivers and water bodies. The people have become bewildered, dejected finding no peace and joy in life.

This gloomy picture of the present earth was exactly the condition of the people during King Vena's rule as retold by mother earth to the king Pruthu, his successor. Mother earth in the form of the wish fulfilling divine cow (Kamadhenu) took away everything into her stomach not being able to bear the oppression of the king and people. Not finding any crop, vegetation and other things, the people starved, suffered miserably in agony and cried for respite from this deplorable condition. The policy makers, political leaders, scientists, technocrats, bureaucrats and above all we are like king Vena wrecking irreparable damage to the mother earth in the name of development and fulfilment of our material desires. Because of the havoc perpetrated on the earth by human beings, the production of crops, vegetables, cereals, medicinal plants and herbs and other things has dwindled. It means the earth in the form of cow has swallowed all. With his heart melted with the entreaty made by the famished and starving people the king Pruthu, the embodiment of Dharma was to save them by any means. The king incensed by their cries and wailings was ready to kill the earth, But the mother earth prayed not to kill her as in His past incarnation in the form of a swine (Baraha avatar) raised up mother earth from the water on the tip of His teeth for the wellbeing of people by killing the demon Hiranakshya. "How can you kill me whom You have saved", she entreated? The very purpose of creation will be nullified. Mother earth suggested to milk her. All people will get their desired things from her to their contentment.

When the king making Manu as the calf milked the earth in the form of cow, streams of milk started flowing and denuded the earth with rains. Crops and vegetations started growing in plenty. People in great joy took the harvests to their homes in great joy. Manu means mana+ u. Mana is mind. U means roaring, making sounds and pervasiveness. Mind is always roaring with various types of thinking. It is always agitated, bewildered and extrovert. Unless it is made steady and still by specific techniques of the control of breath and established in fontanel, it is bound to be moving from one thinking to another. Overpowered by this extrovert mind, man is deluded and bewildered. For this, man moves after money, wealth (production, crops etc.) as his/her mind has been deeply entrenched in Muladhara chakra not being able to rise up to the Sahasrara. If human beings will venerate earth as divine and mother, then it will not be oppressed, exploited and degraded. Otherwise, men will be deprived of crops, vegetations, fruits and other vegetables from the mother earth.

The rishis, saints and sages making their respective God realised masters as calf milked and drank the nectar drops of *Veda* in a plate sanctified by thorough control over senses and mind. *Veda* has come from the root Vid which means to know. To know Thyself is possible when the spiritual persons having thorough control over senses and mind remain engrossed in the fontanel rising above the Muladhara chakra. Human birth is meant for self-realisation. With God realisation all delusion, ignorance and error are wiped out.

The devas (gods) making Indra as the calf milked the cow and drank in a golden plate. The word devata is derived from the root div which means nothingness or infinite sky. God abides in the kutastha of every human being. Kutastha means as our revered Gurudeva Paramahamsa Hariharananda says existence in space. Kutastha and div convey the same meaning and are similar in connotation. Seated on the kutastha God controls our five senses. But human beings deluded by the extroverted five senses tend to forget the indwelling God in the kutastha. Through the practice of jyoti mudra in Kriya Yoga in the midpoint of the two eye brows an effulgent divine light is perceived. This is the meaning of drinking in golden plate. Divine light will be of various colours passing through the susumna within the spine to the Muladhara and then to the kutastha through one inhalation and exhalation. Forgetting one's mundane existence one is transformed into divinity. Sahasrara is the thousand lotus petalled chakra emitting divine light much more brilliant than the million suns but it is as cool as millions of moons. To be established unwaveringly in the fontanel (Sahasrara) begets tranquillity and quietness of mind. In this stage the seeker realises the all-pervading God. The devas milked the cow for yajna karma. The meaning of yajna is to know thyself. Yajna also means breath. To be conscious of breath every moment in one's actions, deeds and thinking is Yajna. Complete union with God through practice of breath control as taught in Kriya Yoga leads to liberation and immortality. This brings in vigour, strength, lustre and glaze to the body. When a river joins the ocean and becomes one with it, the strength of ocean becomes the strength of the river because the river is the ocean itself. Similarly, the seeker by taking complete refuge in God and getting united with Him in each breath in total forgetfulness of the body-mind and mundane consciousness assumes the strength of divinity. To be conscious of and watch every breath in one's deeds and thoughts is real karma. It is prana karma. By this the seeker will not be bound by the fruits of karma.

The demons drank from the cow making Prahalad the calf wine in an iron plate. Impressions from 8.4 million births we have undertaken in the past lives have been stored in us. In that sense we are all born of demonic attributes. Though Prahalad was born in a demon's family he was one of the greatest devotees of the Lord. Rising above the Muladhara chakra he remained fixed in Sahasrara and traversed beyond by the practice of breath control. God took Nrusingh Avatar for his liberation. The demons never followed him though they took pride on his greatness. Our heritage is our divinity. Deluded by the demoniac forces we tend to forget always the all-compassionate indwelling self. Iron plate is symbolic of tamasic attributes. With tamasic propensities we cannot be divine. Lord Krishna said to Arjuna (*Bhagavad Gita*, 16:4):

dambho darpo 'bhimanas ca krodhah parusyam eva ca

ajnanam ca 'bhijatasya partha sampadam asurim

Hypocrisy, fraud, deceit, arrogance, pride, ego, anger, harshness and ignorance are the attributes of those born with demonic nature.

With such attributes one cannot reach Godhood. It is said in scriptures

devo bhutva devam yajeta

krishnam bhutva krishnam yajet

Worship God by becoming God. Worship Krishna by being Krishna

The demons always remain intoxicated with drink of wine. It means the ignorant people are always intoxicated with the wine of worldly delusion. As a drunkard is unable to know the truth and remains always in hallucination and forgetfulness of the reality, the deluded persons forget to know the indwelling self. The seeker remaining always in fontanel and kutastha feels intoxicated with the divinely permeated euphoric joy in all their actions and deeds. A post master, disciple of Yogiraj Shyama Charan Lahiri could not be able to distribute letters to the addresses as he was always remaining intoxicated with divine joy. The *Kaivalya Tantra* says:

yaduktam parama brahma nirvikaram niranjanam

tasmin pramadana jnanam tanmadyam parikirtitam

Absolute merge and absorption in Parambrahma which is said as devoid of all modifications and descriptions endows one with a divine intoxication known as wine.

Through the constant practice of breath control in yoga and meditation one can remain established in God. This exudes an ineffable, indescribable and intoxicating joy.

Other celestials like Vasaba with nymphs drank the milk from the cow in a lotus leaf making Visvabasu as the calf. The milk was full of fragrance, sweetness and beauty. Water in the lotus leaf does not touch it. While in divine quest the sadhakas should remain detached to the world. Remaining detached to the worldly delusion and illusion the seeker should go above the lower chakras and get merged in the fontanel (Sahasrara chakra). Lord Krishna said to Arjuna in *Bhagavad Gita* (5:10):

brahmany adhaya karmani sangam tyaktva karoti yah

lipyate na sa papena padmapattram iva 'mbhasa

Those who perform karmas shirking attachment, and surrendering their actions into Brahmana, are not affected by sin, just as a lotus leaf is not wet by water.

Like a river merging in the ocean becomes the ocean itself, those seekers who merge with Brahman become Brahman itself. They always realise that they are not working it is God who is functioning through them. Any one attaining such a stage is not touched by sin. He is free from it as he has surrendered every action to God. When each and every action is accomplished with God consciousness it becomes divine. Work becomes worship. When a person ascends from the lower centres and heightens his awareness to the crown of the cranium (fontanel) he or she merges in Brahman and forgets the bodily existence and all longings and desires cease to exist. With the manifestation and realisation of the Self the seeker looks beautiful, wafts a sweet fragrance and wears a mien of peacefulness and calmness. Every movement of the seeker is like a dance with ceaseless divine sound producing inner joy. His life becomes a joyful celebration of the divinity within.

The deceased forefathers and mothers making Aryama as the calf drank in mango leaves the consecrated rice as milk.

Perfected in God realisation and self-realised masters making Kapila as the calf milked the cow with pledges for the wellbeing of the people. Those realised masters with being completely merged in Brahman take it as a crusade for the wellbeing and liberation of mankind. They do not remain confined to the caves, they come forward to serve the people even by sacrificing their lives. They perceive that service to humankind is service to God. Bhima Bhoi, a realised master in Odisha many centuries back said, let me be in hell but the world be liberated first. God realised sages and saints make it a mission of their life to dedicate themselves for the cause of the entire humankind irrespective of any caste, class, creed, faith, nation or race. These sages and saints are very endeared to God.

The persons of wisdom (Vidyadhara) making space (nothingness) as the plate milked the cow to drink khecari as milk in great joy. Khecari means kha+chara. Kha means space and chara means to roam. Those in sadhana always remain in space and nothingness are known as khecari sadhaka. Khecari mudra is a yogic practice. In Hatha Yoga it is a technique by which the tongue is elongated and rolled up to penetrate into the epiglottis – the upper passage of air. In Shiva Samhita (verses 53-54), khecari mudra is highly adored as

> mudraisa khecari prokta bhaktanam anurodhatah
> siddhinam janani hyesa mama pranadhikadhike
> priye
> nirantara krtabhyasam piyusam pratyaham pibet
> tena nigraham siddisyat mrtyu matanga kesari

"At the request of the devotees, khechari mudra is revealed; it is mother of all success, and even dearer than my own life. Practice it continuously, and drink the divine nectar daily. In this way one gets the state of inner peace, similar to the one ensures at the end of a war between the elephant and the lion resulting in the death of the elephant" (excerpted from Paramahamsa Prajnanananda, Jnana Sankalini Tantra).

Lion killing the elephant means thorough control over the breath and desires.

Lord Shiva (Iswara) said to Parvati:

> manah sthiram yasya vinavalambanam
> vayu sthiro yasya vinavarodhanam
> drstih sthira yasya vinavalokanam
> sa eva mudra vicaranti khecari

Ishwara said, "the state where the mind is steady, independent of any support, where vayu (the breath) is tranquil and effortless, and where the gaze is still without perception, is khecari mudra".

Mind is the master of senses. Breath is the master of the mind. If breath becomes still by unwavering concentration on the fontanel mind becomes calm and quiet. By remaining established in the indwelling Self, the gaze becomes introvert though others see him look outside but in reality, his look is inward and firmly perched in the kutastha. Such a spiritually unique stage where mind is calm and quiet, breath is still and gaze is inward, is known as khecari.

In this way all living beings starting from the tiniest to the God realised ones and the devas got their cherished things from the wish fulfilling cow as mother earth. The snakes got poison, the animals got grass and carnivorous got flesh and meat, the birds their fruits and nuts, the trees gum and juice and the mountains minerals. Mother earth as wish-fulfilling cow is the giver of all that the living beings want. If the seekers exercise control over Muladhara chakra and rise above it to fix all concentration on the fontanel, they surely will get access to divine wealth. Insatiable search for material wealth can be transformed into quest for divinity which is the supreme and most sought for by the seekers. In the outside world the earth should not be viewed as a resource cornucopia to be exploited for the body comfort and material wellbeing. The way we look at the world defines our life. It must be with a spiritual attitude we should approach to the earth not with a plundering and preying eye.

Stealing of the sacrificial horse for fire ceremony

The ever joyful sages and saints made available all required essentials to the king Pruthu to solemnise fire ceremony on the banks of the primordial river Saraswati. All gods and deities such as Lord Shiva, Lord Brahma and other celestial beings, nymphs, dancers and musicians (Gandharva) assembled there as Lord Vishnu has Himself manifested there as the Lord of the fire ceremony. Along with the entire entourage of the Lord, the siddhas, sages like Kapila, Narada and Sanatkumars, the child of God were all present. Jealous of the fetes and festivities adorning the fire ceremony, Lord Indra, the king of gods was saddened. The mother earth like Kamadhenu (wish-fulfilling cow) provided all resources. The rivers filled with the juice of sugarcane flowed in ripples. All assembled there were satiated with annam (food) mixed with ghee and yoghurt. The bees in the trees showered honey on all. The seas replete with gems, gold, jewels were buoyant with waves. The mountains providing all kinds of food (digestible, chewable, sucking and drinkable) made the king Pruthu very joyful. Indra, the lord of gods thought to himself, "If

Pruthu does hundred times the fire ceremony, he will surely be enthroned in my place. My all majesties will go away with him". After completion of ninety-nine times of oblations to fire ceremony, he stole away the horse meant for consecration in the fire ceremony with the sole objective of foiling the purpose of king Pruthu.

The sage Atri, one of the presiding priests of fire ceremony knew the misdeeds of Indra and directed the son of the king Pruthu to bring back the horse from Indra. The son of the king Pruthu immediately in great rage rushed after Indra with bow and arrows. Fear stricken Indra knowing being followed, changed himself into an ash smeared ferocious person. On finding that Indra's body smeared with ash, the son of the king refrained from killing him. Knowing this hesitancy of the son of the king, rishi Atri said, "Indra has stolen the horse. Do not leave him. Kill him immediately". Spurred thus by Atri, the son of the king ran after Indra with great vigour. In great fear Indra remained in space leaving the horse behind. Not finding out Indra, the son of the king Pruthu brought back the horse into the fire ceremony. The rishis and sages being happy with the remarkable feat of the son of the king named him as Vijitasva. The next morning finding nobody in the altar of fire ceremony, Indra again took away the horse into the space and remained incognito. Rishi Atri sent again the son of the Pruthu to chase after Indra. Indra changed himself into different forms like many in this world to deceive people. Some remain naked and smeared with ash to lead people on unrighteous paths slurring the *Vedas*. The people who followed them fall into the dungeon of hell. Hearing this the king Pruthu, furious and raged in anger with red eyes, was in the wake of fighting with Indra.

At the sight of the imminent war, all the sages and saints reached the spot to dissuade them from the war. They admonished the king, "in fire ceremony it is ordained in *Vedas* to sacrifice animals and no other beings. We will by offering oblations in the holy fire in the name of Indra, take away all his majesties associated with the position of Indra. It is not proper on your part to kill him".

Angered by Indra's ungodly conduct when the sages and saints were ready to offer the ghee as oblations in the name of Indra so that he would fall into the fire, Lord Brahma appeared before them and addressed them:

"O Supreme ones! Whom you are going to kill enjoys one portion of the oblations offered in the fire ceremony. His body is divine. In his body reside all the deities and gods. In whose mouth you are offering oblations is not worth being killed. Dharma is the supreme cause of all creations and their liberation. Indra adopted the path of demonic and your incarnation is meant for the liberation from the demoniac. You are the receptacle of all virtues and divinity. Nothing is impossible for you. All vices and demonic propensities stored in Vena are annihilated by your birth. In obeisance to my words, you liberate the wicked and demoniac".

The subtle words of Lord Brahma extinguished the fire of anger of Pruthu and that of the sages and saints. By offering donations such as annam (food), clothes and cows to the priests, the king was ingratiated with the blessings from them.

Meet of Indra and Pruthu and God's offer of boons

After the end of the fire ceremony God accompanied by Indra appeared before the king Pruthu. Lord said to Pruthu:

"O King Pruthu! Indra has come to you seeking forgiveness for his sin of having created disturbance in the fire ceremony. You are a sadhu. The sadhus have hatred for none. They are not ill disposed to anybody. They see all with a sense of equanimity as the same indwelling soul resides in all. The persons of wisdom perceiving the body as perishable have no attachment to it. They are not like ordinary and ignorant deluded. They view the body as different and distinct from soul. The imperishable soul is self-effulgent and illuminating by which the senses are shined and activated. Not shrouded by even a shred of illusion the soul is not attracted by and attached to the senses. The soul is everywhere and all-pervading not sullied by the attributes of anything. This body belongs to the senses but the soul presides over all these remaining completely detached. The person who perceives the inherent nature of the soul gets liberation. Penetrating the sheaths of senses of gross body and twenty-four prakritis if one dives deep into the Kutastha and perceives the soul dwelling therein, one gets constant liberation bringing an end to all his sorrows and simmering worldly delusion. If the spiritual seeker remains embedded constantly in Me with unshakable love and devotion, he

does not remain bound by sorrows or happiness. Not overjoyed by prosperity and bewildered by suffering the seeker remains calm and quiet".

Addressing him as the son of Vena, The Lord said, "You should *have thorough control over senses and remain undisturbed and unmoved by both sorrows and joys of life. Taking all people, friends and ministers with you, administer them on the path of Dharma. It is the dharma of the king to maintain and sustain the people righteously. The king who is benevolent to the subjects is entitled to earn one sixth part of the heavenly bliss after death. The king who does contrary to what I said, is thrown into the hell. Leading an exemplary and righteous household life you serve the people of the world. The great seers like Sanatkumars will come to your abode and by their grace you will get the knowledge of the self. I am highly pleased with your dharmic conduct and willing to bless you with boons which you are free to seek from Me".*

In obeisance to Lord's words the king Pruthu bowed down at His feet. Beholding this divine scene, Indra fell down at the feet of the king and begged forgiveness for his sin. Embracing Indra, the king pleased him. Drowned in the ocean of joy and with tears flowing down creating divine sensations the king worshipped the holy feet of the Lord and with folded hands prayed God:

O Lord! You offered me boons which I am unwilling to accept. People seek boons for enjoyment. Getting you as the Lord of my ultimate liberation (Kaivalyanath) what more is there in this life to seek? Being a person of wisdom, I seek nothing from You. I do not seek also mokshya. The fragrant and blissful nectar secreting out of Your lotus feet manifested in the form of Your divinely majestic words gives me euphoric and ineffable joy which I seek earnestly and constantly to hear. O Lord of my innermost heart I entreat Thee to bless me with hundreds of ears to hear Thy glory and beauty. Hearing the illuminating glories about the immortal nectar of your lotus feet expressed through the mouth of seers and realised masters dispels the ignorance from the ignoramus and rekindles knowledge about Thee in the seekers. Nothing else than this, is sought by me. You are the Supreme Purusha. Your feet are the store house of all divinities and majesties. Like mother Laxmi I will serve Thy holy feet. Even though, it will incur conflict with mother Laxmi, I will not scuttle serving Your feet constantly. You are very compassionate and kind to your devotees. Who serves your feet with unswerving devotion, seeks no other boon from you. Your offering boon to me is like a beguiling bait dangled before me to fall into the trap of worldly delusion which I seek earnestly to avoid. If You are kind to me like a father to a son, I will be liberated from the world seething with delusion, ignorance and error".

Rejoiced at these words of love-soaked entreaties the Lord said, *"O King! Let your unblemished love and devotion at my feet remain constant, undivided and unshaken. Let your thought and thinking be always on Me. Let My delusive forces not touch you at all".*

Highly pleased with prayer and worship of the king, the Lord disappeared into His eternal abode.

Sermons to the people

The king Pruthu entered into his abode bedecked with dazzling gems, diamonds, gold, and jewels of many hues. From the gate way to the arched portal of his abode the entire path was festooned with mango leaves and lined with banana trees decorated with varieties of flowers wafting aroma and fragrance far and wide and sprinkled with sandalwood waters. The women standing on both sides with burning lamps offered ovations amidst the spray of flowers on him, the sounds of conches, flutes, and long trumpets and recitation of *Vedas* and hymns in paeons of his glory and majesty.

The abode of the king was situated between the river Ganges and Yamuna where he was residing for the complete working out of his prarabdha karma. He was the sovereign of the entire world composed of seven islands. By his strong command everybody from the higher to the lower was obsequious to him.

Teachings of king Pruthu

Once, the king organised a great magnificence with superb grandeur where all gods, deities, celestial beings, brahmarshi, devarshis, royal saints and sages and people were invited. The king adored and worshipped them with all honour and veneration as due to them. If this grand fete resembled a star-studded sky, the king was shining like a moon with the sheen of divinity.

Addressing all assembled in the conclave the king said,

"God has created me as a king for ushering in a just and righteous administration in the world. I am the protector and sustainer of the people. I always lead them on the path of dharma. Nobody can deviate from the path of dharma. Serving the people on this path pleases God. He who pleases God gets liberation. The king who levies taxes and does not lead and teach his subjects the path of dharma incurs all sins and falls into hell. Be always fearful of adharma and learn from me the precepts of dharma. Shunning the habit of speaking ill of others remain surrendered to the Lord. If you all are kind to me, then take complete refuge in Him".

Paying homage to all sages and saints, the king said,

"O venerable ones! You all be kind to teach my subjects on the nuances of dharma. No work is to be performed without surrendering this to the Lord. God, the Supreme Purusha is the treasure trove of the persons who take refuge in Him. He is the true judge and determiner of the fruits of the actions individuals do. All the realised masters, Svayambhuba Manu, the great devotees like Dhruva and Prahlad, Bali, rajarshi Priyabrata, my forefather Anga and Brahma and Shiva have all spoken on the same voice that the Lord is the only one who is the sole determiner and giver of the fruits of one's deeds. My father, the nephew of lord Death was snared by worldly delusion and most unfortunate to be averse to the Lord. The lotus Feet of the Lord is like the holy Ganges. Love and devotion at the feet of the Lord with total surrender makes human mind pure and clean of all debris of mind. With this cleansed and unalloyed mind detachment is rekindled in him to leave him ultimately rested at the feet of the Lord without return to the world again".

He advised the people,

"You all take refuge in God by complete detachment without enmeshing oneself in the snares of delusion. No matter, in whatever stage a human being is (brahmacharya, grihastha, vanaprastha and sannyasa), he is to take shelter in the Lord for liberation. He is the subtlest of the subtle devoid of any attributes (Nirguna). Like fire immanent in the wood, God abides in all in various forms. He is the Guru of all gurus. It is because of Him all are enjoying the fruits of their own deeds. Brahmanas are dearest to God. It is because of His love and devotion for them He has got Mahalaxmi. Those who adore and love brahmanas are dear to the Lord. The joy that the brahmanas get by being fed with delicious food creates joy in the Lord. The dvijas (brahmans) are those who live in seclusion and solitude and are pure and sacred and have self-control and love for and always immersed in God and lead a life that is regulated by the precepts of Vedas. I always carry over my head the holy dusts from their lotus feet. Persons worshipping and adoring the brahmans are always devoid of any sins. Service to cows, brahmins and the Lord with love and devotion paves the way for liberation bestowing on one prosperity, joy and bliss".

At these words of sublime truth of the king, the assembled audience sang in chorus the praises of him with all adoration. The sages and saints showered on him the benediction and blessings for having gratified their life with the words of wisdom by showing them the path of divinity. The people were highly gratified and beholden to him for having taught them how to remain detached to the muddy world of delusion, illusion and error and seek liberation by taking ultimate refuge in the Lord. They said, "*You are the lord of the universe. We are fortunate to have you as our lord. We bow down at your feet with gratitude and devotion. Like Prahalad being the cause of eradication of the sins of his demonic father Hiranyakasipu, you have liberated your father Vena*".

Sanatkumars' teachings to king Pruthu

Directed by God, Sanatkumars shining like glowing suns reached the palace of the king who dancing with euphoric joy, offered them all ovations and adoration. Bowing them at their feet and washing their feet with cold and sandalwood soaked water and providing them very beatified and gold ornated seats, the king took the dusts from their feet and smeared on his forehead.

With folded hands touching his head he prayed, "*O Supreme Ones, it is because of my past virtuous deeds I am being gratified at beholding you in my naked eyes whom the yogis fail to see. You are all unmanifest and nobody can decipher your directions. Like the indwelling soul seeing all and not being seen by them, you all see and know everything. My life has been fruitful today by being ingratiated with your divinely ordained and blessed darshan. What a bonanza of wealth is to a destitute, you are all to me. A rich man can worship with all required ingredients and pure and unsoiled mind and heart. But a poor needs a simple seat made of grass, water to wash feet and drink, ground to seat on and sweet words full of humility. But for these the life is worthless. Such a home resembles like that of a tree inhabited by serpents becoming dangerous. One's life along with fame and prosperity go in vain if in his house the devotees of God do not wash their feet with great joy. What is the use of wealth, material prosperity and fame if one does not serve with love and devotion the sages and saints? Those whose heart is mired in material and sensual entanglement and enticements are always tied with the fetters of worldly delusion".*

The king Pruthu adoring Sanatkumars as the greatest and supreme of all realised masters said, *"it is not proper to ask about your good. What is good or aught about those who are effulgent with the light of wisdom can be asked. With this concern in mind, I am praying you to teach me the ways for liberation. You are traversing across the universe in the form of Yogindra for the liberation of the sages and saints. Having blessed with your divine presence in my place has ensured my liberation".*

Highly pleased with his adorable humbleness and prayerful supplications making himself very ordinary and ignoble, Sanatkumars said, *"O Supreme one! You are a divine being detached to the sense derived pleasures and averse to worldly delusions concerned with the benevolence and good of others. Since you are a person of wisdom and incarnate of all divine propensities, you asked us these questions about what is the worth seeking and supreme goal in life. The company with sadhus, sages and saints augurs auspicious both for this life and after life. Their discourses are the cause of all what is good and blessed in life".*

On the question of final liberation, Sanatkumars said, *"O King! There are three kinds of worshipping and contemplation God. These are tamasik, rajasik and sattvik. He whose mind is not engrossed in the Lord and wavering outside while adoring and worshipping Him is guided by tamasik bhakti (love). His mind is always stained by the colour of worldly delusion and heart is filled with dirt of all negative and demonic tendencies and he is unable to cross the worldly ocean. With one's heart, mind, intelligence and chitta (memory) pure, unblemished and fully detached one can realise the Ultimate who is all pervading, pure and abiding in all.*

Those who are busy enjoying the sense derived pleasures are rajasik jettisoning association and company with these people heralds divinity in one. Away from society and the worldly life those remain in solitude contemplating on God with all love and devotion without thinking anything, are entitled to remain at the Feet of the Lord.

Renunciation, love, detachment and determination not to fall into the trap of worldly delusion with control over mind, senses and self, remaining equipoised, balanced and equanimous in all dualities like pain, pleasure, cold and hot, joys and sorrows are the attributes of sattvik bhakti. To these persons of wisdom (paramahamsa) nothing is seen and nothing comes to their thinking except God, the Supreme Self. By the fire of wisdom and detachment their all negative and worldly delusions are burnt to ashes like fire burns out the trees. To them seer and seen are one. They do not make any distinction between self and the other. It is egoistic mind that sees the difference out of ignorance. Beholding in all the living presence of all-pervading soul brings an end to ignorance and the distinction between self and the other". All dualities born out of delusive thinking perish.

Sanatkumars told, "O king! in the sleep, awakening and dream realise the living presence of God. The whole creation is the dream product of God. It is like seeing in a dream that a person has become a king enthroned with all pomp and ceremony, surrounded by soldiers and military forces and attended to by many a retinues and subjects enjoying a very luxurious and exorbitant life style. But when the dream vanishes and he awakens he feels awkward to find that he is no more the king but an ordinary person. Similarly, the wise person sees always that this world is ephemeral. The entire creation is delusive and like a dream very short living. The only reality and ultimate truth is God nothing else. So long as there is an egoistic I, the distinction between seer and seen is perceived. With the elimination of this egoistic I, soul is manifested with all its effulgence and there is no mind, no senses. Only soul pervades all. If you look to the water and stand before a mirror, only your image and nobody else's will be reflected. Similarly, the entire creation will look like the reflection of the all resplendent, imperishable soul without any attributes. The egoistic I, mind and senses vanish. The soul exists only encompassing all and everything. Streams of all individualities, egoistic identities, titles and attributes mingle with the oceanic Supreme Self (Paramabrahma)".

Sanatkumars continued:

"O adorable king! Total engrossment with the soul and shunning of bad companies and attachment to the delusive world are the two paths for liberation and final crossing of the worldly ocean. The person who is deeply attached to the world, beguiled by senses and mind, sees the difference between seer and seen and is enslaved by egoism, pride, possessiveness, passion, avarice, jealousy and all other *demonic attributes and has lost his conscience. Like the grass and other plants siphoning of water from the lakes, the senses and mind draws his consciousness and memory away from God. With forgetfulness of the soul, his knowledge of the self is also lost. With knowledge of the indwelling self not being manifested in him, he is lost ever completely in the dungeon of worldly delusion. He incurs the sin of killing his own soul. He who for the temporary pleasures heaped on him by senses and objects sacrifices the eternal and permanent is the most ignorant and deluded".*

Reiterating on the importance of rejection of bad company, Sanatkumaras said:

"O king! The renunciant never remains attached to the world and never seeks company with demonic people and attributes. The principal four aspects of life are dharma, artha, kama and mokshya. Out of these four mokshya (liberation) is the supreme. In what is temporary and delusive lies the seeds of fear of death. The final liberation is eternal, blissful and ananda (joy). It kills the fear of death. He who has fear of kala (Time Spirit) lacks divine peace and joy. You and me are nothing but soul. The entire universe is the manifestation of the soul. Those who are bound by the sense of body, senses, mind, intelligence, ego and memory do not perceive the omnipresence of the soul and are shrouded by the mist of maya (illusion). Like air not attached to the space the soul is not attached to the maya. Though the soul is abiding in all but not attached. Twentyfour prakritis (ten karmendriyas plus five jnanendriyas plus mind, intelligence, memory and ego plus five gross elements – earth, water, fire, air and space, are the basis of all karmas (deeds). A person remaining captive to these is deluded and falls into hell. The imperishable soul

is connected with everything but remains detached. He is the Supreme Purush ever pure. With unshakable love and devotion to Him if you take ultimate refuge in Him, you will get liberation. Pursuing the path of Astanga Yoga strewn with love is the only way to get Him. This world is like an infinite ocean wherein senses are living as dreaded crocodiles ever ready to engulf you. Yoga is the fleet by which you can easily cross the worldly ocean, otherwise you can fall prey to the senses and mind swirling in the unending wheel of birth and death. What can give you fearlessness and immortality is the Feet of the Lord Krishna. Taking complete shelter at His Feet with all love, devotion and dedication by following the path of Yoga is the easiest way to get liberation from the excruciating mundane life. Integration of karma, jnana and bhakti by the practice of yoga is the supreme path of liberation".

Overwhelmed with great joy and tears of gratitude the king Pruthu entreated:

"O Supreme ones! by the grace of Lord Krishna I got your darshan. You all came down to me in obeisance to the direction of the Lord. All my doubts vanished by having seen you. My all wishes were fulfilled. I do not know how to serve you and with what things. Everything on the earth including my body belong to you. Nothing is mine. I have no possession over all these. Like a mother giving everything to the child never receives anything back from the child out of love, similarly, you have given everything to me. I keep all these at your feet. I am just a servant of the Lord. I know with surrender of my life, family, throne, power, possessions, kingdom, wealth, the royal majesties and all that exist on the earth I will not be able to please you. You are kind, compassionate and the Lord of Yoga (Yogeshwar) to show

me the path of liberation. By your divine illumination you removed the darkness of ignorance from me".

Highly pleased with the humble adoration of the king, Sanatkumaras left the place and vanished into infinite. The king unwaveringly established in the Lord ruled the earth treating people as his sons and daughters. Peace, joy and happiness prevailed all over the world. As a king he is non parallel. He is worth being the king as he has dedicated himself for the joy and happiness of all. He is as brilliant as the sun in effulgence. He is invincible as a king. He is as tolerant as the earth is. He fulfils the cherished goal of all as one seeks in heaven. He causes rains. He fulfils the prayers of all. He is as deep as the ocean. He is a preceptor like a dharma. He is as stupendous as the Himalayas. He is as rich as lord Kubera. He is a great preserver like an ocean. He is as cool as the moon. He is as prideful as the air. He is angry like Rudra. He is as beautiful as the Kandarpa. He is as ferocious as the lion is. He is as kind as the king Manu is. He is as sovereign as the Providence. He is God realised like a guru preceptor. Like the Lord he has mastery over senses. He is servicing to cows and brahmanas. He is very humble in service and love to the devotees of the Lord. Nobody matches him in treating all as equal. He is creator like Lord Brahma. He is as illustrious and renowned as Sri Rama.

Ultimate liberation of the king Pruthu

Advising people to remain always fixed at the feet of the Lord without any thinking and bequeathing his kingship to his sons such as Vijitasva, Dhumrakesha,

Haryakshya, Dravina, and Brukesha he left the world with his wife Arjee and entered into deep forest for ultimate union with the Lord by following the path of yoga as taught by Sanatkumaras. He went through an ordeal of penance and austerity. Gradually he left food, water and air. Following the techniques taught by Sanatkumaras, he merged the earth element into water, then water into fire, fire into air and air into infinite space and remained immersed in the divine sound of the space. All the five elements along with their attributes like smell, rasa, teja, touch and sound got merged in the infinite along with their presiding deities. Mind, intelligence, chitta and ego were merged in mahat tattwa

Metaphorical interpretation

On the banks of the primordial and the holy river Saraswati the king Pruthu solemnised *asvamedha yajna* (a fire ceremony where a horse is sacrificed). The rivers and mountains that are found in the world in macro forms are subtly to be perceived inside the micro human body. In the human body the north pole is the fontanel and there flows the ida and pingala nadi inside the spine like the rivers Ganga and Yamuna originate from the Himalayas in the north. In Jnana Sankalini Tantra (verse 11) it is pronounced by Lord Shiva to Mother Parvati:

> ida bhagavati Ganga
> pingala Yamuna nadi
> idapingalayor madhye
> sushumna ca Saraswati

Ida is the divine river Ganga, pingala is the river Yamuna and between ida and pingala lies susumna, which is the holy river, Saraswati.

The source of innumerable nerve channels is the cerebro-spinal system with manifold veins and arteries. In the yogic idioms Ida nadi spreads from the left side of the brain to the Muladhara chakra. Pingala nadi originates from the right side of the brain and spreads to the Muladhara chakra. The central channel inside the spinal cord is Saraswati. In the next verse it is said by Lord Shiva:

> triveni samgamo yatra tirtharaja sa ucyate
> tatra snanamprakurvita sarva papairpramucyate

Where there is triveni sangama (the confluence of the three holy rivers), it becomes the holiest of holy places and by taking a bath there one is freed from all sins (Paramahamsa Prajnanananda, Jnana Sankalini Tantra).

The confluence of these three rivers is called the tirtharaj - the holiest place, the royal and supreme among the pilgrimages. For this reason, the king Pruthu selected this place as the holiest one to organise the fire ceremony. Inside the spine the confluence of ida and pingala nadi is the pituitary gland - Ajna chakra. It is the holiest trveni - the union of all three nadis. At Muladhara chakra at the base of the spine these three nadis are separated from each other. That is why human beings are beguiled into the delusive world for wealth, money, sex pleasure, passion, ego and vanity. A spiritual seeker in quest for Self-realisation must raise his or her awareness to the triveni – the confluence of these nadis. Once established and immersed there constantly in each and every moment will herald bliss, joy and peace. From this sanctum to be conscious of every breath is negation of all sins. To forget the indwelling soul in each and every breath is sin. By the proper techniques of breath control as very succinctly practiced in Kriya Yoga the union with the indwelling soul takes place in this confluence. In the Hatha Yoga Pradipika (2:41; 4:12), it is eloquently expressed:

vidhivat prana samyamaih nadichakra vishodhite
sushumna vandaam bhitva sukhat vishati marutah
sushumna vahini prane shunye vishati manase
tada sarvani karmani nirmula yati yogavit

"Through the proper process of breath control and purification of the chakras in the spine, one opens the path of the susumna. The subtle breath flows in the opened passage. Thus, the mind becomes tranquil and still. Then all the actions of the knower of yoga are like life giving nectar. It brings immortality" (translated by Paramahamsa Hariharananda, The Essence of Kriya Yoga).

King Pruthu, an incarnation of Dharma was seated at this holiest confluence in meditation and fully merged with the indwelling soul he was performing all functions surrendering all to God.

Asvamedha yajna

In this sacrifice a horse is allowed to move followed by three hundred guards. If the horse is obstructed in its journey a fight is ensued between the guards and the hinders. When the horse completes its victorious circuit of the earth and returns to the capital, it is offered as a sacrifice and the king who performs the sacrifice assumes the title of sovereign emperor. This is described in details in Satapatha Brahman (XIII,1-5). In yogic interpretation:

Asva is composed of two words a+sva. A means not and sva means tomorrow. What will not remain for tomorrow or future is asva. In other words, not leaving everything to the future, at this moment to be surrendered to God is asvamedha yajna. This world is temporal and transient. Nothing is permanent. Without being deluded by what is impermanent and perishable to resign oneself to the feet of God is true asvamedha yajna. It implies, the worldly sense is to be sacrificed for union with the Lord.

Yajna means to know. To know what? To know and realise Thyself is yajna. Yajna also means breath. It is through breath control the indwelling soul is to be realised. There are fifty types of breath in human body. Out of these 49 breaths are extrovert and drag human beings into the dungeon of worldly delusion. The 50th breath is very short and slow. It flows between pituitary (Ajna chakra) and the fontanel (Sahasrara). If the seeker remains conscious of this slow and feeble breath his/her mind will be quiet, calm and still. The fire is burning in the Sahasrara emitting light more brilliant than millions of suns and cooler than millions of moons. To feel this short breath touching the Sahasrara is the oblation offered to burning fire. When the seeker stays put in this breath with all attention undisturbed and steady like a burning lamp unflickered in absence of wind in fontanel withdrawing himself/herself away from the spur and impetus of demoniac attributes of the lower chakras, he or she attains to the Ultimate. This is asvamedha yajna. Our Gurudeva Paramahamsa Hariharananda used to say every time:

Kuru punyam, ahoratra smar nityam anityam ca. Every moment to remain conscious of the short breath is punya and day and night think of the ephemeral world and the imperishable soul within. On the grave of the ephemeral world is to be realised the union with the eternal and imperishable soul residing within us.

In scriptures it is described whenever any king did meditation or tapasya or any asva medha yajna Indra, the king of devas got wary of this and tried to disturb it by any means fearing that his throne would be usurped. This happened in case of king Pruthu when he was organizing the horse sacrifice. The horse was immediately stolen from the spot by none else than Indra himself. Its real yogic interpretation is as follows:

The other name of Indra is Purandara. It is said:

arinam puram darayati iti Indra.

It implies one who destroys the cities or dominion of the enemies is Purandara. The enemies are within the lower chakras of the human body. These are the demonic propensities reigning the human beings and preventing them from perceiving the truth.

puram nagaram darayati iti purandara.

This human body is pura. The body consciousness hinders human beings' perception of the truth. It is to be replaced by soul consciousness. One who helps destroy body consciousness is purandara.

Another version is

idam drshtva iti indra. Those who see everything as different from themselves are purandara. To perceive indwelling soul as different from body.

In *Katha Upanishad* the senses are likened to horses:

> atmanam rathinam viddhi sariram ratham eva tu
> buddhim tu saradhim viddhi manah
> pragraham eva ca (1.3.3)
> indriyani hayan ahur visayams tesu gocaran
> atmendriya manoyuktam bhoktety
> ahur manisinah (1.3.4)

The atman (indwelling soul) is compared to the owner of the chariot (rathin), the body being the chariot (ratha), buddhi or intellect is the driver (sarathi), the horses are said to be the senses (indriyani), manas is the rein (pragrah) by which the intellect control the senses.

The seeker is to make his or her senses introvert by drifting them away from the sense objects like a tortoise withdrawing its senses inside from outside and divert these to the divine. By this constant practice he or she will be well established in wisdom. The master of the senses is the mind, and the master of the mind is breath. It is through breath control and constant practice with detachment to the mundane the senses are controlled and mind becomes still and quiet. If breath is slow, mind becomes calm and quiet. Keeping attention on the kutastha (pituitary) and fontanel to become constantly conscious of the slow and divine breath flowing between pituitary and fontanel paves the way for anchoring in the divine.

To remain immersed completely in the soul means to elevate oneself from the demonic attributes lying powerful and active in lower chakras to the fontanel. In the funeral pyre of body consciousness is to be clearly realised the union with the indwelling soul. What is eternal and permanent is to be realised as different from what is temporal and transitory.

In the sadhana takes place the fight between the eternal and the impermanent, between the demoniac and the divine. This is the fight between Indra and Vijitasva, the son of Pruthu who ultimately won by taking away the horse from Indra's hand. He is named by sages as Vijitasva it is because he could realise what is permanent and truth and ignore what is temporary and momentary. Sacrificial horse being taken away umpteenth times the king Pruthu went to the extent of invoking the name of Indra as oblation to the ceremonial fire. The demoniac forces will not easily leave the sadhaka. These appear to dominate the divine forces. The sages and saints including Lord Brahma, Lord Shiva and Lord Vishnu appeared and brought him to the right path.

In spiritual path in order to realise God one has to do sadhana himself/herself. Nobody can do it for the other. One has to fight its own battle between the demonic and the divine. Lord Krishna said to Arjuna (*Bhagavad Gita*, 6:5):

uddhared atmana 'tmanam na 'tmanam avasadayet

atmai 'va hy atmano bandhur atmai 'va ripur atmanah

By the help of Self (soul consciousness) elevate yourself from delusion. Do not degrade yourself, for you are your own friend and you are your own enemy.

There is no substitute for self-efforts. It is key to success. Man is the maker of his own destiny. As you think so you become. If man so wishes and tries hard, he can transform himself from Ratnakara to Maharshi Valmika. Keeping undivided and unwavering attention on the soul if one controls the mind, senses, thought, ego, vanity, intellect and body and worldly sense through breath control with deepest love he or she can easily elevate his mind from the lower chakras to the fontanel. Man will be released from the confinement of body cage into the limitless infinite soul. It is through self-effort one can one day be God realised. After the construction of the bridge in the Indian ocean when Sri Ramachandra made the samkalpa (pledge) to kill Ravana by worshipping Mother Durga. To conduct the fire ceremony before Mother Durga who was the befitting priest, Sri Ramachandra asked everyone. All unequivocally answered it was no else than Ravana who was the right person to conduct the puja. Lakshmana was sent for the purpose. Without hesitation accepting the invitation, Ravana came and performed nicely the fire ceremony. After puja as it is customary to give as and what asked by the priest (dakshina). Ravana could have sought Sita as dakshina, instead beseeched that he should be killed by Sri Rama. The significance of this story is that we have to become the sole priest or conductor of very act of subduing all our dreaded demoniac and animal propensities stored in us from the past infinite births. If we do not do this at this moment how our evil forces will be wiped out? Who will do it for us? You have to fight your own war within.

This is the reason the king Pruthu was angry with Indra for the stealing of his sacrificial horse. Why Indra will do it for the king? The king is to do for himself. When the king Pruthu got himself seated firmly in the soul, God brought Indra with Him to the king and asked him to pardon Indra for this. Being highly pleased with sadhana and benevolence of the king, God blessed him that Sanatkumars will come to you one day to teach you the techniques of God realisation and liberation from the worldly delusion.

www.ingramcontent.com/pod-product-compliance
Lightning Source LLC
LaVergne TN
LVHW091709070526
838199LV00050B/2329